GRESLEY'S
MASTER ENGINEER, BERT SPENCER

GRESLEY'S MASTER ENGINEER, BERT SPENCER

A Career in Railway Engineering and Design

TIM HILLIER-GRAVES

PEN & SWORD TRANSPORT

AN IMPRINT OF PEN & SWORD BOOKS LTD.
YORKSHIRE – PHILADELPHIA

First published in Great Britain in 2023 by
Pen and Sword Transport
An imprint of Pen & Sword Books Ltd.
Yorkshire - Philadelphia

Copyright © Tim Hillier-Graves, 2023

ISBN 9781399045070

The right of Tim Hillier-Graves to be identified as
Author of this work has been asserted by him in accordance
with the Copyright, Designs and Patents Act 1988.

A CIP catalogue record for this book is available from the British Library.

All rights reserved. No part of this book may be reproduced or transmitted in any form
or by any means, electronic or mechanical including photocopying, recording or by any
information storage and retrieval system, without permission from the Publisher in writing.

Typeset in Sabon LT Std 9.5/11.5 by
SJmagic DESIGN SERVICES, India.
Printed and bound in India by Replika Press Pvt. Ltd.

Pen & Sword Books Ltd incorporates the imprints of Pen & Sword Books Archaeology,
Atlas, Aviation, Battleground, Discovery, Family History, History, Maritime, Military, Naval,
Politics, Railways, Select, Transport, True Crime, Fiction, Frontline Books, Leo Cooper,
Praetorian Press, Seaforth Publishing, Wharncliffe and White Owl.

For a complete list of Pen & Sword titles please contact

PEN & SWORD BOOKS LIMITED
47 Church Street, Barnsley, South Yorkshire, S70 2AS, England
E-mail: enquiries@pen-and-sword.co.uk
Website: www.pen-and-sword.co.uk

Or
PEN AND SWORD BOOKS
1950 Lawrence Rd, Havertown, PA 19083, USA
E-mail: Uspen-and-sword@casematepublishers.com
Website: www.penandswordbooks.com

Contents

Acknowledgements		6
Prologue		7
Chapter 1	An Exceptional Student	10
Chapter 2	Front and Centre	32
Chapter 3	Innovation or Stagnation	50
	Bert Spencer – A Design Engineer's World in Colour	97
Chapter 4	Pressing Home Their Advantage	105
Chapter 5	To Greater Glory	141
Chapter 6	Aftermath	198
Epilogue		234
Reference Sources		242
Index		244

Acknowledgements

I have been privileged to meet many people who worked on the railways and were happy to paint vivid pictures of the time when steam dominated their day to day lives – engineers, designers, footplate crew, managers and many more. Their number grows thinner each year, but luckily many have been moved to reminisce or write about their experiences. This has created a bank of information for future generations to enjoy and so increase their understanding of a time of which many can have no personal knowledge.

To this we can add many other individuals who have made a huge commitment, personal and financial, to preserve and record so many aspects of railway history. Amongst them I number my late uncle, Ronald Hillier, whose work has helped me write about many railway-related subjects. In preparing this latest book it helped considerably that Ron knew both Bert Spencer and his wife Elsie and occasionally visited them at their home in Devon and recorded many of their memories.

The principal sources of material I have used are listed in the bibliography of this book. Occasionally I have quoted directly from them, mostly because I couldn`t improve on what they have written. In addition, I believe that using contemporary accounts, wherever possible, captures the spirit of the time in which these events took place much more effectively than I could ever do. There is an immediacy about their words, untainted by beneficial hindsight. I thank the authors or holders of this material for permission to use it to enliven this book and give it greater authenticity.

To all the people who have helped me I give my thanks and hope I have done justice to all that they have contributed. Ultimately, though, all an historian can do is to sift and consider all material and reach a judgement that he or she thinks honestly represents history. There will, undoubtedly, be other views or conclusions and even some omissions that someone thinks may be crucial to a story, but that is as it should be. I don`t think there is ever a final word on any subject and new material may be found to allow fresh interpretations to be made.

In producing photographs for this book, some preservation work has been necessary. In some cases their sepia finish, foxing and dilapidated condition could not be entirely overcome. However, because they are often rare pictures or have some historic significance they have been included despite their condition. I hope this does not spoil your enjoyment of the book.

Bert Spencer, in his familiar light coloured hat, stands with two colleagues waiting the departure of 4485, *Kestrel*, to the north in the years immediately before the Second World War. The spectacle of a gleaming A4 was always a draw, but in this case heavily encouraged by professional interest, these engines having absorbed so much time and energy as they gradually evolved from Gresley's 1922-introduced A1s. (BS)

Prologue

To anyone interested in the history of the London and North Eastern Railway and its celebrated Chief Mechanical Engineer Nigel Gresley, the name of Bert Spencer will be familiar. This softly spoken, modest but very talented engineer laboured in the giant shadow cast by his leader, unobtrusively working to support him in his great deeds.

Spencer was a daily presence in the CME's London offices at King's Cross for sixteen years, having spent seven years learning his trade as a draughtsman and designer with the Great Northern and Lancashire and Yorkshire Railways. But such was his understanding of engineering and his leader's way of working that he managed to merge into the background and never sought to steal the limelight from Gresley or embarrass him when his ideas went awry. He quietly went about his business, suggesting improvements and translating often very sketchy proposals to ensure that any schemes reaching the Chief Draughtsman were effectively and correctly defined. He did this with a master's touch despite the debatable influence of other more ebullient, ambitious souls, such as Oliver Bulleid, ever eager to catch Gresley's eye and seek to influence his thoughts and decisions.

In some ways, he may be seen as a 'the power behind the throne', but to do so would be disingenuous and wholly misleading of the man and his motives. He was, first and foremost, someone always prepared to work for the greater good, rejecting any thought of personal reward beyond the desire to see a job well done. Such people are to be valued very highly.

And yet his time with Gresley occupied less than half his working life. Although a period in which they both reached the peaks of their careers, the remaining years were hardly wasted, each filled with many noteworthy achievements. Firstly, he ably assisted Gresley's successor,

Above left: A photo from Bert Spencer's collection that captures the result of Nigel Gresley's great endeavours, ably supported by his redoubtable and astute assistant – a collection of Pacifics showing the CME's evolution of ideas. (BS)

Above right: King's Cross Station in the 1920s as it appeared when Spencer was appointed to the post of Gresley's assistant. He later recalled that it was 'a grimy place to work. There was a constant pall of smoke and dust lay heavily over everything in our offices which daily cleaning did little to shift. After a while each of us developed a cough and wheeze that made us sound as though we were consumptives. Nevertheless, it was a wonderful place to work.' (RH)

Edward Thompson, and met the demands of war and recovery with equal skill and devotion. Then he skilfully supported the LNER's last Chief Mechanical Engineer, Arthur Peppercorn, as he grappled with the after effects of war and the machinations of nationalisation. Finally, there came ten years of active service with British Railways itself, a time in which he played an important role in its test and evaluation programmes, the development of standardised steam locomotives and the introduction of diesels. But wherever he went or whatever he did, the guiding principles he adopted were those forged whilst working with Gresley. To the end of his days in Devon, he never forgot his mentor or allowed any criticism to sully his memory.

Without Gresley, Spencer may not have achieved so much, but I believe Gresley's accomplishments could have been far less without the ever present Spencer. Difficult to prove, of course, but it would be too easy to sweep the younger man's contribution to one side by using the ambiguous epithet 'they were Gresley's engines'. In truth, there were many contributors to his success – Robert Thom, Bulleid, Tom Street and Edward Windle to name but a few. However, I believe the most important, when it came to formulating ideas and ensuring they were followed through to success, was the man who sat beside him for all those years at King's Cross. It was Spencer who was able to judge his moods, assure his privacy when contemplating the future, supported and influenced his creative processes, counselled him when necessary, translated often very sketchy proposals and added his own well-considered ideas.

Like Gresley, Spencer entered the railway industry as an apprentice but, unlike his Marlborough-educated mentor, he did so from a far less privileged background. Born in a poor backstreet of Doncaster, the youngest child of a journeyman cabinet maker in the last years of Victoria's reign, he proved to be a clever, hardworking child and, encouraged by his parents, gained access to the prestigious Doncaster Grammar School. At each stage of his education, he excelled and easily sat at the top of his class across all subjects, particularly the sciences. In an age where opportunities for advancement from such a background were limited, any advantages gained from a good education had to be exploited to the full and this the young Bert did. As a result, this very able boy grew to manhood in the workshops of the Great Northern Railway at Doncaster, as an engineering apprentice, where his skills soon shone and his obvious talents marked him down for a very bright future if he continued to work hard.

Above left: Although an LNER man through and through, Spencer was fascinated by all locomotive developments in Britain and around the world. Judging by his photographic collection, the LMS's streamliners became one class which continued to interest him and on which he rode a number of times. Checking out the competition, perhaps, or simply a love of steam? Here, No. 6222, *Queen Mary*, passes by early in its career. (BS)

Above right: Throughout his life Spencer was an avid collector and taker of railway photographs and was also fairly adept at avoiding the camera's lens himself. Judging by his collection he was regularly drawn to Liverpool Street Station in London, as shown here, where he captured many pictures of BR's new standard Pacifics, in this case the first of class No. 70000, *Britannia*. (BS)

No matter how talented the individual, it helps if there is someone of senior rank to help guide them through the early years of their career. Here Bert was very lucky in being piloted by two stalwarts of the GNR – John Bazin and William Elwess – before Gresley became aware of the full extent of his talents. But this type of help can only prove beneficial if the individual concerned truly has skill and a determination to succeed. There is little doubt that Spencer was so imbued and became a master engineer along the way. This allowed him to sit beside another master of his trade and earn the right to be treated as an indispensable equal. This was something the modest Spencer would never claim for himself, but I believe it to be true, nonetheless.

In the main, the stories of Spencer and other equally gifted engineers are now lost to time. Their achievements have been consumed by the collective mass of history. Their leaders' names now simply grace the engines they helped build and these have become their memorials, though their contributions to this work have largely been forgotten. A few recorded their thoughts to help us understand these events, but these accounts are few and far between and often not written by men close to the action. Then there were a few others, like the LMS's Tom Coleman and Spencer, who did so indirectly or by chance. In these cases, it was achieved through official papers that have survived, or in correspondence or during conversations with friends and colleagues. And in Spencer's case this was supplemented by papers he presented to professional bodies in the 1920s through to the '40s or other people's submissions on which he commented. This has left a rich tapestry of material to consider and enjoy. By some judicious editing this allows us to view many key events through his eyes, with some general scene setting added to help complete the picture.

In a history such as this there are a number of threads to be drawn together if we are to truly understand what happened and the contributions of each person to the success of a project. In Spencer's case this allows us to assess his life and work, but also view and evaluate the relationship that existed between him and his leader and the effect it had on Gresley's work. It was, after all, a relationship central to all that happened in the CME's offices at King's Cross in the truly invigorating years between 1925 and 1941.

It is a story that begins in Victorian Doncaster, in a country where poverty was rife and steam dominated industry. It ends seventy years later in a peaceful coastal town in Devon during the 'Swinging Sixties' where, in a hugely changed world, much that Spencer held dear had been swept away by two world wars and massive social change.

Spencer's life spanned the regeneration of Britain's railways from steam to diesel and electric motive power. He appears to have expressed no feelings either way about the demise of steam and took a keen interest in BR's new diesels, such as the Class 55 Deltics that became common on the East Coast Mainline in 1961/62. He collected or took many photographs of them in the last years of his life. (BS)

Chapter 1

An Exceptional Student

I was born in a typical Victorian terraced house close to Doncaster town centre. My father was a cabinet maker and my mother his third wife, the first two having died a few years earlier leaving him to bring up two children by himself. In the years that followed three more children came along, with me being the last in 1898. Although we did not have much money my childhood was a happy one and being the youngest meant that I was probably indulged more than the others.

So wrote Bert Spencer when retired and living in Shaldon, overlooking the River Teign in Devon. By then in his late 60s he seems to have looked back at his early years with a feeling of contentment. Delivered by the local midwife on 6 May 1898 in a small terraced house in Doncaster, he grew to maturity in the town's backstreets at a time when poverty was endemic. For those who could not make ends meet there was the ever present reminder of what could befall the unlucky or the 'lazy' if they failed, in the shape of the workhouse on Springwell Lane which opened in 1900. This intimidating building dominated the landscape sending out an only too clear message to those living in its shadow. Its only saving grace – it replaced an even grimmer institution on Hexthorpe Lane. Spencer remembered both these institutions until the end of his days, so great was their impact.

His family had not always lived in Doncaster but migrated to the town in search of work during the 1880s. Abel Spencer, his father, hailed from Bradford, and his mother, Frances, from South Leverton, Nottinghamshire. By the time they married in 1883, the twice wed Abel was 36 and his new bride fourteen years younger. His first and second wives, Eliza and Mary, both died very young. This was the lot of many then, where childbirth was a huge risk and many illnesses, virtually unknown today, such as cholera, typhoid and small pox, regularly killed thousands. And then there was the ever-present threat of tuberculosis to contend with.

By the time Abel met Frances he was struggling to find work and raise two young children, both Eliza's – Edith born in 1874 and Ernest three years later. Undoubtedly his family, particularly his brother George and his wife, who lived next door in Undercliffe Street in Bradford, would have helped, but a second parent would have eased his burden considerably. Luckily, Frances proved to be resilient to the ills and rigours of life then. In due course, she would bear him three sons – Fred in December 1884, Harry in 1886 and Bert twelve years later. The youngest Spencer later recalled that his mother called him 'our much blessed after thought'.

Abel is described in census returns of the period as a 'journeyman cabinet maker' and was probably employed in

Bert Spencer when a year old in 1899 and dressed in the style of late Victorian Britain. Being the youngest of five in a small terraced house in Doncaster, life might have been difficult, but he remembered his childhood as a happy time. (BS)

On the back of this sepia print Bert has written 'Doncaster British School in 1907/08. I am third on the left of the first row standing partially hidden by Tom'. (BS)

For the poor, the ill or destitute the 1900 opened workhouse on Springwell Lane in Doncaster might prove to be a blessing. But life within its walls could be a tough, cruel business. The buildings as captured in contemporary photos presented a daunting prospect and sat close to the main centres of housing in the town providing a constant reminder of the price of failure. Bert Spencer, for one, remembered the depressing pall it cast over the lives of those who lived within its shadows. (THG)

one or more of the cotton mills that were common in Bradford then. If so, he followed his father William, who was 'Cotton Overlooker', into the business. But with his marriage to Frances, he looked elsewhere for employment and found better paid, perhaps more regular work with the Great Northern Railway in Doncaster shortly before the birth of his son Fred.

It is not hard to see why he joined the GNR. By the 1880s the demand for carpenters, to support a thriving carriage building and maintenance programme, was growing ever larger. Although the work was hard and demanding it probably paid well, by the standards of the age, and, as an added bonus, could offer greater security of tenure to those lucky enough to be employed there.

The family found a new home at 148 St Catherine's Street, where all three brothers were born, then moved to a larger terraced house, with attic rooms, in nearby Somerset Road. With so many children to support, the extra space would have proved useful. It was here that Abel and

St Catherine's Street in Doncaster at about the time Bert was born there in 1898. (BS)

Frances guided them through their childhood to adulthood, with education occupying an essential position in all their lives. As an artisan in an age where having a trade could offer a passport away from poverty, the value of schooling would have been made clear to his offspring. Edith was the first to benefit from this encouragement and became a teacher herself. When Bert was 3, she married James Spouncer and moved to Scunthorpe and here she remained until her death in 1941.

By then, Ernest had left home. During 1899 he married for the first time and lived in Leeds. The relationship appears to have failed and in 1901 he returned to Doncaster, to be employed by the GNR as a coach painter, where in 1903 he married for the second time. In due course, he was joined in the works by brothers Harry and Fred, one as a Carriage and Wagon Wheel Turner, the other as a clerk in the workshops. So it is perhaps unsurprising that Bert would join them when his time at school came to an end.

In the meantime, a Britain which had undergone two industrial revolutions and advanced its empire throughout Queen Victoria's reign was finding its dominant position in the world challenged. Germany was now a unified nation with the ambitious Kaiser Wilhelm II on the throne, ever eager for an empire to match his grandmother's. A key to his expansion plans was a strong navy – both military and merchant – and so a massive shipbuilding programme had been set in hand. At the same time, the German Army grew rapidly in numbers and quality, rivalling anything potential enemies could put in the field. To guard against German expansionist plans France and Russia began re-arming and Britain's Royal Navy grew stronger too.

Britain also had to cope with growing opposition within its empire from those seeking independence from Victoria's distant rule, most notably in India. But of more immediate concern during Bert's early years was the war in South Africa, which lasted until 1902 and absorbed an increasing number of men from across Britain, but not, it seems, the Spencer family; it was a sad precursor of an even bigger tragedy that lay in the not too distant future.

The beginning of the twentieth century also witnessed a rise in the trade union movement and with it a clamour for better working conditions and pay. With few employment rights and an appalling level of health and safety in most industries, the need for change was a pressing one. But it was a process strongly resisted by many in authority grown used to unquestioning obedience. And so battle lines were drawn and the next fifty years witnessed an often bitter struggle, the old order refusing to give ground and the new order constantly pressing forward. There were some victories though. In 1908, a means tested pension was launched for the over seventies. Three years

The changing face of Doncaster in the early 1900s reflecting, as it did, wider progress across Britain. Bicycles were commonplace by then, but motorised transport was taking a huge step forward, in the process gradually displacing the horse. Trams and buses were becoming more commonplace and a few of the better off could purchase cars. This picture, taken in front of W.E. Clark and Co of Doncaster, and the advert captures these changes perfectly. (DN)

later, a National Insurance Act introduced a system of payments for those who could not work due to sickness or who lost their jobs. Neither scheme paid much, but at least it was a start.

Although something of a political backwater, Doncaster would see a rise in the number of women fighting for equality through the suffrage movement. For many, day to day survival in the face of poor living conditions and poverty was simply enough, but there was a growing demand for change which suffragettes and suffragists pursued in their own ways. With the formation of the Women's Social and Political Union in 1903, the protests became louder and more violent, nowhere more so than in Doncaster. In particular, Kathleen Brown's exploits became well known locally. This Newcastle-born, three times imprisoned suffragette moved to Doncaster where she continued her peaceful and not so peaceful protests. In one well known incident, she planned to blow up Wheatley Hall but the attempt failed. Such was her position in the movement that she was able to attract members of the Pankhurst family to the town to speak at several well attended events. Bert later remembered being taken to one by his mother and being 'roundly impressed by what I heard'.

While protest and the search for equality dominated many elements of life in the years before the Great War, there were many developments in science to observe and admire. Railways still dominated lives – for trade, commuting to work and, increasingly, pleasure – but the combustion engine was beginning to challenge their ascendancy. There were ever increasing numbers of lorries, cars and buses, with electric powered trams becoming a feature of town and city life from 1902 onwards, as power stations slowly grew in number. The creation of a national grid was still far in the future, but by the Great War a number of power stations had been built and were beginning to transform the way people lived.

Few people before the war had seen aircraft except in pictures and this had stimulated a great deal of interest in their development. In 1909, a number of flying machines were brought together for a display at Doncaster Racecourse. The week-long event drew huge crowds, including Bert, his parents and brothers, all eager to see aircraft in flight and racing against each other. There is nothing to indicate that the young man was interested in the design of aircraft or harboured a desire to fly them. Nevertheless, the excitement of the occasion was such as to lead him to purchase postcards of the event and cut out a press report, all of which he kept in an album.

Perhaps, of greater interest was the dominating presence of the railways in Doncaster. With a father and three brothers all employed by the GNR, conversations at home must have strayed on to their work in the offices and shops there. So, from the earliest, young Bert must have lived and breathed the culture and life of the railway. He later wrote:

Above left: Senior members of the WSPU were frequent visitors to Yorkshire and Doncaster – here on one occasion a party including Christabel (second left) and her mother Emmeline Pankhurst. Bert Spencer well remembered being taken to one well attended meeting. (JG)

Above right: One of Bert's souvenirs of the Doncaster Air Show held during October 1909. Fellow attendees included Arthur Peppercorn and W.O. Bentley, then premium apprentices at the GNR Works in Doncaster. Peppercorn, of course, would go on to be the LNER's last CME, and guide Bert's career for a time, and Bentley would later branch out into aero engines and cars with great success. (BS)

> My earliest memories are of being taken to watch trains go past and sitting on the platforms of Doncaster Station with my father or brother Ernest. They would describe each engine, tell me their names and how and where they were built. On several occasions, and before my father died, I was taken round the GNR's workshops and remember very clearly the noise and smell of oil mixed with steam and smoke. Early on I began collecting pictures of locomotives and carriages and read all I could find. I traced some of the engineering drawings I came across and gradually learnt how the locomotives worked. With the GNR the biggest employer in the area it seemed more than likely that I would end up working there, which was a prospect that did not worry me.

Although destined for the Works at some point in time, this does not seem to have placed a restriction on the way he viewed the world and all its possibilities. As is the way with gifted children, he read extensively and had an interest in a wide range of subjects, all of which was reflected in a good all round performance wherever he was educated. Later on he recorded that he attended 'Doncaster British Schools' until August 1911, but gave no other details except to say:

> They taught me the three 'R's', as they called them then, and used the cane very often, but the teachers did encourage me to read and make use of the Free Library at St George's Gate. It became one of my regular haunts, drawn by the books and periodicals and the warmth of an open fire on a cold day. I spent many happy hours there lost in works of fact and fiction.

In 1909, Bert was approaching the end of primary education and his future was probably the subject of much discussion. With reports from his teachers confirming how bright he was there would have been an ambition to attend the best senior school possible. With the cost of private education well beyond their means, the next best option would have been Doncaster Grammar School, which could boast an enviable academic record. Bearing this in mind, it is not surprising that places there were highly prized. Once again there would be a question of cost to consider, which would deter many, but such an outlay was probably more manageable than the cost of public schools. And for the less well-off there were scholarships to help defray the expense.

An Exceptional Student 15

(Top) Doncaster Station – one of Bert's regular haunts in childhood. (Middle – left and right) Two of Bert's souvenirs from the early 1900s – lithographs from old magazines he was given. He seems to have shown as much interest in those who worked on the footplate as to the internal workings of the engines themselves. (Right) A photo Bert collected which he inscribed with the words, 'Marshgate level crossing in 1906 or 1907 with the familiar sight of a Great Northern 0-6-0 saddle tank passing by with coal trucks'. (*BS*)

Above left: Doncaster's British School as it appeared before the Great War. Spencer recorded that he attended this school until August 1911 when he moved on to Doncaster Grammar School. It was situated in Chequer Road a quarter of a mile from his home. (THG)

Above right: Doncaster Free Library, at St George's Gate, as it appeared in the early twentieth century. For many, including the Spencer family, but most notably Bert, this facility was essential to their education and, through reading, firing their imaginations and broadening their horizons beyond the boundaries of the town. (THG)

There was also the issue of class to consider. There would have been an expectation that those attending such a prestigious school met certain standards of behaviour. Here those from poorer homes might stand out and struggle to gain acceptance as a result. Even in Britain today there are still these divisions, but in the 1900s these were even more pronounced, and a child might be ostracised for their accent or the poor quality of their uniform. It was hoped that scholarships for the very brightest would help ease these pupils' passage into school and help overcome any prejudice they might face.

For Bert all this was made more difficult by the death of his father in May 1911. It does not seem to have been an unexpected event, but must have been shocking nonetheless. However, with four wage earning children still at home the financial impact may have been lessened. His death may also have helped encourage the powers that be accept his son's application for a scholarship, which they did that spring. So, in August 1911, Spencer made his way to the grammar school where he would spend the next three years. He later wrote:

'It was a little daunting but I quickly made friends with several boys, including John Forster, who started at the same time. We were fellow cyclists and had much in common. He was a happy boy who loved sport. Like many at that time he did not survive the war, dying, I believe, towards its end.

Doncaster Grammar School as it appeared before the Great War when Spencer became a pupil there. It seems to have been the perfect place for this young man and gave him a sound education, particularly in the sciences. (THG)

With only a comparatively short period in which to make his mark it seems that Bert did not waste a moment of time and made full use of the facilities on offer at the school. His reports reflected the effort he made and his success, particularly in the field of science and engineering. So when graduating in 1914, it was perhaps inevitable that he would pursue a career that might fully exploit these growing skills to the full.

Locally there were a number of options to explore, most notably in the coal industry, with its massive presence in Yorkshire, and in the world of shipbuilding. In fact, one of his close friends, William Crabtree, went on to train as a mining engineer at Brodsworth Colliery with some success, and another as a marine engineer in Newcastle. Added to this there were also various careers in business for enterprising young men to follow, while attendance at university was not beyond the bounds of possibility, though its financial burden, without a sponsor, could be a heavy one indeed. Then, of course, there were many railway workshops around Britain, each eager to recruit promising students as engineering apprentices. And it was in this direction that he chose to move, probably influenced by his strong family connection with the industry and by his continued fascination with railways.

He later recalled that:

> Becoming an engineering apprentice of one sort or another was the aim of many young men at that time because it offered gameful employment for life. The best of these training schemes were run by railway companies and I considered, with the help of my family, a number of options, amongst them the Midland, the LNWR, the Lancashire and Yorkshire as well as the GNR. I chose the last of these because the interview I had with John Bazin, was followed by a brief conversation with Nigel Gresley as Locomotive Engineer, which went well. It probably helped that a local billet also suited my family situation.

Presumably the need to care for his widowed mother was a pressing concern for him.

In due course, he was offered an apprenticeship with the GNR and entered their Works at Doncaster that summer. At the same time, he enrolled in a course run by the local Technical College's Mechanical Engineering Department, presumably directed there by his new employer. With war erupting across Europe as a back drop and Britain's entry into the conflict during August, it was an inauspicious time to begin a career. But being just 15 meant that military service would not be possible until 1917 at the earliest.

Of his three brothers, only Fred seems to have joined up. In 1915 he was attached to the rapidly expanding Royal Army Ordnance Corp and, in due course, he served on the Western Front, being demobbed in 1919. By this stage, many jobs in the railway industry, particularly in

The sprawling mass of Doncaster Works as it appeared in the 1920s when Spencer worked there as a draughtsman. (THG)

the workshops, had been classified as reserved occupations by the government and this meant that both Ernest and Harry were excused military service. It remained to be seen whether Bert would follow suit when he came of age

For the time being though, the GNR beckoned and to their workshops he went on 31 July that year to begin his five-year apprenticeship. A month later, he attended his first classes at the technical college. Of this first year he later wrote:

> There were ten of us starting at the same time, but only two attended college from the beginning. I had stated a preference for learning draughtsman's skills when speaking to John Bazin [Assistant Works Manager] and later the Locomotive Engineer, which they, having questioned me closely, thought to be a good idea. They also looked through a number of drawings I brought along to the interview, having been encouraged to do so by my mother, and seemed favourably impressed.
>
> Over the next five years I spent time in each of the workshops observing what they did and learning to use much of the plant and machinery. It was interesting but not particularly enjoyable. I much preferred the cleanliness and order of an office job. So I was happy when from my second year onwards I spent ever more time in the Drawing Office, where the Chief Draughtsman, William Elwess, closely supervised my education. The classes at college, which included mechanical design and construction, freehand, perspective and technical drawing, advanced mathematics and much more, complimented all that I learnt under Elwess. Throughout the five years Bazin oversaw everything I did and was quick to criticise and encourage when necessary. Despite the difference in rank he became a friend and something of a father figure to me.'

Spencer's comments about 'cleanliness and order' are quite revealing, especially for someone who had chosen to work in the dirt and grime of heavy industry. Later, his wife would observe that he 'was a fastidious dresser and always well turned out, as was his mother, and was neat and tidy in all he did. Not one for digging the garden or heavy manual work except when entirely necessary'. It was a state of mind which Eric Bannister, a future assistant at King's Cross, would capture when he wrote:

> Although Spencer occasionally rode on the footplate to assess an engine's performance he never wore overalls, but a good suit, so carefully avoided getting dirty. He was more than happy for me to take on the grimiest duties and scramble about on or the engines when seeking to spot a problem or correct a fault. I was more than happy to do this.

Clearly, in these early years John Bazin and William Elwess strongly influenced Spencer, with Gresley a slightly more remote figure in the background, due to his senior rank. By this stage both men were vastly experienced, having worked for Henry Ivatt, before Gresley took over in 1911.

Bazin, who was born in London in 1879, was himself a GNR apprentice. Such was his success that early in his career he was singled out for senior rank. In fairly short order, he rose from Assistant District Locomotive Superintendent at Colwick to

John Ralph Bazin Assistant Works Manager at Doncaster when Bert Spencer began his apprenticeship there in 1914. He proved to be a mentor, a good tutor and encouraged the younger man to develop his skills through the acquisition of academic qualifications. (THG)

District Locomotive Superintendent at Peterborough, then, in 1909, he moved to the works post at Doncaster where he took on responsibility for the company's apprenticeship scheme. He was someone who actively encouraged his students and insisted that they extend their qualifications by attendance at the local technical college. There is little doubt that he took a paternal interest in Spencer and encouraged him in his personal studies and, perhaps, other aspects of life. As a member of the Institution of Mechanical Engineers he saw many benefits in membership and actively encouraged and proposed the applications of his best students, including Spencer.

Elwess was an even older hand. He was born in 1867 at Intake Farm, a family concern in Wheatley on the edge of Doncaster. His mother died when he was three and his father, also William, was left to bring him and his two brothers up alone until re-marrying. The 460 acre farm appears to have been a successful business, employing twelve men. But the agricultural life does not seem to have appealed to the younger William and so, in his teens, he sought employment as an apprentice with the GNR, when Patrick Stirling held sway as Locomotive Engineer. Like Spencer much later, he chose to work in the Drawing Office and in 1906 rose to become Ivatt's much respected Chief Draughtsman. As such he would play a key role in the younger man's development and career.

All that happened in his early years in the Works was overshadowed by the war. It cannot have escaped Spencer that at any time after his 18th birthday in 1917 he might be called up and find himself at the front. He would have been in no doubt about what this could mean, having noted the ever-lengthening casualty lists appearing in the newspapers each day. And several friends he'd made at the Grammar School had been killed so providing a an even starker reminder of the cost of war. Being able to claim reserved status because of his work would have provided a degree of reassurance, but also presented a moral question – where does my duty truly lie, at the front or at home?

Spencer did not record his thoughts on the matter or describe any struggle of conscience he may have had, so divining his feelings is impossible now. All we know, for sure, is that he saw out the war without a break in his apprenticeship to qualify with honours in 1919. However, he like many others would have been faced with an ethical dilemma that existed between those who had gone to war and those who had not. For many veterans there was a growing anger and

Above left: Sport played an important part in the life of the GNR and then the LNER, with many events supported by senior managers. On this occasion, a cricket match appears to have drawn together three important men in Bert Spencer's development and career. According to Spencer's writing on the back of this print, Nigel Gresley stands on the far left of the group and William Elwess dead centre in the back row, wearing a straw boater. John Bazin, in cricket whites, sits on the far right in the front row. (BS)

Above right: The Boiler Shop at Doncaster as it would have appeared during the early years of Spencer's career. (RH)

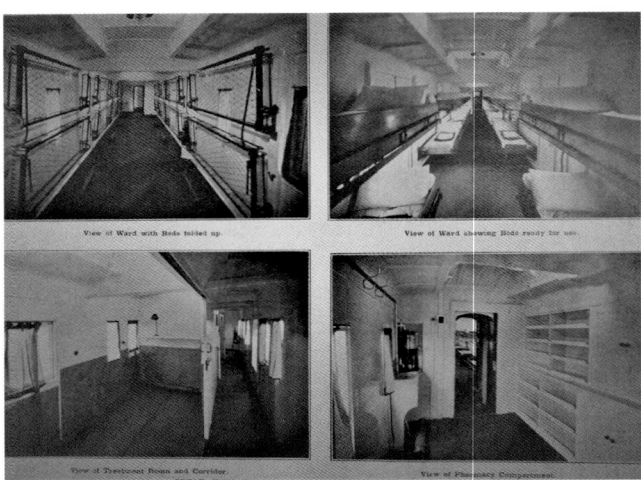

This group of photos, and a written description of the work entailed in fitting out hospital trains, were kept by Spencer suggesting that he may have been involved in this sort of work as an apprentice on the shop floor or in the Drawing Office. (BS)

resentment that the 'stay at homes' had prospered in their careers while those in uniform had suffered and lost out. With recession and hardship following the conflict, it was a feeling that did not dissipate quickly or easily. However, there is little doubt that Bert's mother would have been mightily relieved to have her youngest son safely home, no matter what the moral consequences would have been. And, to be frank, it was probably better to be safe and sound and working hard to rebuild a damaged country than be unnecessarily slaughtered like millions of others on the Western Front, in a war that could so easily have been avoided.

As Spencer's apprenticeship drew to a close, with Bazin and Elwess' backing he spent some months with the Lancashire and Yorkshire Railway's Horwich Works as a draughtsman. One can only guess at the reasons for this, but they seem likely to have been driven by a desire for wider experience. Gresley himself had spent a short time there in 1899/1900, under the tutelage of the company's CME, John Aspinall, so may have encouraged his young apprentice to follow suit. There was also the issue of further education to consider. Spencer's skills were such that attendance at university was a real possibility and an ambition that many were beginning to hold. And it proved to be the case with him. With Liverpool University only a short train ride away from Horwich he took advantage of its close proximity to attend classes and begin the process

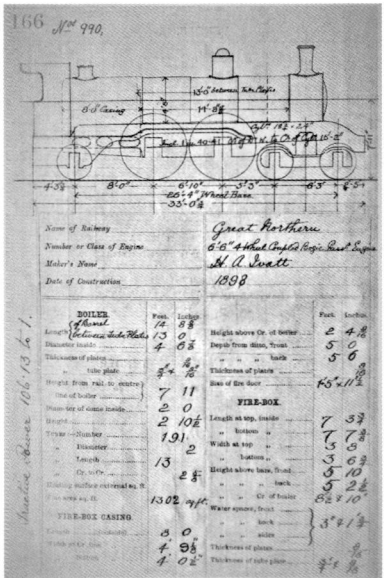
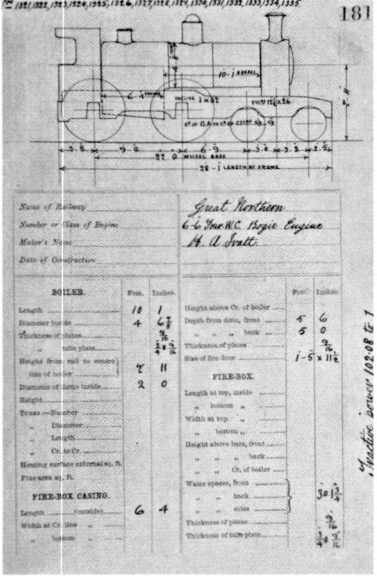

Left and far left During his apprenticeship, and to help in developing his skills as a draughtsman, Spencer kept a journal in which he drew some of the locomotives employed by the GNR – adding facts and figures about each locomotive. It was a good way of learning and it was a practice he kept up throughout his career, though as the pressure of work increased at King's Cross, in much less detail. (BS)

of obtaining an engineering degree. Pressure of work and the need to earn a living seem to have made its completion impossible, though.

Whilst at Horwich, he came under the direct control of the L&YR's talented Chief Draughtsman John Billington and his deputy Edward Gass, with George Hughes as CME having oversight of all they did. There is some evidence to suggest that he became involved in the design work of 0-8-0 tender engines and a single battery powered electric locomotive. This may be so, but his input would have slight and undoubtedly focussed on minor design issues, as they would have been at Doncaster until he was fully qualified.

Spencer's posting was essentially an educational one and in Billington he had a worthy guide. Ernest Cox, who worked at Horwich for a time, later recalled the impact Billington had on his staff and locomotive design in several letters and notes he made for his book *Locomotive Panorama*:

> Of humble Fylde coast parentage, and of short stature and slight build, Billington had a brilliant academic brain [he was a Whitworth Exhibitor]. From an early age he had marked himself for recognition by gaining distinction in the educational field and would go on to become a lecturer at Horwich Mechanics Institute. As Chief Draughstman [he took over from Zachariah Tetlow in 1912] he controlled not only the steam locomotive office, but also the electrical design office in which he made a huge impact ... He was a hard task master and did not suffer fools gladly ... However, he was a born teacher and loved to impart his knowledge to those who would listen at work or in the classroom.
>
> As a designer his ideas were sound and innovative ... He was trusted by George Hughes implicitly to turn out good designs ... He had a preference for big engines at a time when the L&Y's and then the LMS's senior managers were against such proposals. In this he was in tune with Gresley ... History would show them both to be correct in their views. Here Gresley succeeded, but it took until Stanier became CME of the LMS for Derby to change direction ... If Billington had lived [he died in 1925] he might have reached a more senior rank.

By the time Spencer returned to the GNR in the summer of 1919, Bazin, after missing out on two promotions at Doncaster and with the war ending, had looked for a new challenge. He successfully applied for the position of Works Manager to the Great Southern & Western Railway in Ireland and then became its CME at Inchinore two years later. Of his friend and mentor, Spencer later wrote:

> I was sorry to see him go, but there did not seem to be any promotion in the offing for him at Doncaster. He was an ambitious man and was, I believe, capable of becoming a Chief Mechanical Engineer in one of the larger companies, and this is what happened. I suspect but do not know whether he discussed his position with Gresley, but assume he did and this led to his departure. I think it unlikely that there was any animosity between them. Their relationship always seemed a harmonious one to me.

A photo taken in 1912 when a group of 'old boys' from the Lancashire and Yorkshire got together for a reunion. It demonstrates the close link that existed between Gresley and his former comrades at Horwich. It may also explain why Spencer was seconded to the company towards the end of his apprenticeship. (RH)

(Above left) John Billington with his wife Frances. Some considered that the L&Y's young Chief Draughtsman to be one of the great railway engineering talents of the age. Under George Hughes, the CME, who mentored him from a young age, he actively pursued two Pacific designs and much more. Sadly, he died in 1925, before his promise could be fulfilled. (Above right) Billington's capable but less talented assistant Edward Gass, who would direct Spencer on a day-to-day basis whilst at Horwich. (Left) George Hughes, to the right of the schoolboy in a kilt, the L&Y's CME, standing to his right is Guy Granet, General Manager of the Midland Railway who became a leading figure in the LMS. (RH)

(Left) The Drawing Office at Horwich. Spencer's work place for some time. (Right) His colleagues whilst there, Edward Gass fourth from the left front row. (BS)

Above left: A scene typical of life in the Erecting Shop of the L&Y at Horwich at about the time Spencer worked there just after the Great War. 0-8-0, No. 392 is being 'wheeled' as Spencer wrote. (BS)

Above right: Crimpsall Erecting Shop at Doncaster in 1919 at the time Spencer completed his apprenticeship and began working as a draughtsman. The crowded state of the workshop suggests that much was going on in the immediate post war years to reverse the ravages of very heavy use and reduced maintenance during the previous four years. A Gresley Class 01 2-8-0 is suspended under an overhead travelling crane operated by a female worker. During the war years, the number of women employed by the GNR increased rapidly, but just as quickly they went down post 1918 as soldiers returned from the front to reclaim their jobs. (RH)

I was always grateful for the help he gave me and it was him who confirmed my permanent appointment to the GNR shortly before he left for Ireland. We kept in touch for many years.'

When finishing an apprenticeship in those days, there was no guarantee of employment with the company with which you trained. So for a short while Spencer would have lived with some uncertainty over his future. But with the railways seeking to recover from the ravages of four long years of war, there would be a pressing need for experienced workers to speed up the rehabilitation process. In his case, such a gifted student would have been quickly identified as someone worth retaining and this proved to be the case. With John Bazin as advocate and mentor, plus Elwess and Gresley's support, his passage into a permanent job as a draughtsman was assured. There is little doubt that the Locomotive Engineer would have been fully aware of the potential of all his apprentices and been careful to select those with the greatest promise. Spencer, who was rated 'an exceptional student', was clearly one of these.

With his position secure, Spencer could look forward to a long career, but, as always, it remained up to him to work hard and prove himself worthy of promotion. But first there was a need to establish himself and build a solid reputation for good work. And during these early years with Elwess, he found himself being given the 'occasional special project by the CME', as he later called them. This was a sound technique for a senior manager to adopt when dealing with raw recruits. By this simple means they could establish the progress being made and test their potential for higher rank. At the same time, the individual would probably learn many valuable lessons, not least of all how to speak to and deal with those in power. For some this could be a daunting experience, but Spencer seems to have dealt with the challenge well and quickly learnt the best way of dealing with such powerful men. He later wrote of these experiences:

Gresley would often visit the Drawing Office and happily discuss with one and all his ideas. He liked to give tasks to the young and inexperienced men, to test them and see how they

A photograph taken of Nigel Gresley in the 1920s when Spencer was gradually establishing himself as a draughtsman and designer of note at Doncaster. The impression he made on the Locomotive Engineer seems to have been a slowly growing one, Gresley testing the young man out with occasional projects. It was probably a technique he employed with a number of people and the likes of Oliver Bulleid and Arthur Peppercorn undoubtedly benefitted from this early patronage. (RH)

would react. It may have been one of the ways he learnt himself when starting out and it certainly worked. He would set aside time in his very busy schedule to listen to their answers and proposals, with the full agreement of the Chief Draughtsman, who might in other circumstances have felt by-passed.

He believed that learning didn't have a limit and should be pursued as a matter of course through education and the study of other people's work in many fields of research. We were encouraged to join relevant bodies such as the IMechE and ILocoE, participate in their work and keep up to date by reading their journals as well as the 'Engineer', 'Gazette' and other magazines, but also follow the course of various patents, files of which we retained. I was also encouraged, early in my career, by Bazin, to submit and present papers, which I did on three occasions (at meetings of the ILocoE in 1924 – numbers 158,166 and 171) and comment on others. We were also encouraged to attend institution annual dinners where contacts could be made and renewed.

William Elwess and later on Harry Broughton, were also very keen on newcomers getting involved in this way and even encouraged us to raise issues we thought important, provided that we were sure of our ground. Gresley's influence on my career was only very slight at the beginning and was limited to a few special tasks. For example, he asked me to consider the layout of the Pacific's cab. In this I adopted a side-window layout similar to those seen on some Great Eastern engines. I was pleased with the result and showed Sir Nigel during one of his visits. He liked it and ordered it to be fitted in place of a traditional GNR cab. After that the number of small tasks he set me increased.

For Spencer, 1919 was a good time to begin work in the Drawing Office. With the war out of the way there was much to do. Released from the restrictions the conflict imposed, Gresley could begin developing his ideas on locomotive design again, which resulted in a flood of new work for both the draughtsmen and the shop floor workers.

In the years before the conflict, Gresley had not rushed into a major building programme. Instead, he took time to develop his ideas, drawing inspiration from contemporary work being undertaken in Britain and the USA. In particular, he studied the work of George Churchward at Swindon and urged those like Spencer to do likewise, as the young man later recalled:

Gresley was guided by Churchward's work and there was clearly a close link between both men. The subject of locomotives on the GWR and the way their Locomotive Superintendent ran his development programme was a frequent topic of conversation at Doncaster. Gresley would often say 'Look at what they are doing at Swindon and consider how you can apply their practices and ideas to your own work'. When Churchward retired in 1925 there was a notable slackening in the progress being made at Swindon and so our

One of the first engines Gresley built for the GNR following his appointment as Locomotive Engineer in 1911. There were only 10 H2 2-6-0 constructed, the first No. 1630 appearing in 1912, and the remainder, of which this is one, a year later. It was a modest start, but a notable one nonetheless. (*BS*)

interest waned considerably. Nevertheless, Gresley remained in touch with Churchward until the latter died in 1933 and still drew upon the great man's undoubted skills when advice was needed.

Once clear on the direction he wished to travel, Gresley began work on a 2-6-0 design – the two-cylinder Class H2 – which first appeared in 1912. Only ten were built, but it was probably an interesting project on which to cut his teeth and begin the process of trial, error and evolution so crucial to the development of any designer. During 1913, he took the 2-6-0 concept a little further by adding seventy-five H3s. But on this occasion, he increased the boiler size from a 4ft 8in diameter by 10 inches, as he later recalled:

> The power of an engine depends upon its capacity for boiling water. The boiler is therefore without question its most important feature … Mr Ivatt's first Atlantic engine had comparatively small boilers … The larger boilered Atlantics have proved to be much more powerful as express engines and are able to haul much heavier trains and keep time … Later on when the 2-6-0 type was introduced the first ten had smaller boilers. The later ones had boilers 5ft 6in diameter, but the grate area was the same in each case, and the engines in other ways were identical. During the last year's work the ten engines with the smaller boilers consumed about 5lbs more coal per mile than the engines with larger boilers.'

The first two classes of 2-6-0s were followed by an initial attempt at building a heavy goods 2-8-0 locomotive. In 1913, the first of twenty of these two-cylinder Class O1s appeared; a design clearly influenced by Churchward's Class 2800s that were introduced in 1903. Despite these developments, neither the H2/3 or O1s contained the degree of innovation Gresley's post Great War designs would embrace and did not reflect his growing belief in the advantages to be gained from three-cylinder engines, fitted with a conjugated valve gear. It was here that he would make his name and follow a path that would take him on to his celebrated Pacifics.

The first step of this process came in 1918 with the appearance of a single Class 461 2-8-0 engine. Although Spencer seems to have had no direct involvement in this project, he keenly observed the way it evolved and, in 1947, during a presentation to ILocoE members, gave a considered view of Gresley's ideas and the way that they were formed:

> Gresley was a firm advocate of the three-cylinder single expansion locomotive, but contended that if two, instead of three, main valve gears could be used, as in certain four-cylinder engines, one of the principal objections which from time to time has been urged against three-cylinder engines would be removed.

By the time Spencer began his apprenticeship, Gresley had been Locomotive Engineer for barely three years. So, by 1914 he had only just begun to experiment with new designs before the war came and much was put on hold for the duration. The need for heavy goods engines was an important requirement and his first, the two cylinder 2-8-0 Class 01, appeared in 1913. His next version, the single three-cylinder Class 461 (seen above when built in 1918), is deemed to be his most significant design up to this date. In this engine he introduced the idea of a conjugated 2 to 1 valve arrangement, so eliminating the need for a third set of valve gear. It was an idea he continued to refine with Spencer's help for some years with some success. (RH)

His first three-cylinder engine with conjugated valve gear was a O2 mineral engine, No. 461, with 4ft 8in diameter coupled wheels and 18in x 26in cylinders which left Doncaster Works in May 1918. All three-cylinders drove on to the second coupled axle and were inclined at 1 in 8 – the extent necessary to enable the inside crosshead to clear the leading coupled axle – to cranks being at 120 degrees to each other.

Gresley was granted a patent for conjugated valve gears in 1915, there being two forms of gear. In the simple form the three valves are in the same horizontal plane, the middle valve being at the side of its cylinder. Two levers operate in the same plane as the valves, a 2 to 1 lever pivoted to a bracket between the frames and attached at its outer end to one of the outside valves.

The alternative form covered by his patent was the arrangement adopted on No. 461. The Walschaert gear on either side drives the outer rocking shafts which operate the outside valves. An extension of each rocking shaft terminates in an arm to which is attached the levers operating the middle valve.

No. 461 gave rise to much criticism both with regards to the necessity for inclining the outside cylinders and the additional number of joints involved in the conjugated valve gear, as opposed to the number of joints necessary in a third independent valve gear. Mr H. Holcroft [up to 1914 an engineer working for Churchward at Swindon, before moving to the South Eastern and Chatham Railway], who had carried out much investigation into the design of three cylinder engines,[and patented his design in 1909 before letting it lapse] pointed out that horizontal outside cylinders and the simple form of Gresley's gear could be used by displacing the centre crank from the 120 degrees setting by an angle equal to the inclination of the outside cylinder and locating the centre cylinder steam chest horizontally at the side of the inclined cylinder. These changes were successfully embodied in the next 2-6-0 type, the H4/K3.

When recalling these events, Spencer remained fairly non-committal on the direction Gresley's thoughts were going. Yet as a junior draughtsman at Doncaster he must have witnessed first-hand the work as it unfolded, listened to many conversations on the subject and prepared some of the

In 1920, with Spencer now an established member of the drawing office team, Gresley's next key design appeared – the three-cylinder Class H4 2-6-0s. In these engines, he combined a large 6ft diameter boiler with a greatly refined version of the conjugated valve gear. Ten of these engines, of which No. 1001 was the second, were built followed by another 183 by 1925. (RH)

drawings for Elwess and Gresley to consider. He must also have been aware of the controversy that surrounded the use of three cylinders coupled to a 2 to 1 gear. It was not simply that some saw limited merits in adopting this solution, but they then questioned Gresley's right to claim patented rights in the face of Holcroft's earlier development work. Accusations of plagiarism will inevitably arise when two or more parties are seeking to develop a solution to a common problem. While Holcroft was not prepared to go this far, perhaps sensing that the designs were sufficiently different, a suspicion remained in some minds that there had been some degree of imitation.

In describing these events, Spencer maintained a diplomatic stance, which may not have reflected his true feelings on the matter. However, when questioned on the effectiveness of Gresley's work with three cylinders and the conjugated valve gear in 1947, he gave a fairly robust response to one critic, though couched in polite terms as befitted two members of the ILocoE:

> Mr Cox referred to Gresley's policy of applying the three-cylinder design to locomotives in instances where the power required could have been provided by two-cylinders. Whilst the two-cylinder engine may be cheaper and more accessible for maintenance, the three-cylinder engine has advantages which were considered desirable even in the smaller types. The more uniform smokebox draught action of the three-cylinder engine was found to react favourably on coal consumption and the lighter running gear could be more easily handled by the shed staff.

Whatever the reaction of fellow engineers to his three-cylinder locomotives – and opinion remained divided on their effectiveness – in the early 1920s, Gresley was firmly set upon a course that would see most of his new engines built this way. As the years passed and the performance of some of the three-cylinders engines began to cause concern, it would be Spencer who played a

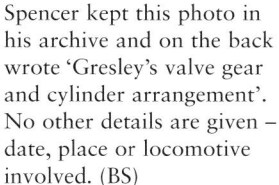

Spencer kept this photo in his archive and on the back wrote 'Gresley's valve gear and cylinder arrangement'. No other details are given – date, place or locomotive involved. (BS)

leading role in helping Gresley resolve them. But for the moment, he was increasing his knowledge and expertise under the experienced, ever watchful eye of Elwess.

With the start of the new decade, Gresley set in motion his most ambitious plan to date, the development of a Pacific class engine. So it must have been with a keen sense of anticipation and mounting excitement that the draughtsman at Doncaster began scheming out the layouts for two prototype locomotives to be ready for service in 1922. Spencer recalled that:

> [My colleagues and I were] aware that something was in the wind and a high degree of secrecy was the order of the day. We heard rumours that the North Eastern Railway were working on their own Pacific at Darlington and we were imbued with a sense of rivalry and wished to be first. Of course, by this stage the GWR's Great Bear had been running for many years, so the GNR's Pacific would not have been the first in the field, but Swindon had abandoned theirs and were only concerned with building more of their impressive 4-6-0s.

The need for a Pacific had been on the cards for some time and rumours had been circulating for a while that the GNR might be producing one. So expectations were high that an engine of this type might soon appear. So some were surprised when Gresley merely introduced his H4s in 1920. No matter how much interest they created, with their large boilers and three-cylinders, it was not the same as a large 4-6-2 rolling from the works to take on an ever-increasing volume of heavy express trains. The sense of disappointment was probably best summed up by Cecil Allen who wrote in the May 1920, 'so the new Great Northern main line locomotive turns out to be not a 4-6-2 Pacific, but merely an enlarged version of the Mogul!'.

But if the railway world was waiting with bated breath for such a new engine, Gresley was in no desperate hurry to oblige the waiting crowd, preferring instead to see how his early experiments with three-cylinders and conjugated valve gear went. If these developments were flawed there would have been little point in risking his reputation and the company's money in such a high profile way. As a scientist, he was imbued with the need to test and evaluate and so it was not until late 1921 that work on the new Pacific began in earnest.

When, in his 1947 presentation, he described this major step forward in design, Spencer played down the impact the A1s had made. In fact, his words barely caused a ripple, so understated were they:

> The increasing necessity on the GNR for an express passenger engine of greater power than the Atlantic type led to the adoption of a 4-6-2 type three-cylinder engine. The first of these engines, No. 1470 *Great Northern*, was the forerunner of the LNER streamlined Pacifics, was completed at Doncaster Works in April 1922. Classified A1, these engines had

Gresley continued developing 2-8-0 types with his 1921 introduced three-cylinder Class 02, the first of which is captured in this photograph. (RH)

6ft 8in diameter wheels and 20in x 26in cylinders. The design incorporated the form of Gresley gear employed on the H4/K3 and later 02 Classes, the outside cylinders being placed horizontally over the bogie, and the centre cylinder being inclined at 1 in 8 and located over the rear axle of the bogie. As in the case of the H4/K3 and 02 Classes, the drive from all three-cylinders was taken by the second pair of coupled wheels.

Other distinctive features were the fitting of a 6ft 5in diameter tapered boiler with combustion chamber and the use of a nickel-chrome steel for the pistons, coupling and connecting rods.'

As the project slowly progressed the working relationship between Gresley and his draughtsmen drew ever closer. He was someone who took a 'hands on' approach and involved himself in the fine detail of the design as Spencer later recalled:

Gresley always paid close attention to all parts of a design, whether large or small. He took a particular interest in the cab arrangements for No.1470 and a full-size wooden model was erected in the pattern shop at Doncaster before the engine was built. This was inspected by all and sundry, but particularly the 'top link' drivers and firemen who were encouraged to voice their opinions, and these we considered in refining the layout. But before building this model there was much discussion over of the most suitable height at which to place the

Amongst his collection of papers, Spencer kept a number of drawings showing the layout and fine detail of the first two A1 Pacifics, far more than any other locomotive he worked on. These are just three of many examples. Although his words when describing this project were brief and understated in his 1947 paper to the ILocoE, the significance of this design may be gauged by the sheer volume of material he kept. The A1s set the pattern for what followed over the next thirteen years in Gresley's Pacific programme. (BS)

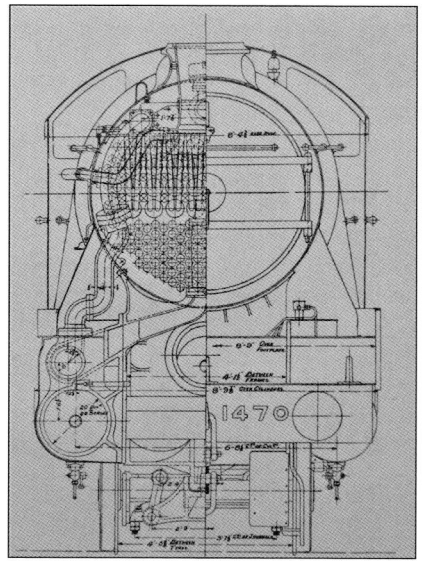
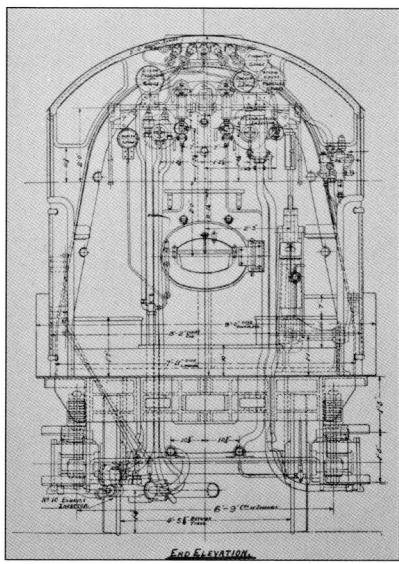
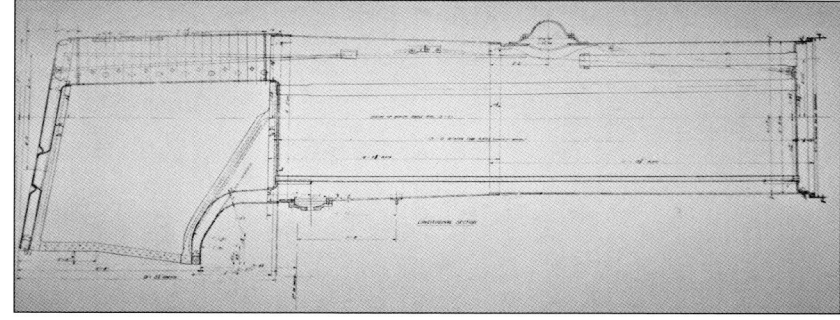

Spencer also kept a series of photos showing No. 1470 being built at Doncaster, each one covering a different aspect of manufacture, testing and assembly. As an up and coming young designer, he was clearly fascinated by the project, was obviously eager to learn from all he saw and play an active part in its development and construction. He later wrote that 'working beside a skilled leader and his team was a wonderful experience and taught me much at an important stage in my career'. (BS)

firehole of the new class in relation to the cab footboards. To obtain a better idea of this Sir Nigel had chalked upon one side of a Drawing Office desk an oval shape representing the firehole. Then towards this he shovelled imaginary coal with his walking stick until he was certain that we had the correct height for a fireman off average build. When the wooden model and then the locomotive were built he would examine them with the same critical eye, making changes as necessary. He was a perfectionist.

Once 1470 was in traffic, followed by 1471 in July, a period of testing quickly followed. Interest in its performance was inevitable and many, including Gresley would have sought time on the footplate to observe how well they worked. Spencer, according to notes he left, managed to get three rides beside the driver on 1470 and a couple on her sister, presumably still wearing a suit:

[I] Handled the controls as instructed by the crew, experiencing the surge in power when the regulator was applied and the wheel slip, which we soon realised was quite common on the Pacifics. For a time, it became a not uncommon sight to see the second engine running under test with a shelter around its front end to protect the engineers monitoring its performance in this precarious position. They were mostly used between Doncaster and London and proved themselves capable of handling 600 or more ton loads of 20 bogie carriages. During these runs the engines averaged 70 mph on the level and could take the steep gradient on Stoke Bank at 45 mph.

Following the successful performance of the first two engines the construction of a further ten was authorised by the GNR, all of which left Doncaster Works in 1923, including No. 4472 *Flying Scotsman*.'

At this stage, Britain's railways were about to undergo a profound change. The proliferation of companies that had existed for so long were deemed by government to be serving customers poorly. With the face of Britain changing in the wake of the Great War, during which the railways had been virtually nationalised, the inefficiencies of the old system were laid bare. However, Lloyd George and his Cabinet shied away from central control and voted to group the companies into four large regionally based businesses where appropriate. And so the GNR became permanently linked with, amongst others, the North Eastern, Great Eastern and Great Central to form the London and North Eastern Railway with its base at King's Cross. And in the jockeying for position that followed, Gresley beat off any rivals to be appointed Chief Mechanical Engineer and to London he moved in 1923 to begin work.

For Spencer, like all his fellow workers, this opportunity brought with it a great deal of uncertainty, which only the passage of time and the security of a job could help assuage. For the moment he remained rooted in Doncaster and awaited events to unfold, hoping they might run in his favour. He probably did not realise that Gresley had undoubtedly 'talent spotted' him and was only awaiting an opportunity to bring the young man into his immediate entourage. But it was a change that would not happen overnight and awaited a period of calm to allow the new organisation to bed in and discover what it needed to do.

(Top) The first A1 No. 1470 *Great Northern* and (Below) No. 1471 *Sir Frederick Banbury*. The first of Gresley's Pacifics as they appeared in 1922 when both were new. Their arrival created a great deal of interest in the railway industry and the press, representing as they did a major step forward in locomotive design. By comparison with what had gone before, they were very large engines indeed, with dimensions that suggested great power. Only time would tell how good they were; until then the GNR could bask in a wealth of good headlines. (RH)

Chapter 2

Front and Centre

In the immediate aftermath of grouping, the most noticeable changes seemed to be at top, with any ripples spreading out from these changes only gently influencing the long established order. But this could not be expected to last, because one of the aims of amalgamation was to remove duplication of effort and make the whole enterprise more efficient. All this would mean changed roles, staff reductions and even closures or redundancies. Such a complex process can take many years to complete, allowing natural wastage to take effect as senior managers decide how best to take an organisation forward. The sense of uncertainty this engenders does not go away, but the passage of time can soften the disruption and the blow when it eventually falls.

For those in the Drawing Office at Doncaster there was still plenty to do, with the first phase of the Pacific programme to complete and other continuing Gresley projects to consider – the O2s, H4s and the J23 0-6-0 tank engines, a programme that began in 1913 and would run on until 1939, by which time 102 had been built as J51/J52s, as the LNER called them. And when it came to future tasks, it may have occurred to some that Gresley might favour his old team over those at Darlington, Gorton and Stratford as rationalisation ran its course. Spencer recalled the uncertainty they must all have felt:

> Few, if any, discussed their fears about redundancies or transfers, but I suspect we all felt this way. There was little the Chief Draughtsman could do about it except to say keep your head down and work hard. Times were different then, of course, and to complain was to mark yourself down as a trouble-maker. For myself it was not so bad. I had a job, I was well qualified and felt that if the worst came to worst I could find another job in the railway industry or shipbuilding at a pinch. There was also the rapidly growing aviation industry which certainly attracted me with its promise of working in a very advanced scientific field, but would have meant leaving my native Yorkshire and my family and girlfriend.

When the LNER came into being, Gresley inherited a large, diverse fleet of locomotives of various types to work with. There was little standardisation and little money to do anything to bring some rationalisation to bear. In the months before the change took effect, Vincent Raven had been pursuing his own dreams of building a Pacific and in late 1922 the first appeared, to be followed by another four by March 1924. With so many of Gresley's A1s soon to appear, it seems strange that the Raven Pacifics, which became A2s, remained in the programme. They were, according to Spencer, 'not much liked at King's Cross and some believed they should have been scrapped in favour of the A1/A3s long before they were'. The A2 shown in this picture, No. 2401 *City of Kingston upon Hull*, was condemned in 1938 and cut up the following year. (BS)

The ex-Great Central Railway's Locomotive Engineer, John Robinson, designed the Class 9P 4-6-0 No. 6164 *Earl Beatty*, which entered service in June 1920, is captured here at King's Cross in the mid-1920s. It was one of six four cylinder 9P express engines inherited by Gresley, which became B3/2s under the LNER's management. Spencer wrote that 'although powerful they proved to be poor steamers when working express services; very heavy on coal and leaked steam from around the piston valves. From the first it was apparent that some modification would be required, but this work was given low priority with only low dome boilers and chimneys being fitted. In due course four were modified with Caprotti valve gear, but the class remained mediocre performers until the end of their lives'. In *Earl Beatty*'s case, the modifications took place in 1939, about eight years before the engine was withdrawn from service. (BS)

Gresley was wrestling with much bigger problems than this though and had been stripped of the infrastructure that had surrounded him at Doncaster for support. To overcome this, he soon started building up a small team at King's Cross and began by recruiting Oliver Bulleid, then Carriage and Wagon Superintendent at Doncaster, to be his Principal Assistant. There is a suspicion that the younger man, once in post, tended to view himself as deputy CME, but this was far from the case. Arthur Stamer, who had substituted for Raven as CME during the war at Darlington, took on the role of Mechanical Engineer at Darlington and Gresley's deputy at the same time. He combined these posts successfully until retirement in 1933 and after which Gresley appears to have let the deputy post lapse.

Bulleid's son Henry, in his book *Bulleid of the Southern* captured a flavour of these early days when he wrote:

> When Gresley and Bulleid moved into the CME's offices along Platform 10 at King's Cross in April 1923 they controlled ten Works employing over 100,000 people and the maintenance and replacement of over 7,000 engines, 20,000 carriages and 300,000 wagons. For this large task Gresley wisely decided to use existing facilities and only direct and check from King's Cross where he therefore set up a small drawing office for scheme and checking work; he himself approved most loco drawings and Bulleid approved the remainder and all the carriage and wagon drawings.
>
> Gresley was meticulous with paperwork and all the important mail was placed on his desk each morning supported by the relevant files ... Preparing the mail for Gresley took a bit of time and Bulleid sometimes grumbled if he arrived early ... They averaged about four of the five-and-a-half working days a week ... Right from the start of the LNER

After Gresley, the next key player in the CME's new Headquarters at King's Cross was Oliver Bulleid (above left in the 1920s) (HAVB). Some describe him as a leading light in steam locomotive design, others that he was erratic and adopted a scatter gun approach to design – one idea amongst many being good the rest being impractical or creating unnecessary distractions. The relationship between him and Spencer was not an easy one, each being diametrically opposed in character and way of working to the other. (Above right) The daily view for the small team working in Gresley's London Offices – in this case a very busy Platform 10 sometime during the 1920s. (BS)

Bulleid was much more of a free agent than Gresley who had to attend many meetings of directors and senior officers and who was also in demand outside the LNER on account of his increased status. So, it was Bulleid who got around the vast new arena more often, who was delighted to know all that was going on, who succeeded in gaining the confidence of the new District Mechanical Engineers, and who already had the knack of keeping Gresley well and succinctly informed.

Sadly, Gresley died before he could write his memoirs and so we will never know how he viewed Bulleid, or for that matter anyone else he worked with. But his ebullient assistant lived long enough to leave a very interesting assessment of his greatly admired leader:

Gresley was the best Chief I had been under and our relations were of the happiest. He was incapable of ill-temper, but what I appreciated most was his wide interest in all engineering. He was always ready to adopt any suggestion, but only after very careful consideration. It could be felt that if he agreed to try anything it would certainly be a success.

He had a wonderful memory, was extremely observant, and amongst other things could read a drawing in a way given to few. Disloyalty was the one thing he did not tolerate. After all the head of a department deserves loyalty, unremitting service and obedience. He has also to be given all possible help to lighten the burden he assumes.

If this is so, later events would show that Bulleid did not always follow his own advice and his relationship with Gresley suffered as a result.

With the CME based at King's Cross and kept busy with myriad often competing demands, Drawing Office staff at Doncaster, long used to his frequent visits, found this had created a void that some missed. Spencer remembered that:

During his career, Spencer was an avid collector of anything connected to the development of locomotives in Britain and overseas. He seems to have been fascinated by the way engines evolved from the very beginning of steam's history and kept many charts, such as these two, which demonstrated their evolution. For obvious reasons, the GNR locomotives dominated this collection, but not to the exclusion of all others. Although there is no record of his visiting North America, like many of his fellow engineers he acquired a substantial amount of information about development work over there, particularly on Pacifics and streamliners. In this he was probably encouraged by Gresley, who looked more broadly as a matter of course. (BS)

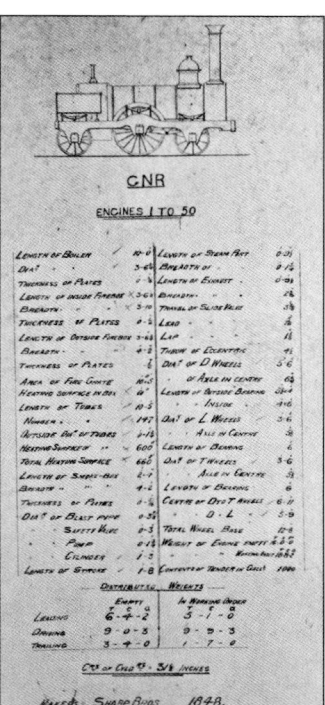
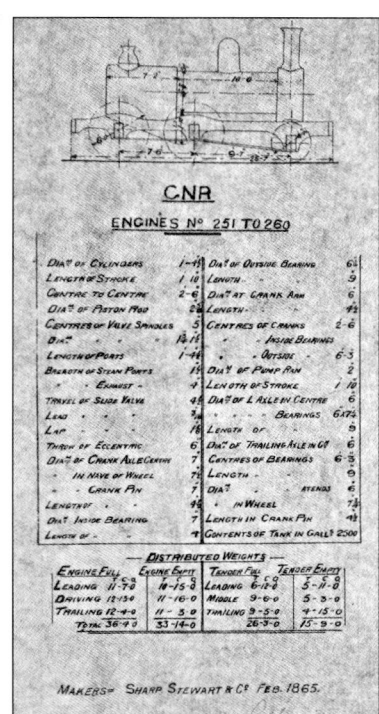

We junior staff lacked the sense of involvement we once experienced when Gresley would drop by to ask questions and test our skills. The older hands were far less concerned and you would hear the occasional muttered 'we can get on with our jobs now' when the subject of the CME cropped up. Now however, whilst there were far fewer visits the Chief Draughtsman received a constant stream of letters, memorandum and minutes giving instructions, seeking progress reports or simply offering advice – some with OVB's initials attached when Gresley was absent. However, as time went on, and his other duties allowed, the CME did pay us the occasional visit to seek information on various tasks current at the time. To me he seemed happiest when sitting with draughtsmen discussing issue of common interest, less so when involved in the nitty, gritty of workshop life. By nature he wasn't a production manager and preferred leaving this aspect of workshop life to those such as Frank Wintour, Robert Thom, Edward Thompson and Peppercorn who were all experts in this field.

It was at this time that Spencer became very friendly with Alfred Willetts, then a senior draughtsman on the carriage and wagon side of business. He later wrote:

Willetts and I worked together in adjoining offices under Harry Broughton, who was deputy Chief Draughtsman at the time and would, in due course, succeed Elwess. Although older than me we had much in common and Alfred's wife Lucy took my bride to be under her wing. Alfred became a specialist on rolling stock design and became the Carriage and Wagon Chief Draughtsman in the late 1920s. He was a practical designer who had very strong views on the need to strengthen the frames and shells of each carriage to make them stronger and safer. In this he disagreed with Gresley over the use of wood and advanced the case for metal bodies and frames, windows with rounded corners and much more.

There was one subject on which they both agreed – the way carriages should be styled – and wholeheartedly embraced a very modern look. In this they were both influenced by the fashion at the time for art nouveau in fixtures, fittings and colour schemes and developments in the United States. With carriages there was greater scope for this than the locomotives, but even here streamlining, colours and lettering were influenced by these fashions.

Fred remained a good friend until the end of his life and was a tremendous help when I was making my way in the world. He was first to offer advice when needed and he was somone I could always go to for a quiet chat, especially at crucial stages in my career. His knowledge of design was second to none and his work was crucial to the develoment of the Silver Jubilee carriage set that appeared in 1935.

It also seems as though Willetts and his wife Lucy were instrumental in Spencer meeting Elsie Mozley in 1922, shortly after the young woman returned to Britain after spending some time in the USA. She was the youngest of five children and the fourth daughter of William Mozley, who had become District Superintendent of the GNR at Doncaster in 1910, after a long career with the Great Central, and his wife Sarah.

It is unclear when Bert and Elsie first met or the course their courtship took before they married. But with a father and a husband both working for the GNR it seems likely that they moved in the same circles and may have met at some social function, of which there were many in Doncaster. How such a senior offcer viewed the courstship of his daughter and the young draughtsman from the backstreets, whose brothers were craftsmen in the Works, is not recorded, or if there was any friction between them because of their different backgrounds. But it was hardly a whirlwind romance, so Mozley would have had the chance to get used to the arrangement. However, it is interesting to note that the marriage only took place shortly after Elsie's father retired and was living in Cleethorpes, Lincolnshire.

While this relationship was flourishing, Spencer became even more deeply involved in locomotive design and seems to have relished the opportunity to observe and analyse Gresley's work at close quarters. He later wrote, 'Bill Elwess and the senior draughtsmen encouraged me to get involved in all aspects of locomotive design, spend as much time as possible on the footplate observing engines working first-hand and think for myself in finding solutions to the day to day problems we faced.'

It is not known to what extent Gresley encouraged Spencer in these endeavours or, for that matter, whether he was even aware of the young man's developing talents. All we know for certain is that by 1923/24, the CME's small HQ team was increasingly hard-pressed to meet his needs. Gresley had a sufficiency of administrators, but not engineers. Put simply, he needed specialists who understood design and construction, who could follow his train of thought, develop the

Although larger engines attracted much attention and designing them held greater kudos, the lesser locomotives, such as this 1907 N1 0-6-2 tank engine No. 1552, employed on suburban commuter services around North London, proved of equal attraction to Spencer throughout his career. His papers contain many reports about them, plus photos such as this, and many pages of notes about their performance. He seems to have undertaken a special study of the type, whether directed to do so by Gresley is unclear. One thing is certain, though – he often travelled behind them, when commuting into London daily from New Barnet, from 1925 until 1941. (BS)

concepts he championed, produce drawings, then help smooth the passage of his ideas through the main drawing offices and workshops. In addition, working so closely to the centre of power called for men who were diplomatic, yet confident in their ability to deal with senior managers, often in very stressful situations.

When candidates were being considered for the London office, some might have been surprised to hear Spencer's name being mentioned in connection with the post. Here was a man who was only 24 years of age and still a junior draughtsman learning his trade. By any standards, such a promotion could come with some risks, not least of all selecting someone for such an important position who could not manage the stress or pressures. Luckily, Spencer seems to have been made of sterner stuff and would soon prove that he had all the necessary skills Gresley needed in an assistant.

It was during this period that Spencer became active in presenting papers for publication by the ILocoE, which he joined in 1919/20. For such a clever, innovative engineer this is not surprising, but the volume of work he produced in 1923/24 is. It was a feat he never repeated in a long career and in fact only produced one other paper and this was his 1947 eulogy to Gresley. It is hard to understand why this was so, but the most likely reason is that these papers were written and presented to help establish his name, encouraged by Elwess. For a confident, outgoing, intelligent man such as Gresley, writing and presenting learned papers came more easily. Spencer was cut from quite different cloth so he would have found the whole process much harder. At all times he displayed a natural reserve, so while writing a paper would have posed no insuperable problems, presenting it to a large audience of fellow professionals was quite another matter. In addition, when he became Gresley's technical assistant, often working six days a week and late into the evening, he would not have had time to do anything but serve his leader.

It may have been a short-lived output, but it was an interesting one, nonetheless. In late 1923, his first paper (No. 158) tackled 'Features of Locomotive Design'. During his brief presentation, he advocated the use of the Belpaire firebox and the Walschaert valve gear, but did not stray too far into the thorny question of three-cylinders or Gresley's conjugated valve gear. He then went on to discuss the differing views on hornblock and axlebox slides, concluding that 'in many cases it would be possible to unite the left and right-hand axlebox slides in one casting and form an effective frame stay'. In so doing it would 'reduce the intensified forces and the bending of frames caused by increased axle loading and journal lengths as locomotives became bigger'.

His conclusions did not receive wide support, although neither Gresley or Elwess were present, the audience appearing happier to maintain the status quo and avoid too much change. But the CME and Chief Draughtsman would have undoubtedly applauded his efforts and supported his wish to try something new. His next two papers, in 1924, elicited a similar response. In the first of these, No. 166, he tackled the question of piston valves and superheating. Then in paper No. 171 he produced a robust argument in favour of the Walschaert Valve Gear over the Stephenson version. Once again, he attracted a negative reaction from some in the audience. In his response, he seemed unfazed by this criticism and remained adamant in his views, a response which the equally innovative and inventive Gresley probably noted with some interest.

Exactly when Gresley recruited Spencer to work directly for him is not clear. There seem to be two possibilities here. One is that he took on these duties at Doncaster shortly after Gresley became CME in 1923. The other, which seems more likely, is that the transfer took place in 1925 when Spencer moved his home from Yorkshire to London. Either way, it followed an interview with Gresley once the extent of the work to be undertaken by the HQ team had been established. On this issue, Spencer provided no clue and Bulleid, who would surely have been part of the process, left no word either. So the only information we have comes from Geoffrey Hughes, who, in his book *Sir Nigel Gresley*, recorded that:

In his interview with Gresley, which led to him being appointed to the CME's staff, Spencer said that Gresley talked for a long time about the Pacifics, and was very interested when

The changing face of King's Cross in the 1920s as Gresley's Pacific programme came to fruition and most express services along the East Coast Mainline were served by these engines. Only five or so years earlier, this scene would have been dominated by Ivatt's Atlantics. (RH)

Spencer mentioned he had looked into the possibility of modifying the valve gear. The topic was further discussed when he was installed at King's Cross. The impression seems to be that by 1925 Gresley was aware of the need to alter the extent of the valve movements, but with the engines still being built, this was not the moment to decide on an expensive modification.

Hughes' account is interesting because it suggests a reason why Spencer was chosen for such a demanding post – his knowledge of the Pacific programme and how these engines might be made even better. If this is true, and there's no reason to think it is not, such a view would have had to be expressed carefully. Gresley was known to be very sensitive to criticism of his three cylinders and conjugated valve gear, so Spencer was possibly on dangerous ground when bringing the matter up. It says much for his honesty, tact and growing reputation that the conversation took place at all, was deemed to be a positive contribution and selection followed. And so he became the CME's Technical Assistant on matters concerning locomotives.

In his book *The Gresley Influence*, Hughes described what Spencer found when arriving in London:

'The CME's HQ staff was miniscule by today's standards ... Overlooking the old main departure platform 10, Gresley worked with a small personal staff of whom the senior was Oliver Bulleid, dealing with special projects and outstation staff. Bert Spencer was there as technical assistant on locomotive design and Frank Day as carriage and wagon assistant. The Electrical Engineer was Henry Richards, who came from the London, Brighton and South Coast Railway in 1924 and there was a small clerical staff (led by Bill Massey, then Harry Harper).'

Apart from his input on technical matters, Spencer also became a keen observer of the way the HQ team worked, its dynamics and its frictions. Late in his life, he recorded some of his memories in a series of letters. One in particular is of note because he described the relationship between Gresley and Bulleid:

They were like chalk and cheese. Each skilled in their own way, but without the CME's careful handling his assistant could have wasted much time on work that probably would not have led anywhere...There were disagreements and lively discussions, as you would expect from two such forceful men who held strong opinions and could produce fresh ideas with little apparent effort. I think Gresley used me as a filter to keep Bulleid's ideas in check.

During his career, Spencer was an avid taker or collector of photographs, mostly of trains, but not exclusively. Other subjects included architecture, street scenes particularly in and around London, the countryside and much more. Here a photo from his collection captures C8 (ex-NER Class 4CC) 4-4-2, No. 730, awaiting departure from an unidentified station in the north. This engine was built by Wilson Worsdell, the NER's CME, but is thought to have been the work of his Chief Draughtsman Walter Smith. This locomotive would have been of particular interest to Spencer because it was one of two prototypes built during 1906/07. They had four cylinders but were fitted with different forms of valve motion – 730 adopted the Stephenson type and 731 the Walschaerts. They were both fitted with Schmidt superheated boilers in 1915. In service they were based at Gateshead from where they hauled express services until 1933. (BS)

> Sir Nigel had the ability to absorb ideas and vast amounts of information very easily. Then in carefully prepared submissions took people along with him to such an extent that they came to feel that the idea had been theirs all along.

From these words it would be easy to assume that the modest, self-effacing Spencer played little or no part in these developments, just observed the evolution and supported the CME where he could. But in building up Gresley's role during his 1947 presentation, he minimised his own contribution, which was considerable. Yet to fully understand why he did this we have to appreciate the nature of this unassuming man and the way he saw his role as Gresley's assistant. Late in his life he wrote:

> I believe that one of my main roles, and that of the Chief Clerk, was to support Gresley by providing him with an outer office that kept disturbances down to a minimum while maintaining a degree of confidentiality. Men of his great intelligence need time to think without the many distractions that inevitably come their way. Beyond that I would assist him in refining the technical ideas he was constantly developing and converting his rough sketches into a more formal specification for the Chief Draughtsman to consider.

He later added:

> I kept many of his sketches and remember well him calling to me, 'Spencer here's something I want you to look at, get me out some drawings will you!' and then being handed several sheets of paper often lined, covered with rough sketches. A few days later we would pore over these plans and gradually his ideas would take shape at which point he would call in the Chief Draughtsman and Bulleid to get their point of view. More often than not he wouldn't give them any forewarning of what he would lay before them, believing that first reactions were always more revealing.

Eric Bannister, who would later assist Spencer at King's Cross, observed the way the two men worked and Spencer's astute understanding of the CME's needs and his own role in smoothing the passage of many ideas that flowed from Gresley's HQ:

> HNG was a pleasant man to work for. He did not like interruptions to his train of thought, so BS and I waited until he asked us – with the well-known twinkle – for our opinions. We presented the facts as we found them, knowing HNG would make some comment which would automatically cause a re-assessment of opinion and so lead to another conversation. He would always consider carefully before reaching a decision and we were never kept in suspense because of the 'third copy procedure'. When I first went to King's Cross, BS warned me that HNG did not appreciate criticism of his marine big-end nor his conjugated valve motion, but otherwise he encouraged original thought.'

So here we have a highly intelligent, highly trained engineer with sufficient wisdom to understand a great man and support him in the best way possible without thought of self-promotion or reward. In so doing, he gained Gresley's trust and earned his undoubted respect.

Another day and another locomotive to photograph. While the glamourous express trains were a great draw, Spencer still sought out more mundane engines on lesser duties. Each picture tells a story and for an astute engineer it could provide a wealth of information to study and assess. On this occasion, B16 4-6-0, No. 1460, is photographed on frieght duties at an unrecorded location. Thirty-eight of this class, then known as S3s, were built by Vincent Raven for the NER. Post grouping, another thirty-two were constructed under Gresley's management. In due course a number would be rebuilt as B16/2s and B16/3s, projects in which Spencer probably took a hand. Ths class lasted in service into the 1960s. (BS)

One of Spencer's roles as Gresley's assistant was to make sure technical information was distributed to all parts of the CME's organisation. Much of this was achieved by a series of Circular Letters, which were, essentially 'advise and inform' documents. It could be a laborious, time-consuming task, but it was key to ensuring business was conducted effectively and safely. This example was produced by Spencer in early 1925, it is one of many that appeared each year. He kept copies of them of which this is an example. (BS)

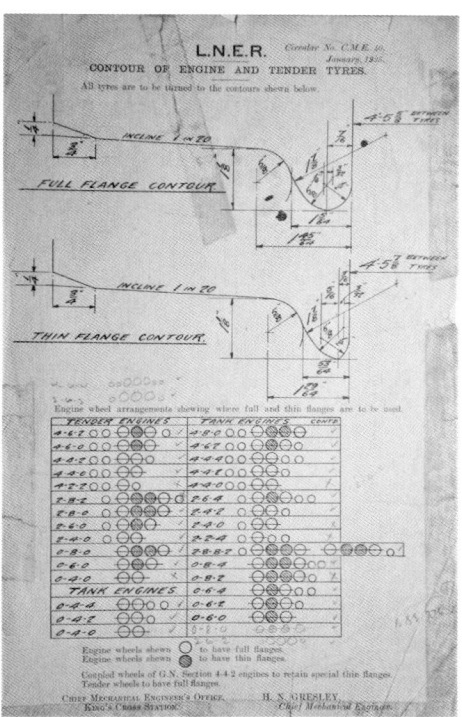

However, in forming such a close rapport with Gresley there was a danger that this might cut across the CME's relationship with Bulleid or even cause some friction between them. From the way Bulleid described his working relationship with Gresley – being a free agent, acting as his eyes and ears, providing a focal point in the office, sifting and prioritising mail and much more – it seems fairly certain that he relished this way of doing business. Whether he could manage all these tasks satisfactorily is quite another matter, of course.

Then Spencer arrived and all of sudden there was another gifted engineer, capable of taking on much of Bulleid's management and advisory role on the locomotive side of business. Perhaps he did not see this as a threat to his position; it did after all free him from many of the more mundane tasks, leaving him time to pursue more interesting projects. For such a dynamic and ambitious man this could be a huge advantage, but he had to accept that this might reduce his contact with the CME and so undermine his ability to shape events in the way he once did.

Some idea of the relationship that existed between the two assistants may be gained from the fact that Bulleid resolutely failed to make mention of Spencer when recalling the twelve or thirteen years they spent in adjoining offices at King's Cross in the accounts he left. And then when commenting on Spencer's well-considered ILocoE paper of 1947, in which he described Gresley's work, his first words were couched in somewhat caustic terms. 'The author has missed an opportunity of describing some of the little troubles and little touches which he might have included in the Paper ... Any discussion of the Paper must be somewhat sketchy, because there was so much about which one could talk for hours.'

He then went on to describe locomotive developments in which he had played a leading part, something he seems to have believed Spencer covered in insufficient detail, presumably to Bulleid's detriment. This may be so, but as the presentation was about honouring the memory of an exceptional engineer and leader, its purpose was clear. And in two hours there was little time to do anything more. But the absence of wider recognition of his part in these events seems to have played on Bulleid's mind, others in the team less so, judging by the comments made by them over the years. One, Harold Harper, who had for a long time been Gresley's Chief Clerk and confidant and personally witnessed these events from close quarters, felt moved by Bulleid's words to praise Spencer for the author's own contribution to the Gresley legend:

I think it ought to be known that the author should have some credit for the introduction of the long lap valve gear on the LNER Pacific engines as, although he himself had not said so, it was largely through his efforts that the decision to alter the gear was made.

From this it seems likely that Bulleid and Spencer did not enjoy an easy relationship. The essence of this was probably captured best by Eric Bannister who wrote:

> A very clever man, Bulleid was rather eccentric and he had some strange ideas. Indeed, he seemed to have a new one every week and of those one a year would be brilliant ... BS used to say, 'What other mad idea has he got?' His ideas, many of which wouldn't really work, are typical of some of the Southern engines that he produced. Some of these were good in many ways but, like him, a bit eccentric!

For the mild mannered and reserved Spencer, these were critical words indeed. There was, undoubtedly, respect for Bulleid's engineering skills, but perhaps not for his working methods, which seemed to lack the self-discipline and the team working abilities of Spencer. But despite these obvious differences, they had to work together and support Gresley as best they could. Yet, in the long term, it was arguably the consistency and reliability of Spencer's unselfish contribution that would prove of greater value to the CME as he tackled many difficult issues. Despite their differences, though, they probably both agreed on one thing – Gresley was a man worth following and supporting to the best of their abilities. Despite their differences, in character and approach, the three of them together made an exceptional Headquarters team, each bringing their own particular skills to bear in achieving a creative dialectic of great strength.

And so Spencer settled into this new world in London. At first he occupied temporary accommodation very close to where both Gresley and Bulleid lived in north London, but this changed on 3 December 1925 when he and Elsie were married in Cleethorpes. After a brief, very wintry honeymoon on the Continent, they soon settled into their new home at 93 Longmore Avenue, New Barnet, where they would live until 1941. Of these early years together, Elsie later wrote:

> We were very happy there, but Bert worked very long hours, quite often six days a week. On many occasions he did not get home until very late at night, having waited in the office for the CME to return from a trip or simply to complete a pressing piece of work. He admired Sir Nigel tremendously and felt it was an honour to serve him. He never complained.

At home he set up a small office equipped with a drawing board and library and would quietly work there when the opportunity arose. He would often show me very detailed drawings of the Pacifics, particularly the streamlined engines and much more, often adding the words 'Gresley wants these out very quickly'. Work was his relaxation, although he enjoyed regular trips to the cinema as well, comedy films being his favourites – Buster Keaton, Laurel and Hardy, who he met some years later, and Will Hay. This was something of which he became fond when growing up in Doncaster and continued to do so for the rest of his life. He also regularly bought *Punch* Magazine which would help pass his daily journeys to work and

Thought to be a picture of Elsie Mozley (front row seated wearing white) and members of her family just after the Great War. Elsie was a well-educated and well-travelled young woman. Before marrying, she spent a considerable period of time in the USA. (BS)

New Barnet became the Spencer home from 1925 to 1941 and Bert and Elsie appear to have led a happy life there. (Top left) One of Spencer's photos showing New Barnet Station. Many of his pictures simply caught the atmosphere of a station and were not concerned with passing trains. (Top right) Their home at 93 Longmore Avenue as it appears today. It is only a short walk to the station. (Bottom) A view of New Barnet from Longmore Avenue, as it appeared between the wars, captured in a postcard from one of Spencer's albums. (BS)

back. He kept several cartoons and had them framed to sit on the wall in his office at home. Each, of course, had a train theme.

He also discovered photography very early on in his life and learnt how to take and develop pictures when attending technical college. Throughout our married life he would often be found at New Barnet Station taking pictures, or, for that matter on any of the mainline stations around London. He would always study designs and assess performances, even when we were on holiday in Yorkshire, Scotland, Wales or the West Country. He was a true devotee and enjoyed attending meetings of Institutions, dressing up for many formal dinners. For such a shy man he could be quite forthright when assessing fellow engineers or when it came to the business of building locomotives. He was a perfectionist in all he did.

Sadly, we were unable to have children, which was a sorrow to us both. We both came from large families and enjoyed having siblings, though Bert being the youngest by some way did not enjoy having brothers as playmates of his own age.

As he settled into a happy personal and professional life, Spencer's thoughts often returned to the work he had begun at Doncaster into ways the new Pacifics might be improved. With so many in service, any shortcomings would have become quickly apparent with the valve gear being of particular concern to him. From the first, Gresley seemed loath to change, no matter how much his new assistant urged him to do so. So it was not a quick process and only came about because of Spencer's ingenuity, sound reasoning, dogged determination and an incident during 1925 which cast a shadow over the A1 programme. In his 1947 presentation, Spencer briefly described what happened. 'In April and May of 1925 an event took place that had a far reaching effect on the development of LNER locomotives. An exchange of engines took place and trials were carried out on both the LNER and GWR lines between Gresley's Pacific and Collett's 4-6-0 type Castle.'

FROM THE GENERAL TO THE PARTICULAR
Young Lady (who has never travelled by this line before). "Do you go to Kew Gardens?"
Booking-Clerk. "Sometimes on a Sunday, miss, on a summer's afternoon!"

REGULAR IRREGULARITY
Passenger (in a hurry). "Is this train punctual?"
Porter. "Yessir, generally a quarter of an hour late to a minute!"

It is said that one sure guide to a person's character is their sense of humour. According to his wife, Elsie, Bert Spencer found these two *Punch* cartons so amusing that he had them framed and hung on his office wall at home. The wit is dry, gentle and work related, suggesting a mild sense of humour and the ability to see fun in the world around him. (BS)

Why the LNER's board felt it necessary to sanction these trials is unclear, because the two companies did not compete over the same primary routes. It may simply have been a case of hurt professional pride. In 1924, the GWR and LNER each had one sample of their locomotive fleets on display in the Palace of Engineering which was a key part of the Wembley Exhibition. So the A1 *Flying Scotsman* and Castle Class 4-6-0 No. 4073 *Caerphilly Castle* sat closely together. Somewhat provocatively, GWR managers placed a large placard on their engine claiming it to be the most powerful class then working in Britain. It was a proud boast, based on the activities of the 4-6-0s working on the high speed Cheltenham Flyer service, and one likely to elicit a strong reaction from their rivals. With the ever-increasing search for good PR a gauntlet had been thrown down that the men at King's Cross felt unable to ignore. Bert Spencer later recorded a more considered view of these events:

At the time it was thought by many to be an unnecessary distraction. The tests were not scientifically based, recording only timings and fuel consumption, so offered little to analyse or compare. There was a suggestion that the full range of analysis then available through the use of dynamometer cars should have been brought to bear, but this seems to have been ignored by all except Sir Nigel. As a result, I do not think he involved himself in the trials willingly, seeing little value in them from a scientific point of view, and so was bowing to pressure from Whitelaw and Wedgwood. However, the issue of the Pacific's coal consumption had become a topic of some discussion, with views being expressed that it could be improved. The GWR trials were seen by some as helping bring this debate to a head.

My personal view was that this problem was more likely due, in part, to the drivers who were more used to the Atlantics and adopted their practice of long cut-off, with the regulator partially open, when driving the Pacifics. There was also an issue, which I raised with the CME, about the valve gear employed on the A1s. He was interested in work I had been doing, under Frances Wintour's guidance in the Drawing Office, on possible modifications to the valve gear [although Spencer mentions Wintour, who was the Mechanical Engineer, he may have meant to write William Elwess or Harry Broughton, who he worked for at the time].

The exchange trials that sought to compare the GWR's Castle Class 4-6-0s with the LNER's A1 Pacifics was an 'unnecessary distraction', or so some at King's Cross and Doncaster thought. They believed its sole purpose was publicity driven, with no true scientific base to warrant such an exercise. As things turned out, it proved even worse than they feared it would when the Castles appeared to outperform the bigger 4-6-2s. (Top left) A1 No. 4474 *Victor Wild* gets underway from Paddington, while (top right) Castle Class No. 4079 *Pendennis Castle* departs from King's Cross with a 475 ton load and (bottom left picture) is captured in md-stride on her way northwards. (Bottom right) A picture of contrasting styles as an A1 joins its GWR cousins (BS)

The CME looked at the drawings I had prepared a few months earlier. It seemed to me that he had been considering changes to the extent of valve movement for some time, being aware that the original design was flawed, but was loath to change the design until the engines were due for general repair. The trials in 1925 did help speed the rate of change though.

The GWR engine, weighing less than 80 tons, proved to be lighter on coal than its 92 ton LNER rival and, as a consequence, Gresley decided to revert to the use of long lap valve gear as it was clear that this feature of the Castle was mainly responsible for its superior performance.

The provision of short lap valves on the A1s was the outcome of early experience with the Gresley gear on the 2-6-0 K3 class. In actual practice the short lap valve gear made it necessary to run the Pacifics at comparatively late cut-offs and towards the end of 1924 consideration was given to the fitting of long lap valve gear to permit earlier cut –off working. The scheme was not proceeded with as it was not felt that the extensive alterations to the outside valve gear then proposed could be justified in view of the successful performance of these engines on main line duties. Early in 1925, however, the centre valve was given an additional 1/16in lap to counteract the effect of over-travel on the centre cylinder output at high speeds.

Following the exchange tests of April-May 1925, Gresley began to experiment with long lap valves on the Pacifics. The valve gear of engine No. 4477, *Gay Crusader* was modified and trials were carried out with valves having 1 5/8 in lap. The results were most satisfactory in spite of the fact that only the minimum amount of alteration had been made to the existing valve gear.

The success of this experiment led to the fitting of the completely redesigned outside valve gear originally proposed in 1924 ... The first engine to be fitted with the new valve gear was No. 2555, *Centenary*, [work completed in March 1927], and in comparison with Pacifics having the original valve gear the average coal consumption with trains of approximately 500 tons between Doncaster and King's Cross was reduced from 50 to 38lb. per train mile.

All existing Pacifics were subsequently altered in a similar manner to No. 2555 [as and when they entered a period of maintenance or repair] and the modified gear was fitted on all future engines of this type. The improved engine performance was an important factor in the successful running of the non-stop Flying Scotsman between London and Edinburgh inaugurated on 1st May 1928 and the high speed trains that went into service some years later.

From these words, it would easy to assume that the modest Spencer played little or no part in these developments, just observed the evolution and supported the CME where he could. But this was far from the case as an impartial review of the available evidence quickly reveals. Let us begin with Spencer's own words on the subject and how he came to identify the problem and suggest possible solutions:

From the earliest it seemed to me there was room for improvement, especially in the matter of coal consumed and the problem stemmed from the short travel valve gear. It seemed to me that fitting a long travel valve gear that increased the expansion ration was the obvious solution. Alternatively, discard Gresley's conjugated valve gear completely and revert to two cylinders or replace the 2 to 1 with three independent sets of Walschaerts valve gear.

So we have Spencer quietly working on ways of improving the valve gear in the years before becoming Gresley's technical assistant. Then we have a change of attitude almost forced on the CME by events and a growing awareness that something needed to be done if his Pacifics were to reach their full potential. It is to Spencer's great credit that he persevered with his ideas and eventually moved Gresley towards them. The difficulties he faced in doing so might have intimidated a lesser man, especially in the face of the 'CME's sensitivity to any criticism of his conjugated valve motion', as Bannister put it. So, to understand how this change of heart came about, we have to move away from Spencer's 1947 account and look more deeply at the way events unfolded in the months following his transfer to King's Cross. But in unravelling this story we face one simple problem – there are several versions that do not, in truth, always match up. In

Spencer later recorded, 'I often wondered around King's Cross station and the surrounding area to observe locomotives in operation, not simply when arriving or departing from the station. You could tell a lot from this'. This photograph captures a scene typical of daily life in the late 1920s, with what appears to be the 1924 built A1 Pacific No. 2545 *Diamond Jubilee* in the midst of preparation for her next duty. (BS)

addition, some detail seems to have grown in an apocryphal, often unattributed way so ensuring that elements of each account are difficult to verify. In this situation it is easy to understand why Spencer chose to recall events in the simplistic, unambiguous way he did in 1947.

All the accounts I have seen seem to agree that Spencer was indeed pursuing ways of improving Gresley's valve gear from as early as 1922 and saw a long travel version as the solution. Likewise, it seems to be agreed that in 1924, Gresley's growing concerns about the A1s led him to increase the steam lap on the centre valve only and in this way hopefully eradicate the problem. As a result, in March 1925 he directed Wintour at Doncaster to fit a modified set of piston valve rings to the centre valve of engine No. 4474, to create a longer steam lap. During the tests that followed, an improvement was noted and so Gresley instructed the Mechanical Engineer to begin modifying all but one of the remaining A1s, with No. 4475 first up so she could participate in the exchange trials.

Despite this, Gresley was still prepared to experiment, perhaps as a concession to his insistent young assistant. So he agreed that engine No. 1477 (soon to be 4477) should be equipped with long travel valves similar to those fitted to the Castle Class, to see how she compared with the other A1s undergoing modification. According to the locomotive's record card, this was completed between 18 and 20 February, but it took until August for the first indicator tests to be carried out. Spencer by all accounts was not involved in this work and is quoted as having said 'it was a botched up job, with more emphasis on using existing components than on getting good valve events'. So it probably came as no surprise that the hoped for improvements were not forthcoming.

Following the A1s' questionable showing during the exchange trials, Gresley again addressed the problem that had taxed him for so long, but still seems to have considered Spencer's ideas regarding long travel valve gear interesting but not necessarily correct. His reasons for this are thought to centre on the belief that the A1s' trouble stemmed from the uneven and excessive wear of the broad piston valve rings and the amount of steam that then escaped. Gresley also seems to have believed that long travel valves would be subject to greater wear, followed by a rapid drop in efficiency. So any benefits that might accrue from their use might quickly be outweighed by other

Above left: When modifications to a design were considered, as they were for the A1s valve gear in the mid-1920s, selection of a locomotive appears to have been a random exercise at times. Spencer later recorded that 'It was generally a case of modifying any engine that was in the works for minor repairs at the time. Only occasionally was a specific engine selected'. So we shall probably never know why No. 4474 (above) was chosen, in March 1925 to have a modified set of piston valve rings fitted to its centre valve in the hope that this would create a longer steam lap and improve its performance. (BS)

Above right: Next up in Gresley's programme of modifications was No. 4475, *Flying Fox*, here photographed at King's Cross. Before being detached for the GWR/LNER exchange trials, this engine underwent the modifications first tried with No. 4474. (BS)

1477, soon to be re-numbered 4477, makes a striking impression when being turned at King's Cross. Spencer's argued his case so well that Gresley agreed to fit this A1 with long travel valves similar to those used by the GWR on their Castle Class locomotives. He wished to see how it compared to the other A1s undergoing modification. Spencer was unimpressed with the standard of work undertaken at Doncaster and so was not surprised when no improvement was forthcoming. (RH)

considerations. All well and good if his modifications to the valve gear had proved successful, but the results were poor, despite more tinkering around the edges. For example, in early 1926 it was decided to fit narrow piston valve rings, the existing rings not producing a steam-tight fit and so the valve travel wasted considerable amounts of energy. As a result, the A1s began being fitted with Knorr type piston valves, which seemed to improve performance, but not as much as Gresley hoped it would.

One can only imagine Spencer's frustration as he observed this happening, but events were moving in his favour. Towards the end of 1926 Gresley finally relented and agreed with Spencer's proposal to set up a modified version of the long travel valve gear at Doncaster for testing purposes. On this occasion he superintended the work himself and paid great attention to the way the work was carried out. So, for example, the connection between the foot of the radius link and the eccentric rod was lowered and the radius of the link foot joint was increased from 1ft 6in to 1ft 9in.

This had the effect of making finer settings at short cut-off possible. Bench testing allowed Spencer to refine the design still further and on 13 December instructions were given to fit the new valve gear to the next Pacific entering the works. This happened to be No. 2555, *Centenary*, which was in the shops for repair to its left hand piston rod and a cracked cylinder. Work began on 30 December and the engine was back in service on 25 March ready for testing. Whereas trials with 4477 had, Spencer believed, been poorly managed with such things as valves being set when cold and no allowance being made for expansion, no such mistake was made with *Centenary*. This attention to detail was crucial and trial running soon revealed that this engine performed better and burned significantly less coal than A1s with the old valve gear – 38lb per mile against an average of 50lb.

Yet even with such obviously good results Gresley still seemed loath to abandon his original idea. But he was not blind to the possibilities and in April ordered that two more A1s, No. 2549, *Persimmon*, and No. 4480, *Enterprise*, be fitted with Spencer's valve gear for use during the very busy summer season. And so, in July they began running and quickly confirmed the favourable

Above left: And so the experiments continued. Spencer was not prepared to give up on what he saw as an essential modification to the Pacifics. After overseeing further refinements to the design, the latest form of valve gear was fitted to No. 2555. Under test conditions this engine performed well and burnt significantly less coal per mile than her sisters. (RH)

Above right: With Gresley still loath to change his design two more A1s – No. 2549, *Persimmon*, (above) and No. 4480, *Enterprise*, were fitted with the modified valve gear trialled with No. 2555. Over the course of the Summer Season that followed, both engines ran well and finally convinced Gresley that the changes pursued so doggedly by his young assistant were of great value. (RH)

impression established by *Centenary*, though Gresley is reported as still being a doubting witness to this accomplishment, even when faced with such clear evidence of success.

According to one account, the CME's position only softened in May 1927 when he took the opportunity to ride on 2555's footplate, from Doncaster to London, to see for himself what she could do. This seems to have been a 'Saul on the road to Damascus' moment. And having seen the light, Gresley moved quickly to implement the ideas Spencer had been championing for so long, seemingly ignoring his own concerns over excessive wear of the broad piston valve rings and the loss of steam this might cause.

It is said that on arriving at King's Cross he immediately sought Spencer out, praised him for his work and directed that all of the Pacifics be converted when they were passing through the workshops. This may be an apocryphal tale, but it is pleasing nonetheless. Spencer remained quite guarded on this point and only wrote that 'the CME when convinced of the validity of a proposal would move swiftly to implement it, as was the case with the long lap valve'.

Wherever the truth might lie, it is a fact that Gresley did issue an instruction on 14 May initiating the Spencer-inspired modification programme. However, it proved to be a slow process and it was not until 1931 that the last two locomotives, Nos. 2545 and 2557, were completed. By then Gresley's A3 'Super Pacific' programme was well into its stride, each of this new class showing the benefit of Spencer's development work. In 1935 they would be followed by the A4s.

It seems clear to me that this issue, and the way Spencer handled it so effectively, established him as a man of great skill and dedication who would, without fear or favour, serve the CME faithfully, no matter how difficult things became. In the highly politicised and competitive world of the railways these were rare qualities that any leader would value highly. And so the scene was set for many years of great achievement and the birth of the Gresley legend, ably assisted by men of substance amongst whom Spencer occupied an increasingly important place. In the meantime, though, the LNER and much of British industry, faced a growing problem that would finally explode with great violence during 1926 with dramatic consequences.

Chapter 3

Innovation or Stagnation

The 1920s were years of great social upheaval in Britain. In a slow burning campaign, begun in the nineteenth century, greater equality had been sought, but progress had been painfully slow. By the time the new century dawned there had been some successes, most notably in the field of employment rights, but so much more waited to be accomplished. As frustration with the lack of government action grew, so did the levels of protest and violence. In a land where wealth,

The General Strike of 1926 which Spencer witnessed first-hand. He collected a number of photographs and press cuttings that recorded these events. (Top and lower left). The police used baton charges and horses to break up protesting groups even when the demonstrations were peaceful or contained children. (Lower right) Outside King's Cross station a man going to work, and deemed to be 'strike breaking', was badly beaten by protesters and severely injured. It was a time when, as Spencer recorded, 'things could have quickly got out of hand and we expected civil war to break out such was the anger and violence often displayed by the police and strikers.' (BS)

privilege and comfort were enjoyed by a lucky few, and many simply lived in abject poverty with few rights, this was inevitable after four years of sacrifice in the trenches. Pressure for change grew exponentially year by year, with the battle for better pay, living and working conditions and women's suffrage being at the centre of the struggle.

The Great War created an environment in which many of these issues could be carefully side-stepped by politicians and the ruling class. But the sacrifice of those condemned to fight in the trenches and those suffering great loss at home sharpened the need for change once the conflict had ended. The extension of voting rights helped release some of this tension, but the establishment was slow in meeting other demands and by the mid-1920s the battle lines had been drawn, with the depth of ill-feeling exacerbated by the severe economic recession that followed the war. As Gresley, Bulleid, Spencer and their small team worked quietly at King's Cross to make their business more efficient, the world around them was in danger of collapsing into chaos.

The spark for the most extreme civil unrest was generated by the mine owners, who, in the face of reducing profits, forced severe wage cuts and longer working hours on their employees. Lives that were already blighted by poor living and working conditions became even harder and protests broke out. When the miners refused to accept lower rates of pay and longer working

While soldiers, tanks and armoured cars patrolled the streets, threatening a level of violence few could ignore, the LNER tried to present a picture of calmness with the slogan 'business as usual'. This is reflected in these heavily romanticised, wholly misleading pictures of volunteers manning the trains. Spencer later wrote of these events, 'it seemed a shame to me that the politicians who showed only aggression to the strikers, who after all had made a strong case for fair treatment, did not demonstrate the same degree of resistance to Hitler a decade later and avoid another world war'. (BS)

hours, the owners simply locked out 1.2 million men and women and suspended their pay. Faced with such heartless action, the General Council of the Trades Union Congress felt moved to act and called for strike action by its members as a means of demonstrating solidarity, but also as a call to government to act. In May 1926, enraged by these callous actions, an estimated 1.7 million workers across many industries joined the miners in what became known as the General Strike. The disruption this caused was extreme over a nine-day period. The railways virtually came to a halt, with even a skeleton service becoming almost impossible to sustain.

In London, soldiers and tanks were on the streets and violence occasionally erupted, especially when some workers or agitators tried to break picket lines. The atmosphere was tinderbox dry and was only one spark away from rioting and mass arrests to begin. These were black days which Spencer witnessed first-hand, especially as many of the clashes took place in and around the mainline stations, King's Cross in particular. He recalled that:

It was a very difficult time and the strikes profoundly affected my brothers who were employed in the Works at Doncaster, which were shut down for a while. None of us knew how long this situation would last and there was a great deal of anger. Although I strongly sympathized with the miners, having grown up in Yorkshire, there was little I could do to help alleviate the suffering. It was pitiful to see how they lived and worked and I fully understood that a 50 per cent reduction in their pay would make things even worse. But it was expected that I would carry on working and I did so, although Gresley left it up to individuals to decide whether they struck or not. However, I did donate part of my salary to a miners benefit fund in Yorkshire.

I do not remember the CME expressing an opinion either way about the strike, preferring to take a neutral stance in public, at least. He was a reasonable man, who believed in a 'fair day's work for a fair day's wage'. But Trades Unions were in their infancy then and few managers had yet grasped how best to deal with them, except by being overly tough. From

For those who carried on working there were medals, particularly for railway employees (above left). For Spencer these events were remembered by a file of photos and press cuttings, such as this copy of the *Daily Mirror*. (BS)

Innovation or Stagnation

this point of view Gresley was probably ahead of his time and seemed prepared to listen and do what he could for his employees. He was a fair man, as were Wintour, Stamer, Thom, Thompson and Peppercorn in dealing with their employees.

Getting to work each day of the strike proved difficult but not impossible, some trains running from New Barnet to King's Cross, although the service was far from regular. The locomotives were crewed by strike-breaking drivers and firemen, some managers and office workers with footplate experience adding their weight. Stories of volunteers from the Public Schools filled the Conservative press at the time and staged photos often appeared, but these were pure fantasy. Having untrained, unqualified men or women on the footplate would have been to court disaster. To prove this point, it was later reported that four people were killed and others injured in five rail crashes during the strike and these were deemed to have been caused by inexperienced volunteers taking on work for which they were wholly unsuited and untrained.

For several days there were scuffles and confrontations in the approaches to King's Cross, with a number of people ending up in hospital as a result. However, the police and some soldiers kept the strikers away from the station concourse and platforms for most of the time. Nevertheless, things were very nasty for a week or so and the threat of violence hung heavy in the air making life very difficult, although I was not personally threatened in any way. It was clear that things could have quickly got out of hand and we half expected some form of civil war to break out such was the anger and violence displayed by both police and strikers.

The General Strike took an even nastier turn on 11 May 1926 when it was reported that some striking miners caused the derailment of the 10am service from Edinburgh to King's Cross north of Newcastle. In an unusual move, Spencer was sent by Gresley to the crash site to assess the damage and likely cause. Sadly, it proved to be a deliberate act of vandalism which, luckily, did not result in any deaths only injury to crew and passengers. These three pictures were part of a group kept by Spencer showing the aftermath of the crash and the clear-up operation. (BS)

Things came to a head, as far as the LNER was concerned, when, on 11 May, an express train from Edinburgh to King's Cross [the 10am service pulled by Pacific No. 2565, *Merry Hampton*] was derailed north of Newcastle by, we were told at the time, striking miners intent on stopping a coal train, but miscalculated. No one was killed, but this was more by luck than judgement. Due to the seriousness of this incident I was sent by Gresley to Newcastle that afternoon to assess the damage and report back to him that day on how quickly the locomotive might be moved. It was a practice the CME followed on a number of occasions in the years leading up to the war. He always took the view that much can be learnt about locomotive design from these sorts of incidents and trusted me to report any issues of note to him. It was a sad duty especially when the accident involved fatalities.

When I arrived at Cramlington Edward Thompson was there not only in his capacity as Carriage and Wagon Manager at Darlington, but also because he had extensive experience of accident investigation. Together we looked over the locomotive which still had not be righted at the time. We noted the damage, the position of the controls in the cab and observed the likely cause, which we concluded was by malicious intent, occasioned by the removal of fishplates, coach screws and a length of track. That evening we were joined by Colonel J W Pringle from the Ministry of Transport who was a well-known and respected figure in railway circles and who we assisted on this occasion. Thompson phoned through a report to the CME and my written report was in his hands the following afternoon. I believe a group of miners were later arrested for the crime, faced prosecution and were jailed.

It was rumoured at the time that strikers or agitators had attempted to disrupt services on many other occasions by damaging signals or leaving old railway sleepers or metal posts on the track to cause delays and accidents.

In the aftermath of the derailment, eight miners were indeed arrested and prosecuted for their part in the incident. The twelve carriage Flying Scotsman had set off late from Edinburgh at 10.09 hrs that morning with driver R. Sheldon in charge, assisted by two volunteer firemen. At Berwick, the train stopped and was joined by a second very experienced driver, Thomas Wedderburn. This seems to have been a precautionary measure because trouble was thought to be possible as the train passed through mining areas where agitators were known to be operating. This proved to be the case, and a group of miners, stirred by an inflammatory speech made earlier that day by William Golightly, a local miners association committee member, in which he uttered the words 'let no wheels turn', were moved to action.

Near Cramlington, words were turned into deeds and a group of forty or so men removed a section of track which caused the derailment. However, by this stage the train was travelling more slowly than usual due to the threat of action from strikers known to be operating in the area. This precautionary action may well have saved lives, but the locomotive was still travelling fast enough to leave the track and turn on its side, taking five carriages with it. The police soon opened their investigation, aided by local informers. In early June arrests began and eight men were found guilty at the trial that followed at Moot Hall in Newcastle. Soon they were sentenced to between four and eight years for their part in the crime, each still pleading their innocence. By this stage, the strike was over, though the bitterness it had generated would not disperse so easily. For Spencer, and many others, the end did not come soon enough but was accompanied by very mixed emotions:

> I was glad when the strike came to an end, but saddened that these actions did not lead to better conditions for miners and their families. The hunger marches during the 1930s continued to show how difficult life was for many in the North of England, something that the powers that be seemed happy to ignore to their great discredit.

It seemed a shame to me that the politicians who showed only aggression to the strikers, who had after all made a strong case for fair treatment, did not demonstrate the same degree of resistance to Hitler a decade later and avoid another world war.

At the time of the strike, Spencer's brothers Ernest and Harry were still working as craftsmen in the Carriage Works at Doncaster, and his other brother, Fred, had become a junior manager. Bert did not record whether any of them went out on strike – voluntarily or involuntarily – but with the Works seemingly closed by the industrial dispute, the confrontation would have profoundly affected their lives. It was a battle that could easily have divided many families and Spencer's reference to 'a great deal of anger' suggests some tension close to home. For all concerned it must have been a relief when the strike came to an end and things returned to something near normal, though it may have left a residue of reserve or ill-feeling that could have proved difficult to mollify.

For the moment, though, normal business resumed, which for Spencer meant developing his role as Gresley's assistant. Here he was greatly assisted by the CME who actively encouraged him to extend his knowledge and make new contacts within their profession. By nature, Gresley was a good mixer and moved easily amongst people of all ranks and classes, but especially his board of directors and others in authority where things are decided. In this way, he developed many close links in this country and overseas that he could exploit to good effect when developing his ideas. He was also an astute politician with a deep understanding of how business worked and the nuances of managing in such a high profile post.

Although not essential for success in his chosen field, he realised very early on that these skills could help smooth the passage of his ideas and convince those in power that his proposals were sound and should be financed. Some senior engineers lacked these broader skills and many projects failed at the outset because they had not understood the political or economic climate, or prepared their cases well. And then there was the impact of professional bodies to consider. Here he found people of great skill ever eager to share their thoughts and knowledge with those of like mind and ambition.

Scientific discovery inevitably works best when a community openly shares knowledge and generates a creative interaction – I have an idea, you have an idea and from this we create a third idea. For example, no one person created all the elements necessary for powered flight, but the

The 1920s and '30s were years of great contrasts between the haves, who were few, and the have nots who ran into millions. For Spencer, this was no better demonstrated in his papers than these two photos plus press cuttings from the time showing the juxtaposition of hunger marches and the affluence of luxury rail travel which he kept together. Here was a man with a strong social conscience who seems to have been thankful for having a good job and good pay by the standards of the age. (BS)

Wright Brothers brought a number of discoveries together to achieve this aim at Kittyhawk in December 1903. And so it was with locomotives. Gresley saw this very early on and was able to assimilate the work of many leading scientists of the age in producing new designs.

Amongst these close contacts he numbered Professor William Dalby, a noted academic, who had a detailed knowledge of engine balancing. Then there was Frederick Johansen, a specialist in aerodynamics who worked for the National Physical Laboratory, and Professor Thomas Turner, an expert in metallurgy. To these eminent scientists Gresley would add men from his own industry such as Andre Chapelon, the French locomotive engineer, and Dr Richard Wagner, his opposite number with the Deutsche Reichbahn-Gesellschaft. But this was just the tip of an iceberg when it came to a broad and very active list of collaborators. So, it was inevitable that he would encourage those who worked for him at King's Cross to establish their own list of contacts, enjoy the collaborative work of learned institutions and absorb as much as they could. Spencer later described the effect of all this on his work:

> All this greatly extended my knowledge and gradually made me more confident when dealing with the many senior officials, from within the LNER and other bodies, with whom I came in almost daily contact, if Gresley or Bullied were there and, more importantly, when they were absent on business when answers to many pertinent questions were required at short notice. This was particularly so in the case of Ralph Wedgwood, the Chief General Manager, who was a regular and much liked and respected visitor. On these occasions Gresley trusted me to act on his behalf and then report to him what had happened at the earliest opportunity.
>
> Early each week we discussed progress on a number of tasks he had given me and our small team of draughtsmen. In addition, he expected me to have an up to date reports on work being undertaken at Doncaster, Darlington and the rest of the workshops on locomotive construction and maintenance programmes. This I based on reports sent to me late the previous week by the Mechanical Engineers allowing me to compile the data the CME needed to see first thing on Monday morning. He then gave me a list of instructions to pass out to the workshops the same day in a series of memos, selecting a few of the important ones on which he would write or telephone himself.

Judging by photographs he took or collected, street scenes in London were of great interest to Spencer, especially when they captured scenes such as this with their emphasis on transport systems. Thick cloying fog, as any Londoner knows, was a common feature of daily life well into the 1960s when smokeless fuels became the norm. (BS)

(Left to right) Professor Thomas Turner, Professor William Dalby and Dr Frederick Johansen who all became long term associates of Nigel Gresley and in so doing worked closely with Bulleid and Spencer on locomotive design, in varying degrees. Turner, having begun his career as a mining engineer, became a specialist in metallurgy, Dalby developed a very detailed knowledge of locomotive balancing and Johansen was an expert in the sciences of fluid flow and aerodynamics. Turner's son, Thomas Henry, followed him into the field of metallurgy and was employed full time by the LNER as Chief Chemist under the CME. (THG).

Three overseas engineers whose work either influenced or challenged Gresley's work helping him drive forward his own ideas, in so doing bringing Spencer into this wider sphere of interest. (Left to right) Dr Richard Wagner of the DRG whose cutting edge steam designs and work on high powered diesel railcars set a trend for others to follow. The rise of Nazism would in time colour his relationships with Gresley and many others. Andre Chapelon, the highly gifted French engineer, remained Gresley's friend and colleague until France's defeat in 1940. The cleverness of his ideas on design were of constant interest to the Englishman. Meanwhile the Italian born designer Ettore Bugatti, who made a name for himself as a leading car designer, then turned his attention to rail vehicles when the world recession hit car buying. Gresley was deeply interested in his diesel railcar and his ideas on aerodynamics, having already journeyed into this field with the help of Frederick Johansen. (*THG*)

Any successful business likes to reflect on the priogress it has made and publicise its successes. This was none more so than the LNER as this picture reveals. A preserved Stirling 4-2-2 Single, No.1, is posed beside Gresley's A1 No. 2579, *Robert the Devil* at Old York Station in 1927. Any comment about comparative sizes is superfluous. The results of Gresley 'big locomotive policy' are only too apparent. (BS)

By late 1925, Spencer had probably established himself sufficiently to begin making a more substantial contribution to Gresley's work. As such he would have been more active in supporting Bulleid as well. In fact, his arrival seems to have been a catalyst for change in the senior man's career. With a good young assistant in place, Bulleid could be released from the day to day grind of office life to focus on more important matters. For example, in October 1925 he was invited by Gresley to attend meetings of the highly regarded Association of Railway Engineers (ARLE), which since the 1890s had become an authoritative body in the industry. Its aim was a simple one, 'to discuss the locomotive practice in force on the railways'. In particular, it had considered such things as 'the standardisation of locomotives in mechanical engineering matters' in the war and post-war years.

Up to 1925, the group's meetings had simply been attended by current and former CMEs, but then it was proposed that membership be extended to include other leading figures in the railway industry, such as Bulleid. However, Gresley was quick to restrict the level of authority vested in these newcomers. He was concerned that they might conceivably band together and overrule the CMEs, which is something he would not tolerate and with this proviso agreed, membership was considerably increased. As things turned out, Gresley's concerns prove unfounded. The ARLE's

Ralph Wedgwood (far right), the LNER's Cambridge educated Chief General Manager from 1923 to 1939, was one of Gresley's strong allies and a regular visitor to the CME's office at King's Cross and Spencer became used to dealing with this erudite and very experienced man in the CME's absence. He is captured here at an event held in Manchester accompanied by four of the LNER's directors whose names are not recorded although the figure second from right may be Alexander Henderson, Lord Faringdon who was Deputy Chairman until he died in 1934). (BS)

Innovation or Stagnation

contribution to locomotive design was muted at best, but the opportunity to assemble regularly may have allowed its members to compare notes on items of common interest. And discussing current projects, problems being faced and much more would undoubtedly have led to some sharing of information and experiences. In this it replicated the work of the learned institutions so had some academic value, but this became less so when grouping took place.

At the same time, Gresley decided to broaden Bulleid's brief by sending him to France to study the work of designers there, particularly the advances they were making on compounding. Undoubtedly Bulleid was chosen for this task because he was fluent in French, having worked for 1¾ years as a Test Engineer, then Assistant Works Manager at the Westinghouse Works at Freinville, near Paris. He then moved to Brussels to be part of a group entitled the British Exhibition Overseas before returning to the GNR at Doncaster in early 1912. So his personal and professional credentials made him ideally suited for this new liaison task. In addition, Gresley or Bulleid attended monthly conferences in France during which the CME's opposite numbers from the key railway companies there discussed issues of common interest. And with the very talented Spencer now working at King's Cross, the CME probably had as much specialist engineering and personal support that he might need on the locomotive side of business. To this Spencer added a brief but telling note:

> Someone as gifted and ebullient as Bulleid needed careful handling. A settled daily routine wasn't for him. His life was a constant search for new schemes to explore and subjects to study. He was a restless man who could so easily have engaged all around him in quests for the next big idea, some proving to be distractions from the business at hand. This interest only really applied to steam locomotives and rolling stock, he was far less concerned with diesel or electric traction, unlike the CME.
>
> It seemed to me that Gresley managed Bulleid by giving him special tasks that would keep him fully engaged and out on the road for much of the time. This seemed to work well for such a gifted man with boundless energy and possibly created a more harmonious atmosphere in the offices at King's Cross at the same time.'

Above left: Spencer continued to show great interest in all aspects of railway operation, as captured here as work proceeds on fitting or refitting, the moving parts of a turntable. These sort of infrastructure projects naturally impacted on locomotive operations, but his interest seems to have gone well beyond this, suggesting an underlying fascination with civil engineering issues. A1 Pacific No. 2559, *The Tetrarch*, provides a suitable backdrop to such work. (BS)

Above right: Even when Pacifics became more commonplace on the LNER, the company still had to rely on its smaller engines for many heavy duties. This resulted in a high level of double heading, which increased running costs and was a primary driver in the development of bigger engines by Gresley and his fellow CMEs. In this case, 4-4-0 No. 4312 appears to be under considerable strain while Atlantic 4-4-2 No. 4418 seems to be making slightly lighter work of the load as it departs from Peterborough during the 1920s. (BS)

From these words one can sense some impatience with the way Bulleid worked. Of course, we shall never know to what degree, if any, Gresley shared this view and, if so, how it affected him or his immediate entourage. One can only assume that the positives outweighed the negatives and the CME gained immeasurably from the plusses and coped as best he could with the minuses – Spencer less so, never having the authority to overrule or ignore Bulleid. One detects that a polite truce of sorts prevailed, with each choosing to ignore the other as much as Gresley's overriding needs would allow.

While all this was going on, Spencer carefully studied Gresley at work, learning much from him in the process. But he was also a keen observer of the way the CME was allowed to work by his superiors, which considering the tight financial constraints imposed by recession, was quite remarkable, reflecting as it did the high regard with which he was held. The Chairman, William Whitelaw, and Chief General Manager would also have been conscious of the fact that Gresley was a major figure in the industry and one who would attract some interest from rivals. So, if he was not given a degree of freedom to experiment and develop his ideas, he might well seek a greater challenge elsewhere This was something that neither Whitelaw nor Wedgwood would wish to have seen happen as they sought to build the company into a successful business. Spencer caught a flavour of this when he wrote:

> This was a very important period in which Gresley was given free rein to test and evaluate many ideas. Some of these were simply experiments with the aim of extracting the last few ounces of performance from steam locomotives, but others looked more broadly at other forms of tractive power. The war curtailed much of this activity, but he, even when very ill and increasingly confused, saw this as a temporary matter and used the pause to think more deeply about the future. To him steam was not the be all and end all of locomotive development and he foresaw its demise.

The locomotive programme was inevitably hindered by cost considerations and for most of the 1920s and '30s funds were restricted as the country sought to hold inflation and recession in check. And things only worsened when the rampant speculation that led to the Wall Street Crash of 1929 sent a tidal wave of unsecured debt and more economic turmoil around the world. No country escaped its effects, but some were hit much harder than others. Germany, which had hardly begun to rebuild its economy after its loss in the Great War, was again plunged into a chaos from which Nazism emerged. In Britain, things had been difficult for many years, but at least some growth had been possible, though any small advantage gained was soon reversed by this latest calamity.

At King's Cross, this meant that while Gresley was allowed to extend his Pacific project, modify existing designs wherever practical and carry on with building programmes initiated by the constituent companies, he had to rein in any other ambitions he may have harboured. Spencer captured the essence of these problems and the limited options open to the CME when he wrote:

> The early years were difficult. With so many different types of locomotives to operate it was impossible to establish how well they met the company's needs. There were more than enough in number but not necessarily of the right type. So from the beginning Sir Nigel continued building those introduced before amalgamation until the future became clearer. Forty more A1s were built between 1923 and 1925 – twenty of these at Doncaster and another twenty under contract by North British – as well as another three more of Raven's Pacifics at Darlington in 1924. In addition, there were more N2s, O2s J50s and H4s (now re-designated K3s). If my memory serves me well new construction of these engines totalled 80 in 1924 and 63 in 1924. This period was noted for being one of hard work on new designs but also of the need to convince those in charge that all was not well and could be improved.

So, any advances made by Gresley during this period were incremental in nature and based, for the most part on well-established design principles. The development of new technologies such as diesel or electric traction simply fell by the wayside no matter how strongly Gresley felt about it. And it seems he was a firm believer in the benefits of electric motive power. He had inherited some examples developed by Vincent Raven when CME of the NER and seen for himself what they could do. But funds for the massive capital investment needed to take these projects forward simply did not exist, no matter how hard Gresley pushed his chairman to release the purse strings.

Nevertheless, his enthusiasm for electrification remained a key feature of his work as Spencer recalled:

Gresley was fascinated by the electrification projects which had begun to appear in the North East, across in Lancashire and around the South of London. So it came as no surprise when he recruited Henry Richards from the Southern Railway to keep development work going even though there was little prospect of getting any other line electrified in the foreseeable future. Richard's, who was a specialist in this field at a time when very few others existed, sat near us at King's Cross. He brought with him a considerable bank of information, collected when he worked for AEG then the old London, Brighton and South Coast Railway as their Electrical Traction Engineer, which he shared with us. In time Richards would have the able support of three electrical engineering assistants – Harry Swift, Alexander Emerson, who was an ex-Gresley

Above left: Engine No.727 approaches Darlington Bank Top in the late 1920s, demonstrating the mixture of engines Gresley had to work with as CME. This locomotive was a member of Vincent Raven's forty strong three-cylinder Z Class 4-4-2s, which first appeared in 1911. Post 1923 (now designated C7s) these engines were gradually replaced by the Pacifics on the heavier turns, but still occasionally appeared on the premier services often double-heading. Gresley and his team modified these engines in a number of ways. For example, the class were fitted with his conjugated valve gear, some received ACFI feed water heaters and so on. Two, including No. 727, were fitted with boosters to their rear bogies. So it is hardly surprising that a number of photos and drawings of these engines were kept by Spencer in his archives. The last of them remained in service until 1948. (BS)

Above right: Electrification on the LNER – a missed opportunity? When becoming CME, Gresley inherited an advanced electric transport system, which had begun to show true merit, from Vincent Raven. Engine No. 13 (above in 1925 when displayed as part of the commemoration for the Stockton and Darlington Railway), which was built in 1922 as a prototype for use on the mainline between York and Newcastle, was one result of his work. Financial constraints are often cited as the main reason for these projects being shelved in the early 1920s, but some also believe that postponement was a short-sighted aberration on the part of Gresley, who seemingly preferred to continue developing his steam locomotives instead. The truth seems to have been that the external constraints placed on him were massive, coupled to the fact that the power grid was not extensive enough to support an electrified network then. When things improved, the CME was ready and willing to invest heavily in these schemes and but for the war would have overseen massive advances. (BS)

apprentice who I had known at Doncaster, and Alfred Hopking. In the meantime, until they arrived late in the 1930s, I and the draughtsmen at King's Cross supported him and became actively involved in the work he was doing, though most of this was theoretical in nature.

It was not simply lack of money that held up these developments on the LNER, but the lack of national grid and a balanced supply system across our network. The major cities were well served by new power stations, but there were large areas between them where this did not exist and wouldn't do so until the mid-1930s at the earliest. The CME was aware of this and took a realistic view which meant focussing on steam until the 1926 Electricity Supply Act could be fully enacted.

Gresley seemed less keen on diesel motive power, for reasons he never made clear to me, though cost would have been a factor. Any consideration of diesels was, as a result, limited though he took careful notice of developments in France, Germany, the USA, Italy and Holland in the 1930s.

With these alternative forms of transport unlikely to advance far for at least a decade, Spencer's main effort was inevitably directed towards steam and Gresley's plans to modernise the fleet and advance their design whenever he could. But even here the CME faced some criticism from fellow engineers that he did not embrace the question of standardisation as fully as he might and reap the benefits of such a policy. Instead, as H.C.B. Rogers wrote in his book *The Last Steam Locomotive Engineer,* 'Gresley, great engineer though he was, embarked on a policy which was the antithesis of the Churchward school … he never attempted any standardisation. His engines were frequently tailor made to meet local conditions.'

Nothing is ever quite as clear cut this, though and the reality was rather more complex than Rogers describes. Some idea of where Gresley stood on this issue can be gauged from a presentation he made to the ILocoE in Leeds on 11 May 1918:

> Now I am going to touch upon dangerous ground. As to the future, the subject that is claiming the attention of locomotive engineers today is the suggested standardisation of Locomotives in England.
>
> The question was brought into prominence by the remarks of the late Sir John Barry when he delivered his James Forrest lecture twelve months ago….I have a lively recollection of the caustic remarks made to me subsequently by some of my friends who were there.
>
> He stated that the locomotive engineers were responsible for the absence of standardisation, and attributed the lamentable fact to these causes – that every British Company kept its own type and acted on the supposition that each railway must have engines suitable to its own traffic conditions, but he confidently submitted that there was nothing to support such a contention. In India a broader view has been taken. The movement has been a great success, and has saved India a very large sum of money, and it is very much hoped that, if more centralisation of Britain's railways became a fact, the locomotives in this country would be dealt with as they had been in our great Dependency.
>
> Now let me say at once that I am a strong advocate of standardisation in principle, but not necessarily of standardised locomotives, but the present is not the most opportune moment for the introduction of the standard engine. After three and a half years of the greatest war the world has ever known, we are hard put to it to carry on the railway transportation of the country. The continued and increasing restrictions in the railway service are sufficient evidence of the difficulties with which we have to contend. To add to these by the introduction of several new types of standard engines, having new standards for such parts as brake blocks, firebars, valves, piston rings and a hundred others, which constantly require renewal, and of which stocks have to be kept in the various depots all over the country, would be the height of folly and could only result in disaster.

Spencer's photographic collection continues to capture daily scenes of interest to him, many involving the process of engine servicing – in this case an unidentified Pacific at Doncaster Works, which he frequently visited pursuing any issue raised by Gresley. (BS)

> Supposing for the sake of argument that the type of one railway company were adopted. That company would be no better off from a maintenance standpoint than they are today; possibly they might get their new engines a bit cheaper; but every other railway which purchased or built any new engines would have to provide in its works new patterns, templates, flanging blocks etc, and its running sheds would have to keep complete stocks of the spare parts ... You have only got to think of it. It could not be a more inopportune time to start.

Gresley made these comments when the war was still raging, so was clearly aware of the limitations the conflict imposed on all new developments. But even allowing for this, his views were expressed strongly enough to suggest that he would not be for turning when the railways ceased being subject to the constraints imposed by war. Spencer later added his own views on the matter:

> The CME saw little merit in standardisation and believed that it would only work if all the railway companies were nationalised, which for a time in 1918 seemed likely. He felt that the centralised control this introduced might be able to produce a standard range of locomotives to cope with most needs over a period of twenty years or more. But he believed that this depended on two things – a substantial injection of capital to fund a very large construction programme and acceptance of the need to scrap a considerable number of engines long before the end of their useful lives. Once it was formed the LNER could have pursued such a policy by itself, but Gresley saw little point in adopting a major programme such as Churchward had attempted at Swindon, on cost grounds alone. However, he accepted that when building new classes of locomotive that some standardisation might be possible, though did not see this as being a matter of overriding concern. Better to have engines that met the company's needs, ran effectively and economically with few lost days between periods of maintenance than allow commonality of spares to dominate his thinking. Essentially his was a very practical and pragmatic response to the situation in which he found himself.

Throughout his career, Gresley expressed his views very clearly and with some force when the need arose. But he was also a man prepared to listen to engineers he respected and learn from what they were doing, when he saw some benefit in doing so. To sit beside him must have been both a fascinating and, at times, a frustrating experience, especially for those such as Bulleid and

Spencer who were considerably skilled themselves and had minds of their own. On balance, the positives seemed to have outweighed the negatives, a fact confirmed by Spencer when he wrote that:

> With Gresley every day was made more interesting by his constant search for new ideas and ways of doing things. In this he and Bulleid were similar, though the CME was, perhaps, more realistic in his approach. Although we did not agree on some fundamental issues, such as the use of the Belpaire boilers, it is true to say that he was always prepared to listen to any alternative view I put forward and act on my proposal once he had been convinced of its merit. However, it was rarely a quick process and acceptance had to be based on service trials and comparisons between competing solutions. By the 1930s, as his trust in me grew, the process became easier, although the level of questioning remained unchanged.
>
> By adopting his methods of examining a problem from all angles I learnt a lot. It was a process that first began when I was an apprentice, but took on added weight when I listened to his speech to the Leeds Branch of the ILocoE in 1918. As suggested by John Bazin, I took copious notes, and followed this practice for the rest of my career. On this occasion Gresley outlined his beliefs in a such a cogent way that it made me think very deeply about a wide range of engineering issues. These included superheating, which he strongly advocated when saying that it had 'greatly accelerated' the evolution of locomotives. He then added that its 'full advantages have not yet been fully appreciated' and by adopting a higher degree of 'superheat beyond anything at present attempted, it will be possible to obtain much greater benefits from its introduction'.

By the mid to late 1920s, the LNER Publicity Department had established the company's name in the public eye, helped by the introduction of Gresley's Pacifics. Every opportunity was taken to photograph these engines, whether pulling the premier services, or simply being prepared on shed before going out on the mainline. Small boys seem to have been a staple diet for photographers on these occasions. Here, two unidentified Pacifics are captured in photos soon to be released to the press. (BS)

To this he frequently added an exhortation to 'move away from judging an engine by its tractive force. Instead focus on its capacity for boiling water and its ability to supply the necessary steam for long and continuous service'. In support of this he would quote the case of a boiler that can supply steam when set at 20 per cent cut-off, but fails to do so when let out during a long incline. As a result, it has to work at 50 or 60 per cent cut-off to keep going. This shows that it is too small for the cylinders on that type of work, though might be sufficient for lighter shunting or intermittent duties.

In addition to this, he would confirm his commitment to the use of wider fireboxes, especially when matched to larger boilers. He felt, as I do, that they were 'more economical from the point of view of life, and from the point of efficiency'. As proof of this he would point to the work of his predecessor, Henry Ivatt, and his Atlantic engines, which he greatly admired.

There were also more general issues discussed regularly, ease of access to all the moving parts, including the outside cylinders and valve gear for servicing, being one of them. He strongly believed that it is 'possible to secure better cross-bracing of the frames, to say nothing of easier oiling, inspection and maintenance of motion' by doing this. And he concluded that 'with such an engine it is not necessary to put it over a pit before leaving the shed and the essential parts can be better examined in a good light... you cannot see well underneath an engine in a shed, and light is a great advantage'.

He frequently talked about the problem of overheating and the consumption of lubricating oil, emphasizing the importance of mechanical lubricators for axleboxes to 'simplify the work of the enginemen, the oiling of all the boxes being controlled by one lubricator'. And to this he added that:

'There has been a marked decrease in the number of hot boxes and an economy in the consumption of oil due to the fact that when an engine is standing no oil is being used. It is an important point that the mechanical lubricator should be connected to a point in the motion which has constant travel and not to the valve spindle, of which travel is reduced as the engine is notched up.'

As a measure of his commitment to these and many other theories he continued exploring the potential of each class of locomotive available to him, particularly the Pacifics, but not to the exclusion of other new developments such as marine boilers, turbines, feed water heaters and the uniflow system.

Throughout my time with Gresley there were many ideas considered, tried, tested, accepted or rejected, but one central topic did not change. Locomotive testing and the lack of a well-equipped centre, with rolling road, was a matter of some concern to him. He was not a man easily moved to anger, but the tardiness of the powers that be in approving then

The changes Gresley began to introduce as CME and the problems he inherited when so many diverse companies came together in 1923 are only too apparent in this picture of Doncaster Carr Loco Shed. The plethora of types is easily conveyed, with at least three new Pacifics, and possibly a lone P2, showing the way forward. The picture also strengthens the case against any large standardisation programme. With so much rationalisation to be undertaken the cost would have been prohibitive in a time of plenty let alone in a world in the middle of a very deep recession (BS)

funding such a facility always elicited a passionate response from him. But he never gave up canvassing for support at many levels in and outside of the LNER. During this time, he urged me to visit Swindon and view the test facility set up there by Churchward in the early years of the century. Though retired by then I met him several times and was closely questioned, in a gruff way, by the old man, on what Gresley was doing and why he felt the need to pursue his ideas on Pacifics. He clearly felt this was unnecessary and when seeing the GWR's Kings and Castles in operation it was easy to understand why.

Although approval to build a test centre was eventually given, Gresley, although immensely pleased, strongly suspected that it had come too late and its benefits would not be exploited fully. When work began at Rugby in the late 1930s it seemed to many that steam had been taken as far as it could and such a centre had come too late. As it was, the coming of war meant that it didn't become operational until 1948, more than a quarter of a century after Gresley's big push had begun.

Each week we received many engineering and scientific journals which Gresley requested. As a result, there was a constant stream of information arriving in our offices to be read and collated by Bulleid and myself before passing those we thought of particular interest to the CME. This led to many lively discussions and reinforced some of Gresley's ideas or helped persuade him to consider others. In this way we could direct his thoughts on certain issues, though he remained his own master and would gently censure us if he thought we were getting ahead of ourselves!

Journals from North America were always of particular interest to him and influenced many of his proposals – something he was quick to recognise. For example, he once wrote that:

'A few months ago I was reading a very interesting address, given to one of the American Societies, in which the writer said, with regard to locomotives, it has been comparatively easy to make them bigger and heavier, but a greater and far more difficult problem faces us today, that of making every pound of weight justify itself in terms of power. Undoubtedly, engines are approaching their maximum weights and sizes in this country, but are a long way from attaining their maximum power. We can, and shall have to, get more power per unit of weight.'

In all matters he took a broad view of the engineering world and believed that ideas should be shared wherever possible. His pragmatism on this issue may be assumed from his often expressed words, 'when you run out of ideas then copy the best'. It was sound advice which I followed throughout my career.

In his letters and papers, Spencer has only selected and discussed a few of the issues Gresley considered important to locomotive design and construction. There was much more, of course, but there is sufficient here to help us understand how working alongside the CME helped develop the younger man's engineering and management skills. As the 1920s drew to a close, and the extent of the problems the LNER and Gresley faced became only too clear, the scale of the task and challenges ahead must have seemed quite daunting. Yet they had to start somewhere and the development of the high profile Pacifics lay at the centre of this work. But behind it lay a whole raft of other plans and proposals to improve the less glamorous elements of the fleet.

Of course, Spencer's work in sorting out the Pacifics' valve gear and long lap valves had significantly improved these engines, but did not complete their evolution, which would soon be taken to a new level, in line with Gresley's thoughts on boilers size. In the growing knowledge that a pressure of 180psi, plus 32 element superheaters, may not be sufficient for their needs, it was decided to experiment with boilers producing a higher rate of pounds per square inch. Spencer later described what this meant in practice:

In order to obtain information as to the actual economies which would result from the use of a higher working pressure two A1s, Nos. 2544 and 4480, were, in July 1927, fitted with new boilers carrying a pressure of 220lb./sq.in [Gresley had been given permission to convert five locomotives initially as part of a programme to build some additional spare boilers]. The only differences between the new and original boilers were an increase in the thickness of the barrel plates, a closer pitching of the firebox stays and an increase in the number of superheater elements from 32 to 43. The cylinders of No. 4480 were not altered, but those of No. 2544 were reduced to 18 ¼ in. diameter (to give the high-pressure boiler a tractive effort approximately equal to that of the standard 180lb. Pacifics), the tractive efforts being 36,465lb. and 30,362lb. respectively as compared with 29,835lb. on the standard A1 Class.

Engine No. 4480 proved highly successful in service, the increased power due to the use of the higher pressure with 20in. diameter cylinders enabling the engine to be worked at relatively early cut-offs on the heaviest trains.

Comparative trials were carried out between A1 class No. 4473, 'Solario', with 180lb. pressure and No. 2544 with 220lb. pressure (during February 1928, over a two-week period on the hardest duty of the time – the 1051 from Doncaster to King's Cross and return at 1600 hrs). Both engines had long lap valve gear. Engine No. 4473 made six return journeys on consecutive days (312 miles per day) and engine No. 2544 made five return journeys the following week.

Whilst the coal consumption per mile and per ton-mile showed a substantial economy in favour of 2544, there was little to choose between the two engines when comparing coal and water consumption on a horsepower basis. Engine No. 4473 did more work during the trials owing to greater wind resistance which adversely affected its coal and water

A1s Nos 2544, *Lemberg*, and 4473, *Solario*, were used for comparative trials during February 1928 to gauge the benefits of fitting a boiler with a working pressure of 220lb to members of the class. 2544 was so fitted while *Solario* carried the banner for the original 180psi boilers. Spencer was directly involved in this task and in reporting the results to Gresley. This work led to the development of the A3s. (BS)

In the absence of a well-eqipped test centre that could be used to monitor engine performance more effectively, dynamometer cars were of great importance in establishing how well a locomotive was standing up to the pressure of operations. This photo, though probably staged for publicity purposes, does at least capture the nature of the work and its comparative comfort. Only very recently, engineers undertaking this work would have been working behind a crude wooden shelter precariously attached to the engine's front end. Spencer would later write that this method of testing 'was not for me, I much preferred the comfort and cleanliness of the dynamometer car'. (BS)

consumption per mile and per ton-mile, these comparisons giving no credit for the extra effort due to weather conditions.

In his report Spencer makes no reference to his own part in these trials, but later added:

Because I had been closely involved in the long lap valve issue Gresley asked me to superintend this boiler development work and be closely involved in the trials that followed. As the Works readied the first three engines, two of which would be used, the choice of which to use being mine, I worked out the trials programme and agreed the use of a dynamometer car. In some ways I would have preferred to use engine No. 4480 with her 20 in. diameter cylinders, but this engine seemed much more prone to slipping than the others and so we left her to one side just in case this problem coloured the test results. However, I think it true to say that No. 4480 would probably have proved the best of the trio and proved to be so in general service, especially if the driver worked her with a 'light hand'. During the trials I was unable to be present on all twenty-two runs, but rode on the footplate on two occasions and in the dynamometer car on three others. The benefits of the changes made were only too obvious as my report to Gresley made clear.

It was during the February trials that I first became aware of my

COMPARATIVE TESTS BETWEEN "PACIFIC" ENGINES WITH 180 AND 220 lb. per sq. inch BOILER PRESSURE

Made between King's Cross and Doncaster: February 1928.

Particulars	Engine 4473	Engine 2544
Boiler pressure lb./sq.in.	180	220
Cylinder diameter x stroke	20" x 26"	18¼" x 26"
Tractive effort at 85% B.P.	29,835 lb.	30,362 lb.
Average coal consumption:		
Lb. per D.B.H.P. hour	3.07	3.11
Lb. per mile	38.83	35.37
Percentage reduction on 220 lb. engine	—	8.9
Lb. per ton mile (excluding engine)	.092	.083
Lb. per sq. ft. of grate per hour	49.62	46.8
Average water consumption:		
Lb. per D.B.H.P. hour	25.17	25.45
Lb. per mile	317.5	288.8
Lb. per ton mile (excluding engine)	.752	.675
Average evaporation:		
Lb. of water per lb. of coal	8.18	8.17
Average speed in M.P.H.:		
Doncaster to King's Cross	54.93	56.84
King's Cross to Doncaster	50.73	52.54
Average weight of train behind tender:		
Doncaster to King's Cross	435 tons	428 tons
King's Cross to Peterborough	491 ,,	506 ,,
Peterborough to Doncaster	331 ,,	348 ,,
Average work done in H.P. hours per single journey	1970	1770

The trials results as recorded in February 1928 and presented by Spencer to Gresley for consideration. The gap in overall performance was a small one but sufficient benefits were gained to support a case for converting all A1s as they fell due for boiler renewal. (BS)

growing interest in locomotive testing. Up to then I had been on the periphery of this work, my other duties in the drawing office or as Gresley's assistant taking priority. Over the years, other opportunities would arise, but these were always secondary tasks to my main role. If working for the CME had not been so interesting and busy I would certainly have moved into this area of work much earlier.

Spencer then touched on another issue Gresley and his team had considered as they decided whether to proceed with a boiler producing 220lb per sq inch of pressure or not:

> There were concerns over the comparative maintenance costs between boilers operating with different pressures – higher pressures costing more or having shorter lives. Thom had presented a short paper on the subject to the A.R.L.E (Association of Railway Locomotive Engineers) when Gresley was President between 1926 and '27. He compared 180 and 200lb.psi boilers and this led to a great deal of discussion by members each describing their own experiences. With the likes of Gresley, Thom, Stanier, Fowler, Beames and Bulleid in attendance there couldn't have been a more expert group of people, but even so no final conclusion could be reached. However, the consensus, led by Stanier, seemed to be that there would be no appreciable difference in maintenance costs and the benefits of running with a boiler with higher pressure would outweigh any small difference, if it existed at all. With that assurance Gresley felt able to argue the benefits of conversion.

The boiler's psi was only one issue Gresley revisited when addressing the A1s performance. The question of superheating held equal importance, reflecting comments made by Gresley in his 1918 presentation in Leeds. However, on this issue Spencer did not record a great deal, suggesting it was something of lesser importance than the question of boiler capacity or the valve gear. His only comment of any note came in 1947 when Lt Colonel K. Cantlie asked him about experiments carried out by Gresley with different types of superheaters during 1925/26. In response, Spencer focussed on the relative merits of each system available and recalled that Gresley had been disatisfied with the degree of superheating being generated by the Robinson 32 element heaters carried by the A1s and the two P1 2-8-2s built in 1925, so had looked for an alternative solution. On the advice of engineers working for the Superheater Company in New York, who had supplied booster engines for the P1s, he acquired two of their type E superheaters for experimental purposes:

> [These were] fitted to one of the P1 2-8-2 type engines, No. 2394, and to one of the A1 Class Pacific engines, No. 2562 [both in place of superheaters with 32 elements]. Comparative trials were carried out in May 1926 between engines No. 2562 and A1 Class engine No. 2570 fitted with a 32 element Robinson superheater. The total average superheat temperatures for the twelve trips made with each engine were 584 degrees and 553 degrees F for the type E and the Robinson superheater respectively, the highest temperature recorded with the type E being 650 degrees and with the Robinson type 595 degrees.
> The comparatively small increase in superheat obtained with the large increase in superheating surface on the type E was probably due to the fact that on the Robinson type the superheating surface is concentrated in the most effective part of the boiler.

The later Pacifics were fitted with boilers carrying a working pressure of 220psi in conjunction with a 43 element superheater and no further experiments were made with the type E design.'
Armed with the results of these tests and after much thought, Gresley obtained the LNER's Locomotive Committee's agreement to modify the remainder of the A1s, as and when each engine's boiler came up for renewal. This proved to be a slow process; the last engine, No. 2567,

Sir Visto, only being fitted with its new 220psi boiler in 1947/8. By this stage she had been rebuilt as an A3, like fifty of her sisters and been joined by twenty-seven newly constructed A3s between 1928 and 1935. These were hardly speedy programmes and undoubtedly reflected the constant battle for funds and the general effectiveness of the A1s as built.

Although regarded as one of Gresley's great achievements, Spencer made little of the A3 development programme in his 1947 presentation, passing over this important moment in railway history with the words:

'The experience gained with engines 4480 and 2544 led to the introduction of the A3 class Pacifics in 1928. These engines had the identical design of the 220lb./sq. in. 6ft 5in diameter boiler fitted to the trials engines, but the diameter of the cylinders was increased to 19 in., thus raising the tractive effort to 32,909lb. Late engines, commencing with engine No. 2500, *Windsor Lad* had boilers fitted with a steam collector in the form of a steel pressing, integral with the dome, fed by a series of slots ½ in. wide in the top of the barrel plate.'

Yet without Spencer's involvement in the design of the A1s and their subsequent modifications, they may not have advanced so far. As a team player, he was not prepared, then or later, to claim any credit for his part in the project or his ability to gently persuade Gresley that there was a better path to take at critical moments. However, it cannot be denied that his role in their development was an important one, perfectly complementing Gresley's own contribution to their success.

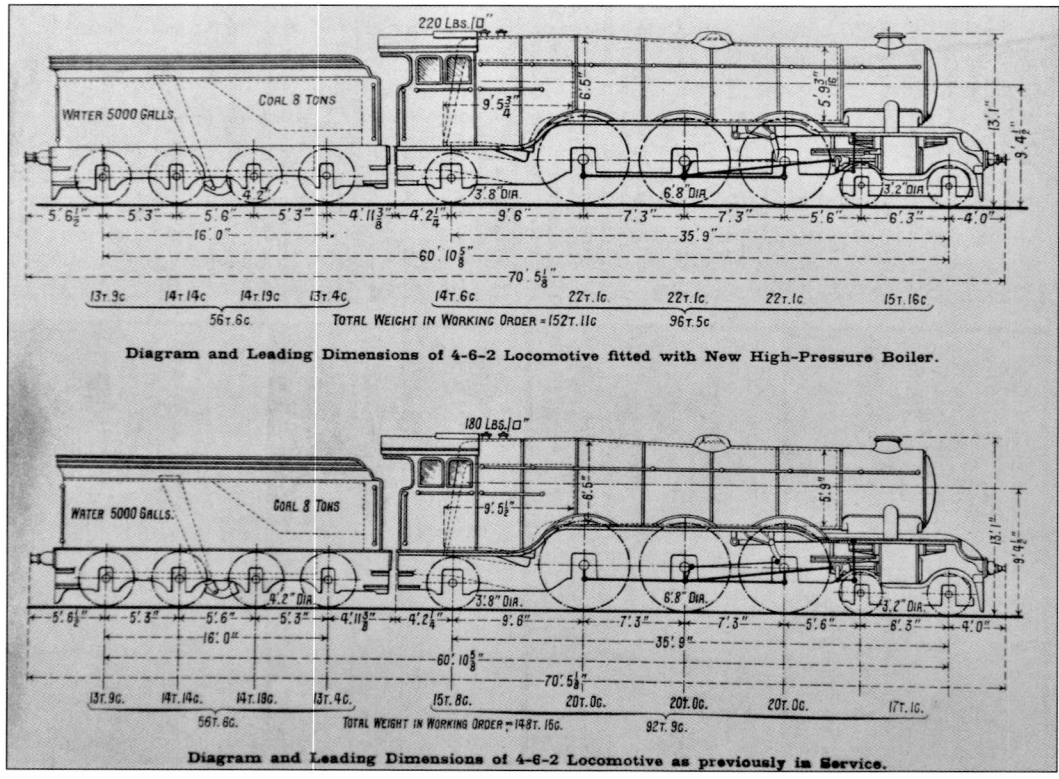

A simple diagram that Spencer kept amongst his papers describing the changes made to the A1 design as it evolved into the A3. (BS)

Innovation or Stagnation 71

11 July 1927 proved to be a very important day in the development of express services to Scotland. Spencer was present on the inaugural non-stop run from London to Newcastle representing Gresley as far as technical analysis was concerned. His report made clear that whilst the A1 could manage the task, its coal capacity did not provide a suitable safety margin for the longer non-stop journey to Edinburgh. He also cofirmed that it was a task beyond the capacity of a single crew operating without a change to manage. Nevertheless the event did attract a large crowd, a great deal of publicity and a host of VIPs. (Above left) 9.50 am and engine No. 4475 *Flying Fox* pulls away with Driver Pibworth and Fireman Mutton in charge. (Above right) The train arrived precisely on time at 3.20pm to be greeted on Platform 8 by 'a dense and enthusiastic crowd'. Here Arthur Lambert, the Lord Mayor of Newcastle, congratulates the crew. (BS)

The gradual evolution of A1/A3s allowed the LNER to pursue a long held ambition – to run a non-stop service between London and Edinburgh. But first the concept had to be tried and in 1927 a test train ran between King's Cross and Newcastle, where it would halt before travelling on to Edinburgh. This long first stage was deemed to be within the capabilities of the A1s with 180psi boilers and on 11 July the service ran for the first time. Spencer was on board, accompanied by Arthur Stamer, who was deputising for Gresley on this occasion. Gresley's assistant later reported that:

The CME instructed me to accompany the train northwards on the 11th to observe how the engine and its crew (Driver A Tibworth and Fireman H Mutton) performed. At this stage there were no A1s with 220lb boilers available and there was some concern that the lower capacity boilers might not cope well with such a demanding schedule. This proved not to be the case, but, I think, this was more to do with the skill of Alf Pibworth and Harry Mutton, who were known to perform wonders on the footplate of Pacifics, and, in Pibworth's case, the Atlantics. During the 1925 exchange trials he had been on the footplate of 4474 when the engine turned in a quite exemplary performance on the mainline to Exeter. So it surprised no one when his name appeared on the roster for the run to Newcastle. By this stage he had become an old friend, but try as I might I could not get him drop the 'Sir' which ended each part of our conversations.

Engine No. 4475, *Flying Fox*, which was thought to be one of the best A1s, left promptly at 9.50am and was scheduled to cover the 268 miles to Newcastle in 5½ hours. She was not long out of General Repair at Doncaster, during which her valve gear had been modified, if my memory serves me well. I do not believe that the other four engines selected to work these trains [4474 *Victor Wild*, 2552 *Sansovino*, 2569 *Gladiateur* and 2575 *Galopin*] had been similarly modified at that stage, although each spent a few days in the Works being prepared for the service. So it was interesting to compare how 4475 performed with the others.

The journey was uneventful and we arrived at Newcastle on time to be greeted by a large crowd, including the Lord Mayor of Newcastle. Later in the day I spoke to the crew and could clearly see how much the run had taken out of them. Alf, who was pushing on a bit by then and not far from retirement, was kept on light duties for a week or so afterwards, such had been the strain. I reported to Gresley by phone and next day we, with Bulleid, discussed these events, with particular emphasis on coal consumption and the way the crew had handled their duties. While 8 tons of coal was sufficient for Newcastle, and provided a good reserve, the additional stage to Edinburgh would cut this to the bone. By some means an extra ton or so of coal had to be squeezed on to the tender. With regard to the crew it was clear that they had been tested to the limit. It was a point Gresley accepted without question, as did Bulleid.

Spencer's assessment must have given Gresley much to think about and the CME's report to the General Manager would have been couched in very positive terms. The issue of the A1s' capability in managing the long non-stop run to Edinburgh and back seemed clear. If 4475, with lower capacity boiler, could manage such an arduous turn then the 220psi versions should do so with greater ease, especially with modified valve gear. All that remained to be considered were the dual questions of capacity – of crew and of fuel – before the new, high-profile service could begin. The answer to both issues was found in the development of a new tender. In fact, it was a practical solution that bears all the hallmarks of Spencer's clever mind working to resolve an operational problem in the simplest way possible. Although making light of his own contribution, he left some notes describing the way the idea evolved:

'There were often debates about the viability of non-stop services and the ability of one driver and fireman to cope with such difficult duties. These discussions came to a head when the non-stop service from King's Cross to Newcastle was introduced in July 1927. With a weather eye to costs some contended that a longer, 7½ hour, journey to Waverley would be well within the capabilities of a single crew. Gresley argued that this would cut the margin for safety to an unacceptable level and proposed having a second fireman on the footplate for the entire journey to share the load, or, as an alternative halt the train mid-way for a fresh crew to take over. He asked me to speak to some of the drivers and gather their thoughts on the alternative solutions. To a man they felt that a single crew would be unable to cope consistently with the turn and having a second fireman would spread the workload, but do nothing to reduce what was a very arduous duty for the driver. Stopping the train for a change of crew was, they believed, the most sensible option, but this was not likely to find favour with the powers that be. With proposals for a non-stop service to Scotland in jeopardy we considered other options.

Railways in this country and overseas could offer no alternative solution, their non-stop services, such as the GWR's Cheltenham Flyer, being operated over much shorter distances and so well within the capabilities of a footplate crew. In the USA longer journeys were helped by labour saving devices such as mechanical stokers and the introduction of oil burners, but neither caught on here. However, an article in an American Journal, some years earlier, about carriage gangway connections on Pullman Cars had caught my eye. On long journeys men would gain access to the locomotive from the first car by leaning out over the coupling and clambering over or around the tender, on a narrow footplate, to reach the cab. As such it had become custom and practice over many years, as well as a regular feature of early cowboy films as goodies and baddies fought for control of the train. It seemed to me a wholly unsafe practice, but did suggest the idea of a tender with a narrow corridor through it linked to a gangway connection to the carriages. This might, if successful, allow a change of crew to safely take place when the train was in motion and remove the need for a midway stop.

The most obvious problem was one of space. The corridor had to be big enough to allow even the largest crew member to pass through, but not so large as to reduce the

Innovation or Stagnation 73

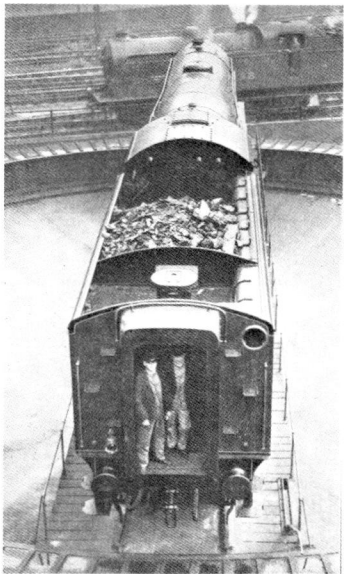

Running long distance non-stop services from London to Scotland was a company ambition, although its effect on the LNER's balance sheet was fairly small when compared to goods traffic. Whilst the modified A1s had the capacity to undertake these duties, the footplate crew would have struggled to meet such a heavy physical demand on a regular basis. Gresley's solution was a simple one – build and fit corridor tenders allowing the crew to be changed mid-journey, thus removing the need for stopping. It was a design task in which Spencer was involved as he later related. He saved many photos and newspaper articles, including those above, that the new tenders and the new service generated. (BS)

Newly built A3s make their appearance. Twenty-seven were built over a seven-year period between 1928 and 1935 in what was a very leisurely programme. But their actual number was much greater when the fifty rebuilt A1s were added to the A3 fleet between 1927 and 1948. Engine No. 2750 *Papyrus*, was the eighth A3 to be built, and entered service in February 1929. Here she is captured on rather a mundane freight duty as far removed from the glamour of express passenger work as it was possible to get. (RH)

space for coal and water. The solution was a simple one and made full use of the loading gauge. I prepared a number of drawings which CME approved and passed to the Chief Draughtsman for further action. The new tenders were slightly longer and higher than the others, could carry 9 tons of coal and fully met our requirement as tests soon proved. It was a matter of some pride to be on the inaugural run and see the tender working well in service, with the much modified A1 in front performing so admirably.'

An order for ten new tenders was soon approved and by mid-1928 seven were ready for service with A1s. The remaining three were allocated to the first three A3s built – Nos. 2743, 2744 and 2745 – and appeared in August that year. It seems that attempts were made to keep their introduction a secret as long as possible, the publicity value of the new non-stop service to Scotland being deemed too good to miss. To this end Spencer recalled:

> 'Rivalry with the LMS in the 'Race to the North' was always strong. Although quite friendly in the way it was conducted, it was inevitable that the company that could manage it as quickly as possible won most plaudits. In late 1927 the LMS were quick to laud its non-stop service between London and Carlisle. With the improved Pacifics available and their range extended by the new tenders, it was clear that the LNER would equal or better this record.
>
> Plans for the new service were kept very quiet, as was the introduction of the corridor tenders. So in some secrecy they were attached to a few chosen locomotives – 4472, 4475, 2547, 2552, 2563, 2565, 2566 and 2569. Some of these were only for a few weeks, others more permanently [for example 4472 was attached for twelve months, 4475 for six years and 2546 for three months]. The intention was to test them quietly to ensure they met all our requirements, with much of this work being undertaken during the hours of darkness. I am not sure if any of this was necessary, but this how it was managed for right or wrong and the trials proved that the tenders were as good as they could be. I recollect that engine No. 2547, *Doncaster*, was the centre of much of this work in April and then reverted to a standard tender in May '28.

While all this was happening, many other operating issues were considered in an effort to ensure the non-stop service would run without undue difficulty. The service from London to Newcastle had revealed no insurmountable problems, but the final 125 miles to Edinburgh threw up one or two problems. Not least of these was a lack of water troughs over the border in Scotland and the greater distance between those in Yorkshire and Northumberland. Prudent management of a locomotive was necessary to overcome this, in terms of water pick up. Tests early in 1928, between York and Edinburgh with an A1 [No. 2582 *Sir Hugo*, pulling a 350 ton load] had shown that on average only 2,000 gallons were scooped up. This was thought insufficient in terms of providing a good margin of safety. Some improvements were made to the troughs and the footplate crew were

Engine No. 4472, *Flying Scotsman*, gets underway on 1 May 1928 on its highly publicised inaugural run from King's Cross to Edinburgh. Gresley and Spencer were just two of the passengers on this memorable trip. (BS)

encouraged to take greater care when using the scoop. In February the trials were repeated [this time with engine No. 2568 *Sceptre* pulling 450 tons] and the crew were able to lift at least a fifth more water.

With these final problems ironed out permission to begin the service was given and the publicity department began releasing details to the press, making no mention of the new tender.

Memorably, engine No. 4472, *Flying Scotsman*, one of five locomotives prepared for the task, pulled the inaugural service northwards on 1 May 1928. Bert Spencer, who was present on this trip, recalled the day in a very brief way:

There were a sizeable number of journalists on board as well as Sir Nigel, some of his family and many representatives from the railway. The journey passed without incident though at one stage it was suspected that a tender axle box might be overheating. But, if so, it didn't slow progress or delay the train in any way. Gresley and I took a number of parties up to the cab through the tender much to the CME's great pleasure, especially when taking the controls for short periods. By this stage he was becoming increasingly concerned about his wife's health and the first non-stop run to Edinburgh provided some distraction.

Although the Pacific programme captured many headlines and would come to represent all that Gresley achieved in his career, they were only one part of a massive locomotive development programme that found its inspiration in the CME's offices at King's Cross. By comparison with the Pacifics, much of this may have appeared mundane or low key but undoubtedly added something to the growing knowledge of Gresley and his team. For example, there was the CME's attempt to create a more effective tank engine, which Spencer touched on briefly during his 1947 presentation:

In 1925 a scheme was prepared for a three cylinder 2-6-4 type tank engine for the GN Section London suburban services incorporating the K3 class cylinders, wheels and running gear, together with the 5ft 6in. diameter boiler used on the GN Section K2 class, 2-6-0 type two cylinder engines. The tractive effort at 85 per cent boiler pressure was to be 28,431lb. It was not found possible to alter the layout at Moorgate Street Station to permit the use of engines of this length in conjunction with suburban train sets and the proposal was not developed.

In 1927 the use of tank engines on the GE Section Southend lines was considered for services usually worked by the B12 class, 4-6-0 type, inside cylinder engines having 6ft 6in. diameter coupled wheels and a tractive effort of 21,969lb. A two cylinder 2-6-4 type tank engine of similar tractive effort was proposed having 6ft 2in. diameter coupled wheels and 20in by 26in cylinders with the 5ft 6in. diameter boiler used on the J39 and D49 classes, but the project was abandoned in favour of additional B12 class tender engines.'

Then there was the LNER's attempt to build a heavy goods engine with the two 2-8-2 P1s that appeared in 1925. Spencer wrote or said very little about them, presumably because he played little or no part in their development when working in the Drawing Office at Doncaster, and then arriving in London, by which time the work was well advanced. So he probably regarded them with an independent, critical eye:

The P1 class mineral engines, Nos 2393 and 2394, were built at Doncaster for working trains of 100 wagons, or 1600 tons, over the GN section between Peterborough and London. These engines were a development of the Pacific type and had the same 6ft 5in diameter

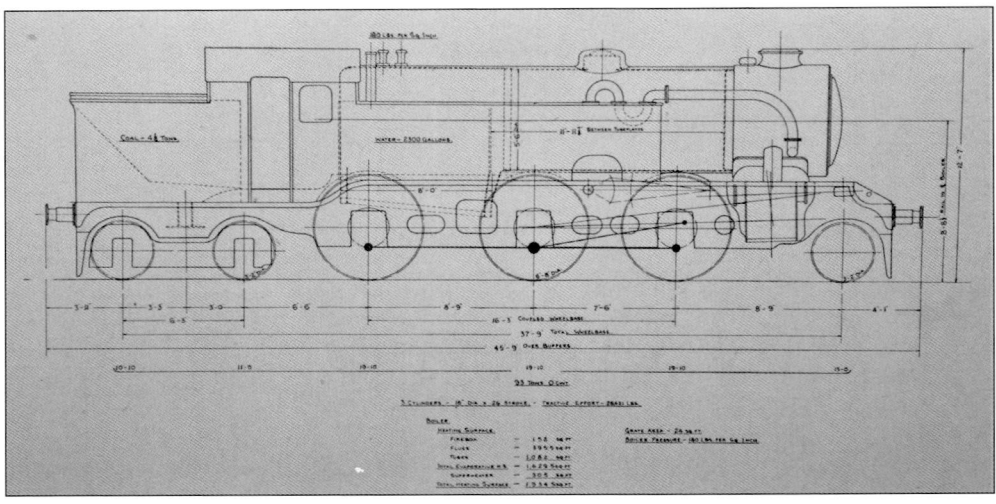

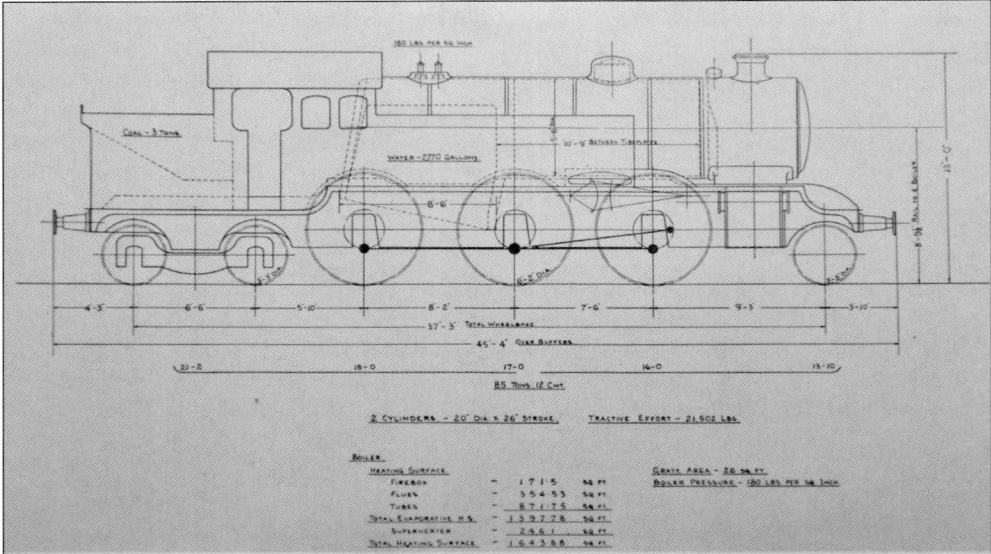

Above and opposite above: The life of any good designer is punctuated by a series of 'what if' questions. What if we tried this or that will prompt many experiments and help lead them to a workable solution to a given problem. To Gresley, Bulleid and Spencer, amongst others, such an approach was second nature. This, plus open enquiring minds, allowed their imaginations to roam free when seeking answers, in so doing they sought to explore what was possible, while recognising both technical and financial limitations. There would be many dead ends and unprofitable avenues to negotiate on the road to success, but this was a necessary part of their work. This process of evaluation, rejection and selection is illustrated by the three drawings reproduced here. Each shows an idea schemed out at King's Cross for various types of new tank engines, all of which were rejected. In reality, Gresley carried on building the successful N2 0-6-2s, introduced in 1920, and then waited until 1930 to begin adding 921 V1/V3 three cylinder 2-6-4Ts to the fleet. On the way he (top) considered this 2-6-4 design for suburban passenger services during 1925, (lower) this was followed in 1927 by a two-cylinder 2-6-4T for use on the Southend Line and (overleaf) a three-cylinder 2-8-2T for colliery work in 1930. None were built but as Spencer related 'each piece of work added something, whether successful or not, which increased our knowledge of design considerably. It was a necessary part of my duties to be directly involved in all this experimental work.' (BS)

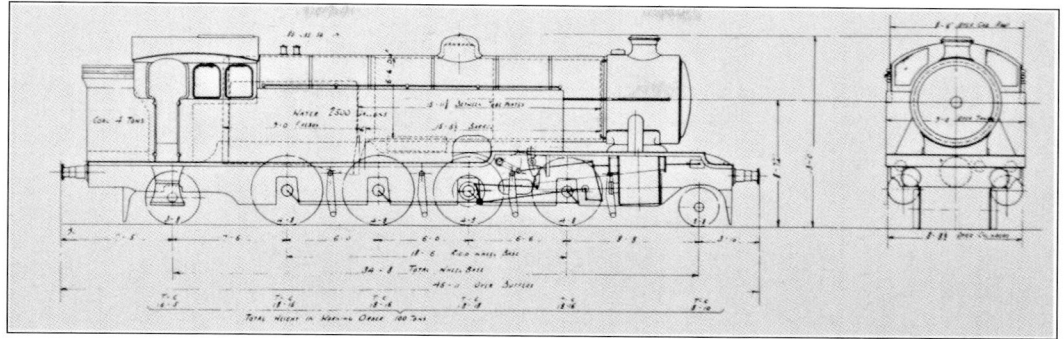

boiler with three cylinders 20in x 26in and coupled wheels 5ft 2in diameter. A booster was originally fitted on the trailing carrying wheels to assist in starting and at some point en route where trains were frequently stopped or checked on rising gradients of 1 in 200.

The great length of the trains the P1 class engines were capable of handling, proved somewhat of a problem for the Operating Department and as more normal loads became usual the boosters were found to be unnecessary and were removed.

Apart from this brief description of their development, Spencer recorded little more about them, but in a letter written much later he added a comment that reveals something interesting about the Gresley-Bulleid relationship:

Much of the planning work for the P1s (and then the P2s) was led by Bulleid who seemed more firmly wedded to the 2-8-2 Mikados than Gresley. The CME was undoubtedly interested but I was left with the impression that for him it was an academic exercise to test a theory and thought its potential for use in Britain was limited. In practice, he demonstrated a greater commitment to the 2-8-0 design, which had wider route availability and were greatly preferred by the crews who had to work either types. As a result, he continued building his Class 02s, with the last group appearing in 1942/43, by which time Thompson was CME. In this choice Gresley was clearly influenced by Churchward, less so when it came to other classes. Bulleid, however, believed that the 2-8-2 concept should be taken further and frequently pressed Gresley to do so, with limited success until the question of more powerful locomotives for the line north of Edinburgh was raised by the Regional Manager.

For the moment, though, this next stage in the development of the Mikados was still some years away. For the time being, there were plenty of other ideas to occupy Gresley's mind. Sometimes these projects were for a new type of locomotive, on other occasions they were simply adaptions of existing classes to test a theory or see if their performance could be improved in some way. One of these involved two old North Eastern Railway locomotives in a project that Spencer later recalled:

The CME carried out a most interesting conversion of two of the C7 type 4-4-2 express passenger engines, built respectively in the years 1911 and 1913. These engines have three single-expansion cylinders driving the first pair of coupled wheels, and they have now been rebuilt and fitted with a bogie placed behind the coupled wheels under the cab, this being the first example of articulation between engine and tender in which the rear end of the front end of the tender are carried on a common base. The arrangement has greatly improved the

The P1 project was an interesting experiment but one that seemed doomed to failure when the massive trains they were designed to pull (up to 100 coal wagons) proved very difficult for the railway's infrastructure to handle. It seems that the Running Department preferred smaller loads which were handled more economically by 2-8-0 engines. Both P1s were withdrawn in 1945. The picture above captures the first of the class, No. 2393, on a duty for which she was designed. Of note is the Westinghouse pump midway along the boiler barrel. The pump supported the booster engine fitted to provide drive to the trailing carrying wheels and help the engine pull away from stop when engaging its heaviest loads. (BS)

The concept of articulated bogies joining a locomotive's cab to its tender and between carriages was a theme Gresley often returned to during his career. It was believed that this arrangement would greatly improve ride quality and reduce lateral movement. For locomotives, as here with one of two C7s converted to this form in 1931, the bogie also carried a booster engine which produced extra power when starting from rest and when climbing a steep gradient. Gresley first tried boosters in 1923 when he converted an Ivatt Atlantic No. 4419 and repeated it with his two P1s in 1925. As Spencer reported 'these modifications proved of great interest but articulation and the fitting of boosters did not catch on, although with carriages, particularly the streamlinded coach sets, the idea found new legs'. (BS)

Innovation or Stagnation

Engine No 234 *Yorkshire* when built at Darlington in 1927 – the first of seventy-six D49s. They had three-cylinders, but in this case the two to one rocking levers were placed behind the cylinders instead of in front. This made it possible for the drive from all three cylinders to be connected to the front coupled axle. Gresley chose to experiment with these engines by fitting different types of valve gear. There were twenty-eight built between 1927 and 1929 with Walschaerts and piston valves, then six more were built in 1928 with Walschaerts and poppet valves, using oscillating cam operated valves (though later rebuilt with poppet valves). The remaining locomotives were fitted with Walschaerts and rotary cam Lentz poppet valve gear. This last group were thought troublesome in service and were, post 1938, rebuilt with ordinary piston valves. Spencer later wrote that 'it was an interesting exercise which involved me in much test work. It took much time to convince the CME that the Walschaert valve gear with piston valves was probably the most effective solution. However, they were never a popular class mostly because of their very rough riding qualities'. (BS)

> riding of the engine and eliminated the relative lateral movement between the engine and the tender. The booster bogie has a side play of 4½ in. each side, controlled by a pair of coil springs, having a compression of 2 tons.
>
> During recent tests with engine No. 727 on a 300 ton train a speed of 19 mph was obtained in 8 minutes on a gradient of 1 in 70 with the booster out of operation. With the booster in operation a speed of 25 mph was reached in 5¾ minutes. On a level road the engine with the booster out of operation was able to start a load of 496 tons, the drawbar pull being 9 tons. With the assistance of the booster, a load of 746 tons was started with a drawbar pull of 12½ tons.'

Another idea of worth which Gresley and his team pursued with great vigour at this time concerned the type of valve gear to be used, which Spencer described in the following way:

> For the lighter passenger services in the North Eastern and Scottish Areas, Gresley introduced the three-cylinder, 4-4-0 type 'Shire' class express engines. The first of the new series, No.234, 'Yorkshire', classified D49, left Darlington works in September 1927. These engines have 6ft 8in. diameter coupled wheels and the three 17in. by 26in. cylinders are arranged in line above the bogie, thus making it possible to accommodate the Gresley gear behind the cylinders. This arrangement avoids the necessity of disconnecting the gear for valve examination and also eliminates the effect of outside valve spindle expansion on the centre valve. The boilers of the D49 class carry a working pressure of 180lb. per sq inch and are interchangeable with those of the J39 class.
>
> In 1928 six D49 class engines built at Darlington were fitted with Lentz poppet valves operated by oscillating cams. The centre cylinder camshaft derived its movement from a

combination of the movements of the two outside Walschaert valve gears by means of a system of rocking shafts behind the cylinders similar to that fitted on engine No. 461 (Gresley's first Class 02 engine built in 1918), but of lighter construction. This arrangement proved unsatisfactory owing to the wear on the various pin joints affecting the accurate movement of the central cylinder and it was replaced by the standard Gresley gear consisting of horizontal '2 in 1' and 'equal' levers located behind the cylinders. Whilst this modification resulted in some improvement the centre cylinder valve events were difficult to maintain and the engines were fitted with piston valves when the cylinders required renewal.

Arising from this work with the D49s, when B17 class 4-6-0s were being designed and built the conjugated valve gear was placed behind the cylinders, as tried and tested on the D49s. They also became the only Gresley three-cylinder engines to have divided drive - the outside cylinders driving on the second coupled axle and the inside cylinder on the first. This arrangement was necessary in order that the weight distribution of the engine should conform to the limits imposed by the engineers. Operational requirements also made it necessary to restrict their overall length and the original GE type six-wheeled tender was therefore provided. Later engines had the larger standard 4,000 galls tender.

Although the D49 class engines were fitted with poppet valves operated by oscillating cams driven from the Walschaert valve gear, Gresley felt that the full advantage of such valves would not be realised unless a simple rotary gear was developed. In 1929 two D49 engines, No. 336, *'Buckinghamshire'* and No. 352, *'Leicestershire'*, were therefore fitted with an experimental arrangement of rotary cam valve gear designed by Messrs. Lentz Patents in collaboration with the LNER.

Engines fitted with each type of valve gear were selected for comparative tests carried out between Newcastle and York in November-December 1929, each engine (Nos. 352, 236, 239 and 352) being tested for five days on the same trains. From the results it will be seen that engine No. 352, with rotary cam operated poppet valves was a little lighter on coal per drawbar horsepower hour than either the piston valve (236) or the oscillating cam poppet valve engine (329).

The first of the B17s as it appeared in 1928, when built by the North British Locomotive Company, who also undertook the detailed design work. Sub-contracting work in this way was not unknown in the industry, especially when there was lack of capacity in the parent company's workshops and design offices. Spencer later recalled that 'I and my small team of draughtsmen undertook a brief study to stablish what was needed in the way of a more powerful engine to work from Liverpool Street into East Anglia. From this we prepared a few drawings and an outline of what was required. When NBL took the work I was a little surprised and during 1927 and 1928 I was tasked by the CME to visit their Works in Glasgow to ensure their draughtsmen were on the right track. Once NBL had produced the first ten the remainder were built at Darlington or the Robert Stephenson and Company workshops in Newcastle.' (BS)

The results of tests carried out with new D49 4-6-0 engines over the course of two months in 1929 as recorded by Spencer and presented to the ILocoE. The purpose was a simple one – to establish the comparative benefits of using different types of valve – piston, rotary or oscillating. (BS)

COMPARATIVE TESTS BETWEEN PISTON AND LENTZ VALVE GEAR.
TYPE D.49 LOCOMOTIVES.

Made between York and Newcastle: November-December 1929.
Engine 352—Lentz Valve, Rotary.
,, 236—Piston Valve.
,, 329—Lentz Valve, Oscillating.

Particulars	Engine 352	Engine 236	Engine 329
Average coal consumption:			
Lb. per drawbar horsepower hour	3.62	3.68	3.69
Lb. per mile	31.55	35.1	34.66
Lb. per ton mile (excluding engine)	.108	.114	.108
Average water consumption:			
Lb. per drawbar horsepower hour	28.17	27.15	27.58
Lb. per mile	245.1	258.5	258.8
Lb. per ton mile (excluding engine)	.839	.842	.811
Average drawbar horsepower exerted	395	430	420
Average drawbar pull, tons	1.46	1.60	1.57
Average speed, m.p.h.	45.2	45.0	44.8
Average steam temperature, deg. F.	576	578	596
Average evaporation:			
Lb. of water per lb. of coal	7.77	7.38	7.46

Spencer then went on to describe all the test results in fine detail and giving any reason for the variations, before confirming that forty more engines with rotary cam gear were then built between 1932 and 1935. However, he passes no comment on the wisdom of doing so, which suggests he may not have been in total agreement with the action taken or others where the CME seemed too innovative. This impression is confirmed to a certain extent by his next statement:

> During development of the three-cylinder 4-4-0 type, D49 class engines, Gresley considered the possibility of constructing a six-cylinder 4-4-0 type geared locomotive, of similar tractive effort, having 6ft 8in. diameter coupled wheels, a boiler pressure of 200lb./sq in and a tractive effort of 21,520lb.
>
> A six-cylinder 'uniflow' engine arranged in 'Vee' form with three cylinders on each side of the smokebox drives twin crankshafts with cranks at 120 degrees was fitted. Rotary cam valve gear operating 3in. diameter double seated poppet valves by stepped cams gives four ranges of cut off in fore gear. The main casting incorporates the crank case, saddle and jackshaft supports … The 'uniflow' engines were to have a crank-shaft speed of 700 rpm at 70 mph and the drive from the twin crankshaft was to be transmitted by bevel gearing to a jackshaft. The provision of a suitable bevel drive presented difficulties and the scheme was not proceeded with.

One can almost hear a sigh of relief in this last sentence. At times working with a strong, dynamic personality can be challenging. The highly creative will always have 'flights of fancy' which will take them in many directions, some of which may eventually prove to be valuable, whilst others become unwanted distractions from the main business at hand. Yet this was part and parcel of Gresley's personality and way of working.

The papers that have survived from this period show how closely the CME involved himself in the process of design and construction, faithfully followed by the ever-present Spencer, both taking an almost minute interest in the fine detail of a project. On many occasions the CME, with or without Spencer's involvement, contacted the Mechanical Engineers at Doncaster and Darlington and the Chief Draughtsman personally on an almost daily basis suggesting changes or seeking updates on work. And to this was added regular visits in which progress was undoubtedly discussed. Luckily, he behaved diplomatically and fully understood the pressures his staff were under, so managed not to ruffle feathers unless absolutely necessary. But at times it must have been a difficult balance to achieve, as Bert Spencer suggested when he wrote:

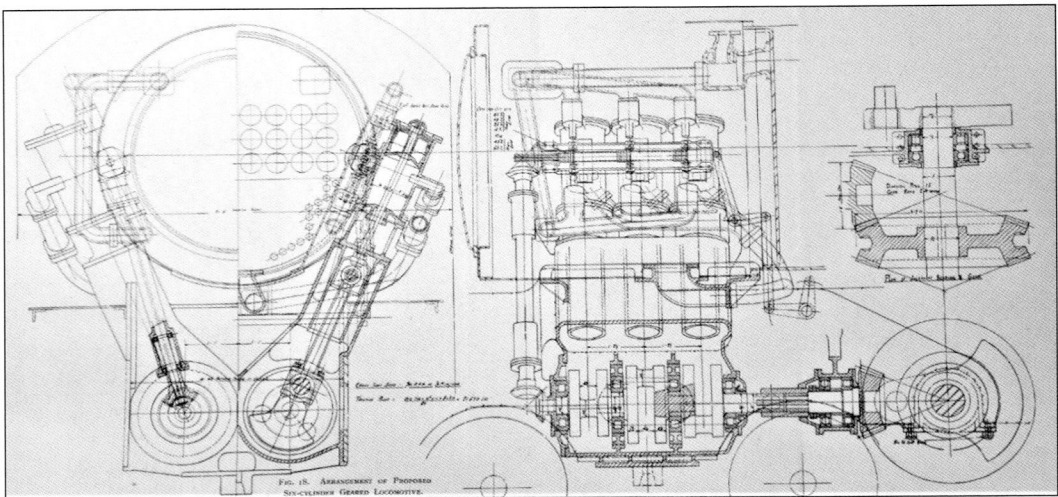

The initial design for Gresley's experimental six-cylinder 'uniflow' engine. Bert Spencer, it seems, took his CME's rough sketches, and scribbled ideas, and produced the drawings that ended up forming part of his 1947 presentation to the ILocoE. Although taking this preparatory action, he reported that the proposal did not get beyond the drawing board phase. A distraction killed off, perhaps, or a far-seeing idea that might have proved a success if not unnecessarily terminated. As with any unusual idea, the weight of other work, plus a degree of scepticism can prove impossible to overcome. It is hard to say how strong Spencer's influence was in these matters, but he does seem to have been a voice of reason and assumed the role of long stop on much that Gresley contemplated. (BS)

> The pace of work was relentless at times. Up to 1929, on an almost daily basis, Sir Nigel would produce new ideas or improvements to other designs in sketches or short written statements as his agile mind appraised all that was going on around him. Many of these were filtered out at King`s Cross or underwent modification before reaching Thom, Stamer or the Chief Draughtsman. But he would also contact them directly on many issues they may already have had well in hand. There was little friction though, such was the high regard in which he was held.

As the end of the 1920s approached the pressure on the team at King's Cross was unrelenting in its intensity and variety. There was much going in the world of design and much to consider as a result. Some ideas were simply observed, considered for a few weeks and put to one side, while others, for some reason, appealed to Gresley's creative mind and were pursued with some vigour. In choosing an idea to follow he was of course guided to a certain extent by good business principles, but he was not afraid to overlook these constraints when he felt there might be long term rewards to reap by being innovative. 'Speculate to accumulate', as Spencer later called it, was a concept close to Gresley's heart, but added that 'when doing so he was generally very selective and took both the General Manager and Chairman with him. He was a sound businessman as well as engineer'.

One idea which interested the CME for a time was the potential of turbines and work that had been carrying on since the the early years of the century in Britain and overseas. Much of this took place before Spencer joined Gresley in London, but as he reported:

> The level of his interest was quickly apparent in all things scientific by the number and variety of files he had accumulated over the years. Gresley was an avid collector and reader of all sorts of scientific papers and amongst them there were many items relating to the development of turbines.

When working in the Drawing Office at Doncaster I had seen first-hand the results of some of this work when the Reid-McCleod condensing direct drive turbine locomotive was introduced in the early '20s (above left). This was soon followed by a version built by Armstrong-Whitworth, but on this occasion driven, if my memory serves me well, by a condensing electric-turbine. I was able to ride on the Reid-McCleod in April 1927, on Gresley's behalf, when running trials between Edinburgh and Glasgow. This work had been going on for six years by then and had still not proved the theory that underpinned its development to be worthwhile. The Armstrong-Whitworth loco (above right) was even less successful and as were several other models. It wasn't until 1931 that the first successful design appeared and this was the Ljungstrom non condensing turbine locomotive, which clearly influenced Stanier as he pursued his Pacific version which appeared in 1935.

Gresley watched all this from a distance and would often engage in discussions with Bulleid and myself on the viability of turbines in steam locomotives. Gresley was not convinced that turbines produced sufficient advantages to justify the huge cost of development at that time, but was not against the idea in principle.'

In the constant search for more efficient locomotives a range of ideas was suggested and considered – some practical, others far less so – many by members of various institutions. Occasionally something most unusual would appear to test the powers of reason and common sense. But as any student of scientific discovery will confirm, these idiosyncratic, unorthodox ideas could prove to be much more than the whim of a daydreamer and hold true merit that only deeper thought and trials might reveal. Just such a case was William Werry's concept for a high speed steam locomotive which, as a report in the *Locomotive* during 1936 recorded, 'Divided the drive between two pistons reciprocating in opposition in a common cylinder, whereby the piston stroke for a given total displacement volume is halved, and as a consequence the piston velocity for any given rotation is similarly diminished.'

How Werry's work came to Gresley's attention is unclear, there being no obvious presentation reported in the records of either the IMechE or ILocoE. However, it is known that Werry did seek out some leaders of the railway industry to discuss his ideas and this may have led him to Gresley. As a result, Spencer, or so it seems from his correspondence, was despatched to meet Werry who 'seemed to be a constant presence in the Marble Arch Hotel, where we met early one morning while the dining room was still being cleared of breakfast dishes'.

Spencer's task was a simple one:

'I was asked by the CME to consider the basis of Werry's ideas and judge whether they warranted further investigation. He cut rather an eccentric figure and was a man I judged to be in his sixties, who launched into his plans without really structuring his thoughts in an organised way. This made it very difficult to follow his arguments or evaluate the data

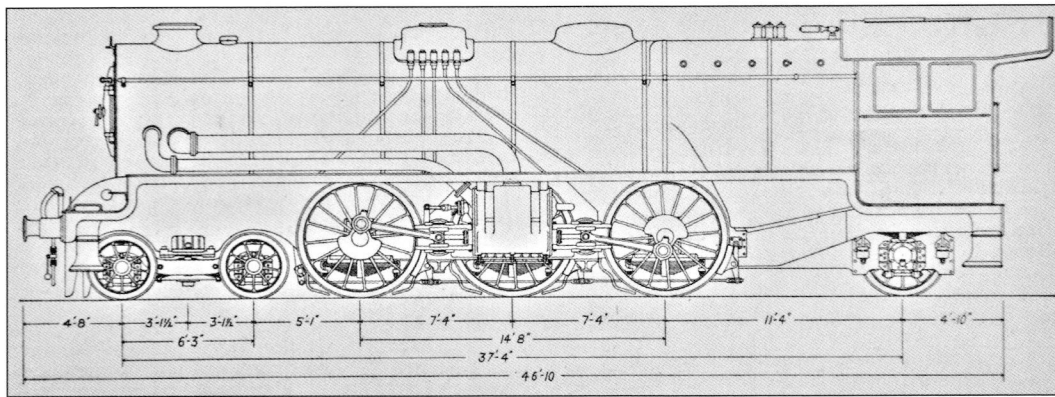

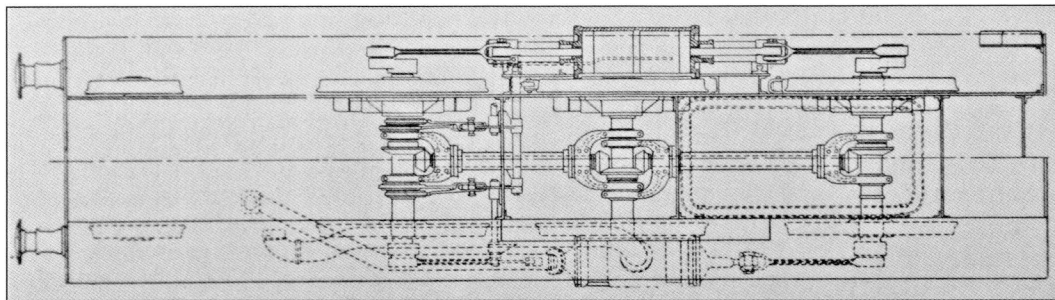

Two drawings produced by William Werry to demonstrate the workings of his design for a high speed locomotive. It seems that Werry was concerned about plagiarism so was loath to hand over more material to the LNER man or anyone else without a firm commitment. In doing so he probably undermined his own case and Gresley took the matter no further. One wonders whether Werry was aware of the debate that had raged years earlier between Gresley and Harold Holcroft over 'ownership' of the two to one valve gear. If so, did this make him overly cautious in dealing with the CME? Perhaps greater openness might have served him better (BS)

he presented, which came thick and fast. He claimed that his design could help reduce maintenance costs by up to 25 per cent over a standard steam engine, generate 25 per cent more speed, improve the power to weight ratio and much more. These were impressive claims, but difficult to verify without more solid test data.

At this stage we knew very little about him or his background, but he gave the impression of being a trained mechanical engineer, who had gained wide experience of marine engineering. He spoke little about his life but did say that he had lived and worked in Australia for a time.

My subsequent report to Gresley, which I did not retain, described some of Werry's ideas and concluded they were probably worthy of further consideration when and if a working prototype had been built and could be analysed. He was not willing to release copies of drawings or specifications to me, beyond some simple diagrams of one engine. If more had been made available Gresley might have been persuaded to look more closely at his proposals. As it was the CME decided to go no further on the grounds of cost but also lack of information. Nevertheless, I followed the remainder of Werry's career with some interest and met him several more times in a personal and professional capacity. I am told by others who knew him that he was greatly angered by his lack of success in selling his ideas and felt that others may have copied them for their own benefit. This may well be so but it is difficult to judge such issues when a number of people are developing similar ideas at the same time.'

Werry remains something of an enigma in engineering circles. He was born to George and Mary in Cornwall during 1862 and emigrated to Australia, with his parents and brother, in 1870. His father appears to have been a tin miner who sought a new life in Steiglitz, Queensland, as a gold prospector and miner but died shortly after their arrival. In due course, William would follow his father into the mines, possibly as an engineer. In 1882 he married Sarah Jane Trembath, in Lefroy, Tasmania. They had three children who all died within days of their birth, and she followed them in 1890. A year later he married Rosa Sewart, and together they had at least seven children many of whom survived into adulthood. Before returning to Britain in the early 1900s, he is reported to have been working on the Victoria Railway in Australia, as a porter, then as an engine minder at a mine in Bendigo a hundred miles or so north-west of Melbourne. However, records do not reveal if he attended college at any time, undertook an apprenticeship or obtained some formal engineering qualification which might have underpinned his scientific credentials and ambitions.

In 1904, local investors, who had been suitably impressed by a demonstration of a small prototype compound engine, built to his design by Ferguson Engineering, decided to bankroll further development work. This led to the creation of the Werry Engine Company and thoughts of rapid expansion if customers could be found. But in a country with a small population and minimal industrial muscle or military might, the opportunities for such a company were limited. So, with his investors' backing, he eventually journeyed to Europe where business conditions were thought to be much better.

Time passed and in 1911 he is recorded as being a widower living in London at the Marble Arch Hotel, with his professional status given as Marine Engine Engineer. At this stage, he is reported as trying to get the Admiralty interested in a design for a balanced, vibration-free steam engine for use in small naval vessels. As a result, he was commissioned to design a steam engine for a 50ft boat being built by the Thames Ironworks Company in support of the much bigger construction of a mother ship, in this case the battlecruiser HMAS *Australia*. His proposal for a steam engine mounted horizontally, with two crankshafts linked by bevel gears and rods to propeller shafts, was accepted. Despite success in the trials that followed, the Admiralty were at a technical crossroads. By this stage internal combustion engines were reaching a more advanced state of development and these were beginning to offer the Navy a far better, more user friendly

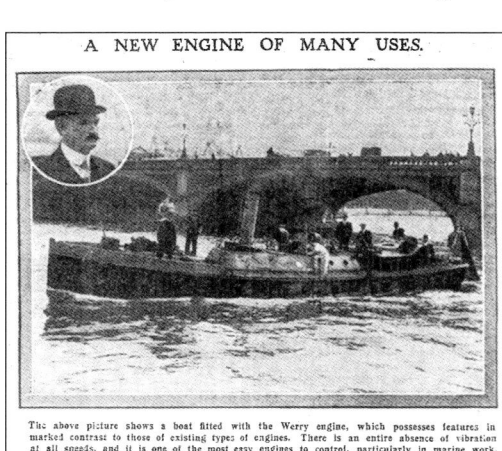

Judging by several press reports that have survived, William Werry developed something of a reputation as an inventor – boats, motor bikes and aircraft being amongst his list of accomplishments. Yet despite his hard work he never seemed to achieve a major breakthrough with his designs and did not enter the mainstream of engineering in Britain or get the recognition he may have thought should have been his. (BS)

source of power than steam engines. So this side of Werry's business faded away, but with steam still dominating the railways there remained this market to exploit.

Over the years he is recorded as having designed many locomotives, beginning in 1906 with the 'flyer' powered by an 'opposed piston, uniflow engine'. From there he moved on to a 4-4-2 design and in 1913, a Pacific. In 1922, there appeared proposals for a 4-10-0, 4-12-0 and 4-14-0 freight engines. In pursuit of this dream, his ideas came thick and fast, pausing only in 1914 when the war pulled him in another direction. But despite his hard work and good intentions, success eluded him, perhaps because his ideas were too far from the norm and so came with great risks. It seemed at one stage that there might be a breakthrough. In 1924 the North British Railway Company produced two Werry inspired designs when bidding for a contract to build engines for the South Australia Railway. In the event, Armstrong Whitworth won the contract and Werry's chance of success soon passed. Undeterred, he doggedly continued seeking someone who might finally make his ideas come to life. And so, in time, this led him to a meeting with Bert Spencer at the Marble Arch Hotel, a sympathetic hearing, a report to Gresley, and another lost opportunity.

Yet, inventive often radical ideas did occasionally manage to pass through Gresley's door, none more so than in the early 1920s with the birth of an ambition to build an engine powered by a high pressure marine type boiler. In a constant search for new ways of improving locomotive design, the CME had, before Spencer became his assistant, observed the construction of such an engine by the American Locomotive Company (ALCO) for the Delaware and Hudson Railroad company in the States. It was designed by John Erhardt Muhlfeld, the former Superintendent of

(Above) John Muhlfeld's two-cylinder combined simple/compound designed high pressure 2-8-0 engine which, according to Gresley, was built in the ALCO Works in Schenectady, New York during 1923/24, for the Delaware and Hudson Railroad Company. On entering service in December 1924, the locomotive was given the number 1400. It was a fairly successful engine and bred three successors but was not mass produced and did not find wider application in the States. However, it helped convince Gresley that the theory was sound and encouraged him to build his own high pressure locomotive. (Lower picture) No. 1400's most unconventional boiler. (BS)

Motive Power of the Baltimore and Ohio Railroad, and subsequently consultant engineer to the D&H RR. He is not well known in Britain but was a prolific designer who probably equalled Gresley in his output – quantity certainly and quality possibly. There is an unconfirmed rumour that they met in 1929, but history has yet to reveal whether this was so or not.

The most unusual feature of this two-cylinder 273 ton high-pressure triple expansion, cross-compound, booster fitted engine and tender, which was given the number 1400 and named Horatio Allen, was its watertube boiler which could produce a very high operating temperature and 350lb per square inch of pressure. The barrel of the boiler was of conventional design with fire tubes and superheater, but the firebox was enclosed by four steam drums, two at the top and two at the bottom. Five vertical tubes connected the top and bottom drums on each side of the firebox. The lower drums extended the length of the firebox, the upper reached farther forward over the barrel. In addition to this a version of the Young valve gear was fitted which allowed an unusually high maximum cut-off of 90 per cent plus if required. In service the company recorded that the Horatio Allen 'could produce a tractive effort of 91,565lb in simple mode and 68,920lb when operating as a cross-compound engine. It gave good fuel economy, but maintenance was greater than expected, later developments [Nos. 1401, 1402 and 1403] being better in this respect'.

In many ways, Muhlfeld's work was following a path already taken by Yarrows, the shipbuilders, in the late nineteenth century when developing their own version of a watertube boiler known as the 'Yarrow Boiler'. Following the company's move from London to Glasgow in 1906, work to refine and develop the concept moved on apace. Such was the progress they made that different versions of these boilers were soon installed in ships of many sizes. In service they proved particularly effective and, as they did so, new applications were considered. One of these was in the power generating business. As electricity supply companies grew in number, they looked for suitable boilers to drive their generators and the 'Yarrow Boiler' was deemed to be suitable for this task and orders soon multiplied.

As the design could be adapted for both mobile and static uses, and could vary in size and capacity, it was hardly surprising when someone in the rail industry thought that the 'Yarrow

A scene typical of Yarrow's Works in Glasgow during the 1920s and '30s, By this stage, the company had gone from simply being shipbuilders to supplying boilers of all sizes to other industries, most notably electricity generation. In the 1880s, they developed and patented their water tubed boiler, which was installed for the first time in 1887 to power a newly developed torpedo boat. Further refinement and development continued and a later version of this boiler would form the basis for Gresley's single W1. The photo above shows six much larger types of boiler being assembled for use in new Southern Region cross channel ferries. The two in the foreground are only partly assembled, the four behind are nearer completion. (BS)

Boiler' might be adapted for use with steam locomotives. And, so, up stepped Gresley as a potential client.

Even before No.1400 had rolled out of the works in New York, the CME had, it seems, opened up a dialogue with engineers at Yarrows, many of whom he would have met through the IMechE. However, it would not be a quick process with both Yarrows and Gresley fully committed to so many other projects. But the die had been cast and though progress was slow there was, at least, some forward movement as both companies found time to consider the development of a prototype engine. In this, Gresley was aided by Arthur Stamer who had, as Bert Spencer recalled:

> Developed a close association with Yarrows over the years and much of the planning for the W1 was undertaken at Darlington. He and Sir Nigel were both fascinated by these ideas and, I believe, Stamer visited the United States at some point in time to see the American engines at work. There was certainly a great number of papers circulating from him with many of his comments attached. He then played an important role in getting the new boiler manufactured and then engine No. 10000 built at Darlington and tested. There was concern in some quarters that the engine was something of a red herring, but both I and Bulleid believed it was a worthwhile experiment that might have borne fruit. Gresley's trust in the new system can be gauged by the patent he and Harold Yarrow submitted in December 1928 [No. 303,284 which was submitted on 17 January 1928 and accepted a year later], to which they gave the title 'Improvements in Locomotive Boilers'. I don't think it earned them any money.
>
> In terms of providing rough and outline sketches and drawings for the engine much of this work was undetaken at King's Cross by myself and the small team of draughtsmen. This was because the CME wished to keep the whole project as secret as possible, not because, as he said on several occasions, he wanted to keep competitors at bay, but in case the problems proved insuperable and he did not wish to see any failure widely advertised. There may also have been a question of development costs, which tend to rise swiftly for such projects and soon draw unwanted attention from chairmen and directors when they do so. With funds always in short supply during the '20s and '30s cries of 'we cannot afford it' would soon be heard. This, I think ,was Gresley's big experiment, just as 'Fury' was for Fowler, 'Turbomotive' for Stanier and the Leader Class for Bulleid. In each case the CME involved did not wish to be baulked in their ambition to build something truly unique and pioneering in its originality.

Gresley made clear his fascination with high pressure locomotives during a presentation he made to the IMechE in January 1931 – a presentation he had spent many months preparing with my support in the wake of his wife's death. In it he explained the basis of his work by relating that:

Arthur Stamer, who would play a leading role in the development of W1, was born in 1869, the fifth child of Sir Lovelace Stamer, Baronet and Rector of Stoke on Trent, and his wife Ellen. Educated at Rugby School, he became an engineering pupil at the Manchester Works of Beyer Peacock. Rapid promotion in the industry followed and in May 1895 he was appointed Supt of the Southern Division of the NER and, in due course, rose to become Vincent Raven's deputy and Mechanical Engineer at Darlington. Post amalgamation he became Gresley's much valued deputy. He retired in 1933. (THG)

Twenty years ago it was thought that the steam locomotive had attained practically its maximum development…The radical changes necessitated by the adoption of extra high pressures seem to have opened up a new era. Not only do these changes render possible an increase in tractive effort, but should increase the overall efficiency.

In Great Britain alone there are 23,000 locomotives and a sum of £45m per annum spent on their maintenance, renewal and running … 25 per cent is the cost of fuel burnt and another 25 per cent has to be spent on their maintenance and renewal. The purpose of novel forms of locomotive, which have been introduced over the last five years, has been to effect economies in fuel consumption and maintenance.

In striving for economy by the use of higher pressure, designers of locomotives are only following the lead which has been set by the designers of large stationary plant and marine engines. Their problem, however, has been made more difficult by loading gauge and weight restrictions, and for these reasons they are unable to take advantage of condensers and have had to extend the pressure gradient upwards to a greater extent. However, whilst high steam pressure gives greater economy in fuel consumption, it demands complication in design, and care must be taken that the economies in fuel are not absorbed in the increased cost of maintenance of the boiler and of the machine as a whole. Simplicity of design is an important factor, because simplicity generally results in accessibility. Time alone can prove which of the designs, if any, that have been recently produced, will result in such overhead economies as will justify their general adoption.

When presenting these findings to the IMechE his 4-6-4 high pressure engine was still in the early stage of development, but a number of test runs and trials had been undertaken. It is true to say that the benefits, even then, were hard to discern and pressure was building on him to bring the experiment to an end.

While this development work was going on, Gresley faced a much greater challenge over which he could exert no control. For some time, his wife's health had given him cause for great concern and finally a diagnosis of cancer was confirmed. Despite surgery, she died on 5 August 1929. Spencer recalled the impact of Ethel's death on her husband:

For some weeks Sir Nigel was rarely seen and Arthur Stamer took over many of the CME's duties. The reason for his absence was known by some, but was kept to a very small circle. When his wife died the impact on him was profound, as one might expect. In all the years I had known them they appeared to be a devoted couple and her loss must have seriously exhausted his reserves of energy and blunted his sense of purpose.

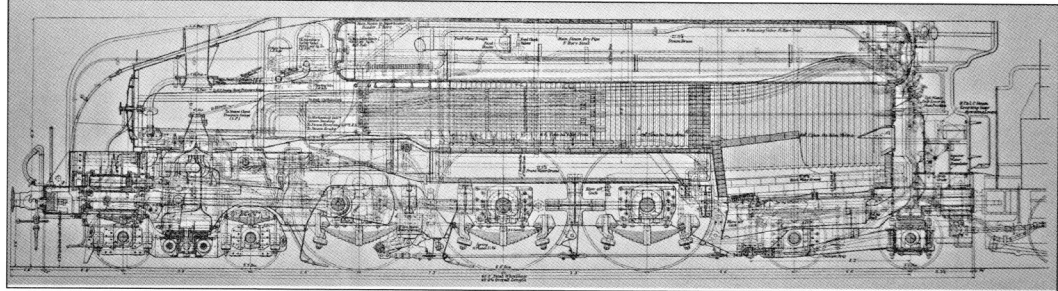

The W1 as it appeared in 1929 with a streamlined casing that revealed another of Gresley's growing passions – the application to locomotives and carriages of developing fluid flow/aerodynamic principles. (BS)

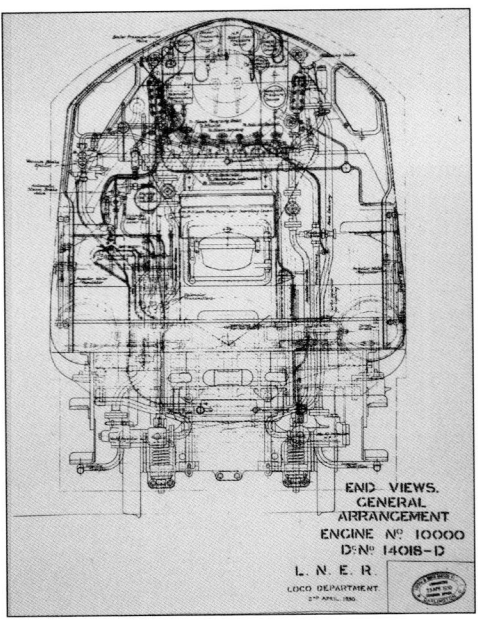

As W1 evolved in great secrecy, as far as the outside world was concerned that is. Spencer played an active role in its development and helped prepare many of the drawings. In his personal archive he kept a large file containing many of them (including the four shown above), plus notes that described the day to day changes made and instructions issued to the workshops. He did the same for the A1/A3 development programme and would do so again for the A4. During Gresley's three month absence in North America, following his wife's death, he appears to have taken instructions from Arthur Stamer and visited Darlington on many occasions to see the work in hand and resolve any queries that arose. (BS)

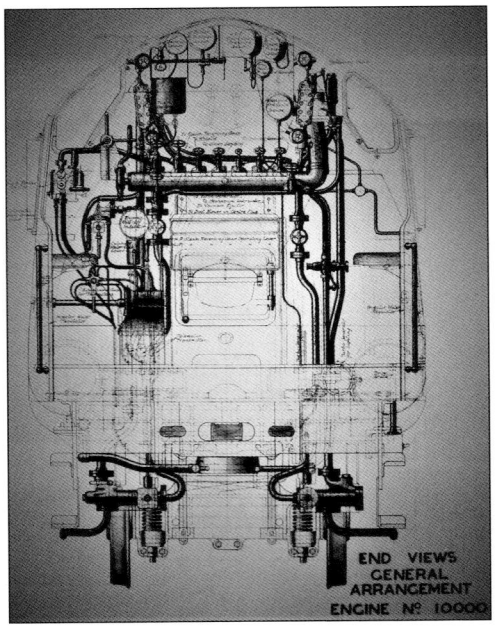
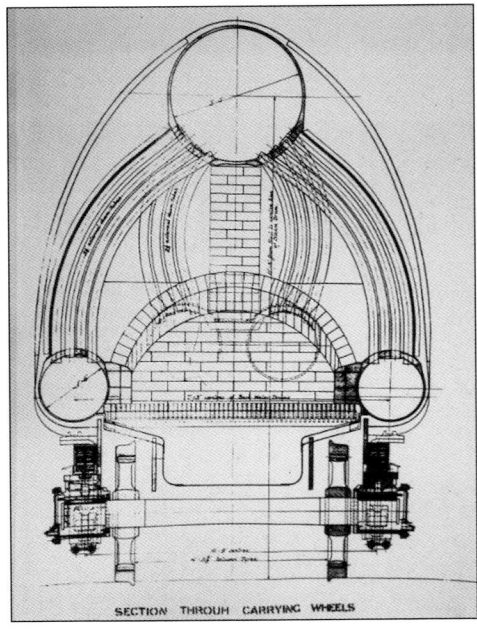

In the aftermath of Ethel's death, Gresley took the advice of family and friends and booked passage to North America for himself and his daughter Violet to enjoy a long holiday together. They departed on 31 August it seems with no specific plan in mind or a specific return date. In many ways it was a pilgramage he had long planned, but which his work and home commitments had made impossible to achieve. Having studied the work of designers on the other side of the Atlantic for some years, he was finally going to get the opportunity of seeing these engines first hand and perhaps even meet some of his American counterparts. But the tour must have been tinged with great sadness and Spencer was probably first to note changes in his esteemed leader:

> When he returned the changes in him were plain for us all to see. He recovered to a certain extent, but never again displayed the same energy or vitality. For many months there were rumours that he might retire and there was much speculation about who his successor might be. It seemed to me that W1, which was nearing completion in the latter part of 1929, provided him with a brief distraction and brought him back into the fold. Its development had interested him for many years and seeing it so close to completion in the Works fascinated him, as it did us all.

Gresley was back in harness for the final stages of W1's production and would have agreed the launch date and the tests that followed. Having been closely associated with the engine's evolution, and by now a very experienced trials engineer, Spencer was directed by the CME to involve himself in the evaluation of *Hush Hush*, as it had become known in railway circles as a nod to the secrecy that had surrounded its birth. With so much riding on this project, not least of all his professional and business reputations, having a dependable and talented lieutenant in such a key position would help ensure all ran well, and, if not, help find solutions to correct any deficiencies in the design that might appear. And if all this was to no avail and the locomotive fell far short of expectations, Gresley had a trusted and honest right-hand man, without bias and wisdom, to help guide his thoughts and actions.

When the CME spoke to members of the IMechE in 1931, this process was very much in its infancy and so these words reflected his hopes that all was set fair and the concept capable of further development:

> The locomotive has worked trains of over 500 tons' weight for long distances at express speeds with constant success and reliability, and although it has not been possible so far to carry out any extensive trials, there is every indication that it will prove more economical in fuel consumption than express engines of the latest normal types. Any economy effected in maintenance cost will only become fully apparent after the engine has run for a few years.
>
> It has been ascertained that the cost of a water-tube boiler similar to that fitted on this engine will not be appreciably greater than that of the ordinary wide firebox type as fitted on Pacific engines. The most expensive components of the water-tube boiler are the solid-forged steam and water-drums. These are not subjected to the action of fire, and consequently may be expected to have a long life. On the wider firebox type of ordinary boiler the copper firebox is the most costly section, and it is well known that its life is short and its renewal an expensive item. Again, in the ordinary type of locomotive boiler tubes and firebox stays are sources of trouble involving costly maintenance and occasional failures. In the design of boilers under consideration there are no stays; the tubes are more effectively secured, and are not subjected to variations in temperature and stress at the points where they enter the drums.

During the manufacturing and assembly of W1, which was split between Yarrow's Works in Glasgow and Darlington, Spencer, with or without Gresley, was a frequent visitor to both places. As a result, he either took or collected fifty or so photos (including this group of six) that recorded each stage of the project. These he later gathered together in an album, to which he chose not to add a written commentary. However, most pictures, including these six, are, to a certain extent, self-explanatory though confirmation of dates and places would have been helpful. Of particular interest is the application of a streamlined casing reflecting Gresley's growing interest in the aerodynamic effect of these things on his express locomotives. (BS)

In conclusion, I submit that, with the moderately high pressure and simple design, which I have adopted, economy both in fuel and maintenance costs will be secured and at the same time the reliability so characteristic of British locomotives will be fully maintained.'

When these words were spoken, two more years of testing lay ahead, with measured trials taking place in December 1932 and August 1933, following periods of maintenance when various modifications were made. In between times she ran normal duties on a variety of lines, including,

On the back of this battered and faded print Spencer has written. 'King's Cross – the engine's first visit to London to be greeted by the CME and a large crowd, including reporters and newsreel cameramen. During turning a small group including Gresley and myself watch the manoeuvre with great interest'. (BS)

on occasions, the Flying Scotsman. And gradually conclusions were reached about Gresley's great experiment, best summarized by Bert Spencer in 1947:

> The evaporative heating surface of the boiler was small for the usual smokebox vacuums and satisfactory steaming only occurred when the engine was developing high outputs at long cut-offs with a smokebox vacuum in the region of 6 in., at which figure the smokebox temperature was too high. Some improvement was effected by fitting twin blast pipes.
>
> The engine was weak during acceleration when working compound after a stop as the superheat took some time to build up and, as a consequence, the LP cylinders could do little work owing to condensation and the HP cylinders were unable to provide sufficient power alone.
>
> Difficulty was experienced in maintaining the airtightness of the boiler walls owing to the variation in the temperature of the plates, and this frequently led to steaming troubles owing to air being drawn through the defective joints instead of through the grate. Considerable modifications were also made to the arrangement of the baffles to ensure that the flue gases came into contact with the whole of the water tubes, as experiments with a full size model of the forward portion of the boiler revealed that short circuiting of the gases had taken place.
>
> Notwithstanding the various alterations carried out, the use of high pressure and compounding on engine No. 10000 did not prove economical and in general working the engine was burning considerably more coal than the standard Pacifics. In 1937 it was therefore decided to rebuild the engine as a three-cylinder simple and substitute a boiler of a similar type to that used on the P2 class.'

Despite Gresley's drive and determination, the high pressure engine project proved very difficult to sustain. To have taken it further by building other engines of the type required an unequivocal statement of benefits demonstrating that there was much to be gained by doing so. Sadly, there were few overriding benefits to be derived from this ambitious but apparently flawed programme. Eventually, even the most optimistic person has to recognise that there is nothing more to be gained and admit that a project has not lived up to expectations. As it was, Gresley managed to keep the experiment going for longer than was truly necessary and only authorised W1's conversion to a more traditional form, albeit streamlined, seven years after it had entered service.

Six of the many W1 photos Spencer kept in his archive. From the sheer volume of material, it is easy to understand how important this project was to him and suggests a high degree of personal involvement. Once again, he wrote no details of time or place, but the top four pictures appear to have been taken on a very overcast, misty 8 January 1930 at King's Cross, two with Gresley and family members looming large. (BS)

With the pressing demand of a railway seeking to survive financially at a difficult time, such a costly experiment would be viewed by some as an unnecessary and costly distraction. Nevertheless, Gresley must have been disappointed when a halt was called to such cutting edge work, but there was some compensation in the fact that he still had more conventional designs to investigate. And, with a government finally taking action to boost the national grid and subsidise developments in various industries, including the railways, electrification was on the agenda

Innovation or Stagnation 95

Two photos Spencer kept showing W1 under test – static and mobile. The second picture has been annotated by him and reads 'At speed heading south near Royston in Cambridgeshire with the fireman, who has built up sufficient steam to meet the engine's needs, enjoying a breather. I was on board timing the engine and assessing its performance'. The date is unclear but is thought to be Sunday, 25 May 1930 and the photo may have been taken after the engine had spent two days in Cambridge 'on exhibition' there. (BS)

again. Raven had made a good start before huge financial pressures necessitated a postponement, but now Gresley could focus his undoubted skills on the task and take it to a new level as funds were gradually released.

In my book *Gresley and His Locomotives*, I surmised that the CME was above all:

> An inventor and anyone with these skills wishes to take the lead in the process of change, if possible, by making a leap of the imagination that considers fundamental principles and questions perceived wisdom. The common man will say 'stay as we are, all is well', the scientist will ask why and perceive a future that can improved by their talents and wisdom. Whilst in the middle sits business which tends to follow a star if it quickly brings a pot of gold to the coffers. Gresley understood this and attempted to take a path between these conflicting views, using all his skills to reach into the future and find new and better solutions to perennial problems.

With government backing and subsidies, Gresley had a new target to pursue which may have assuaged any disappointment he felt when his experiments with W1 came to nought.

In recalling W1 Spencer simply wrote that:

> No further high pressure engines were built by the LNER but it undoubtedly proved to be a very valuable piece of research, or so I believe. Such an experiment always adds something, whether successful or not, to our increasing knowledge of design engineering. It was a necessary part of my duties to be directly involved in all this experimental work and I gained immeasurably from doing so. When later I worked for Edward Thompson I discovered that he was a strong advocate of the high pressure locomotive and would have pursued it himself if he had been CME. Coming from someone thought to be a severe critic of Gresley this was high praise indeed.

With the start of the new decade, Gresley still had much to engage him and many ideas to explore, but he was clearly deeply affected by Ethel's death and the scars ran deep. All this was very clear to Spencer, who seemed happy to remain the CME's faithful assistant while the challenge remained and his efforts were appreciated. But there is always a danger that such a willing and able man might feel taken for granted, come to believe his efforts were not fully appreciated and be tempted to seek another position where recognition and rewards might be greater.

The sleek shape of W1 stands in stark contrast to the more traditional Pacific beside her (in this case A1 No. 2576 *The White Knight* which underwent some modifications to test the benefits of ACFI feed-water heating, which in this case gave her an unsightly bulge above her smokebox – made necessary by the need to protect pipework). For some, streamlining was a publicity stunt with little scientific merit when applied to steam locomotives. For others, including Gresley and Spencer, it was an important field of research to explore – on one level to reduce such operational problems as drifting smoke, on another to improve efficiency and economy. The 1930s would see the CME push these theories as far as he could. (BS)

For the moment, though, there was much to occupy him and the King's Cross team, beyond the immediate needs of the W1 programme. There was the continuing evolution of the Pacifics and Gresley's growing interest in streamlining. Then there was the next stage of the 2-8-2 programme and the development of a number of other classes of locomotive. In addition, there were always myriad engineering issues to consider in the hope that any one of them might take design forward in a new and perhaps unexpected direction. Even though Gresley's life had been turned upside down by his wife's death, scientific curiosity and experimentation remained a cornerstone of his life and personality, so would always provide encouragement and an interest to engage him. And then there would always be a pressing business imperative driving him and his team to new heights.

This photo appears to be the last Spencer collected of W1 in service, judging by its position in his albums. He has not provided date or place, but clearly the engine is running at speed with a heavy load behind. (BS)

Bert Spencer – A Design Engineer's World in Colour

Bert Spencer carefully archived much material during his career and in so doing left a unique record of his time with the GNR, LNER and BR. In the following pages I have displayed some of the photos, drawings and other items from his collection that have some personal connection to him or simply reflect his profession as a mechanical engineer and assistant to Gresley, Thompson and Peppercorn, then as a senior manager with British Railways.

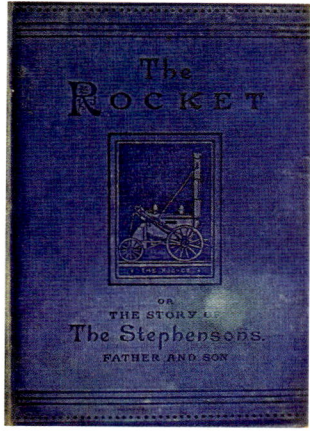

Spencer was an avid collector of postcards and photographs as a child and throughout his career, each one displaying his fascination with locomotives. This picture of an Ivatt Atlantic class locomotive in GNR livery is just one of many hundreds from his archive. (Above right) Spencer's much thumbed copy of H.C. Knight's book *The Rocket*. (BS)

The slide rule was an essential aid to an engineer's work until the advent of electronic calculators. Spencer kept a number of them including this one with his name still visible on the leather pouch and stamped on the back of the rule itself. (BS)

Above and right: Spencer kept several boxes of draughtsmen's equipment including this well used and partially restored selection which his wife presented to him shortly after they married in 1925. (BS)

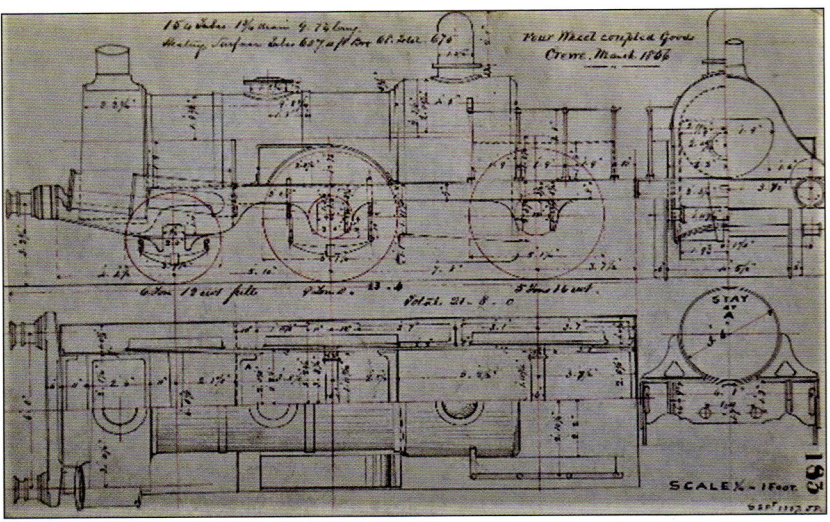

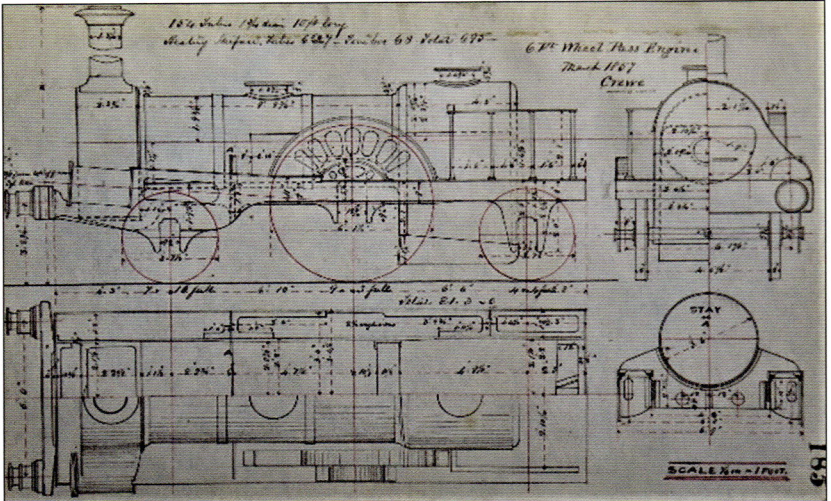

Left and below left: During his apprenticeship, and to help in developing his skills as a draughtsman, Spencer was tasked with producing drawings of existing locomotives. These are just two of ten examples of his work from this time that have survived. For someone so early in his career he demonstrates great skill, so it is little wonder that he came to the notice of senior managers including Gresley. (BS)

 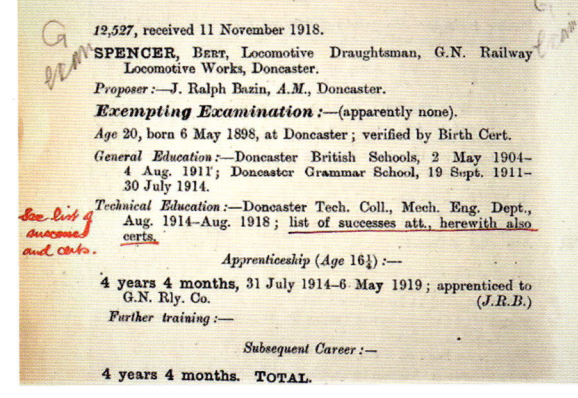

(Right) A mechanical engineer's bible, in this case Spencer's personal copy. (Far right) In 1918 he unsuccessfully applied for membership of the IMechE. There was a second failed attempt, but when he was Thompson's assistant at Doncaster, the CME encouraged him to apply again, wrote a glowing testimonial and he achieved this long held ambition (BS)

In 1922, having finished his training, Spencer was working in the Drawing Office at Doncaster. He recorded that he undertook design work on the A1's cab layout and this is one of his drawings from this period. It was his work on the A1s that is reported to have brought him to Gresley's attention. As he did this work, his thoughts turned toward improving the Pacifics' cylinder/valve gear arrangement and his developing thoughts on the 'long lap' issue. (BS)

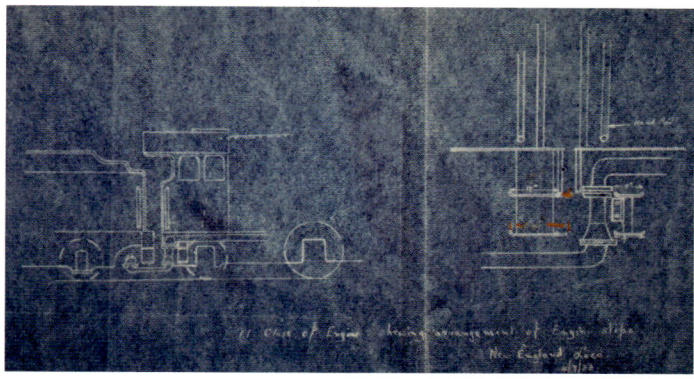

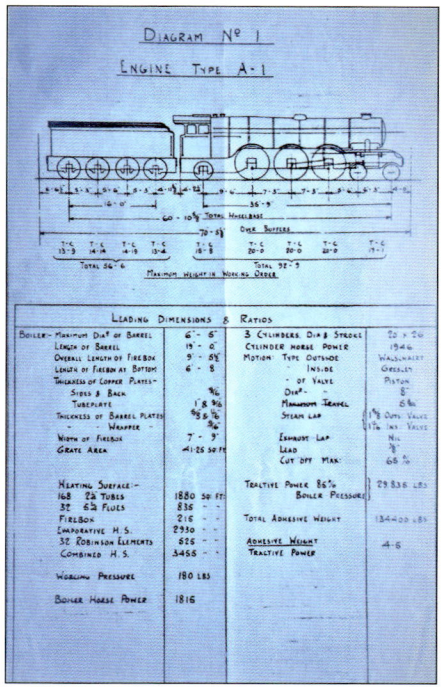

(Above) The result of Gresley's 'big engine' policy is made clear in this postcard of King's Cross, post the creation of the LNER in 1923 – one of a number of pictures that Spencer kept of such scenes over the next thirty years as steam domionated the East Coast Mainline and finally gave way to diesel. (Right) An early Diagram of the A1 that Spencer retained and may well have prepared himself. (BS)

Throughout his career, Spencer produced and kept in a small brown folder mini diagrams such as this showing an A1. By the time he finished in 1958, there were more than 100, of which a few examples are shown in this section (BS)

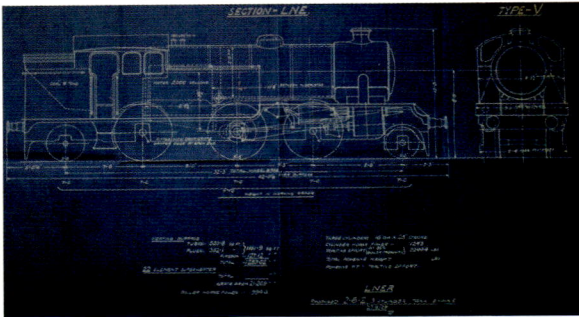

Left: One of many blueprints Spencer kept, this one with his initials suggesting the work, on a 'Type V' 2-6-2 engine may have been his. (BS)

Below: Amongst his papers, Spencer kept many drawings of the cylinder/valve gear arrangement preferred by Gresley, whether he prepared any of these is difficult to determine now, but he was clearly fascinated by the concept but clearly saw ways in which it might be improved and pursued these issues with great, but diplomatic, vigour. (BS)

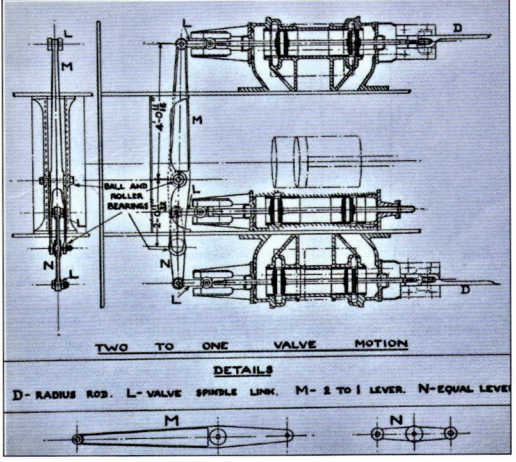

Below left and below right: Spencer recorded that he 'kept many of Gresley's sketches and remember well him calling to me, "Spencer here's something I want you to look at, get me out some drawings will you!" and then being handed several sheets of paper often lined, covered with rough sketches. A few days later we would pore over these plans and gradually his ideas would take shape at which point he would call in the Chief Draughtsman and Bulleid to get their point of view.' Here are two examples that Spencer retained. (BS)

Bottom: Spencer's record of the A3s which began being introduced in 1928. For some reason, he has scribbled the number 2795 (*Trigo*, which entered service in February 1930) on the diagram. (BS)

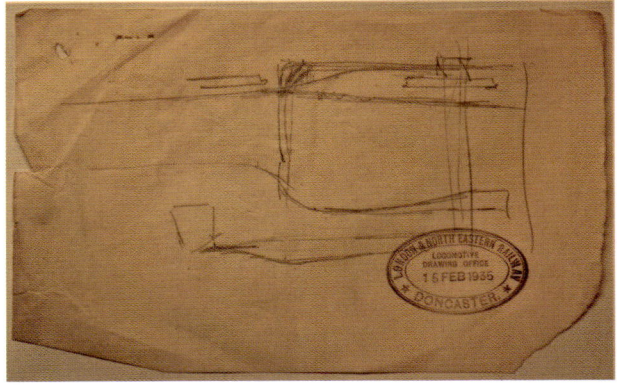
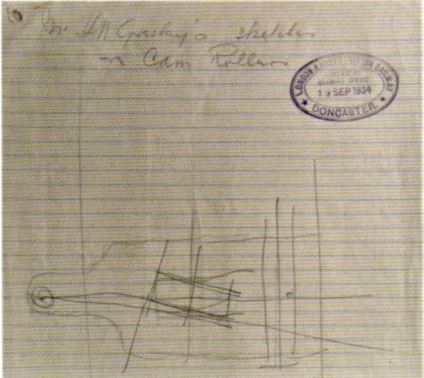

From the mid-1920s, photography played an increasingly important part in Spencer's life and the railways featured large in the subject matter he pursued. Two of his cameras have survived – a Kodak Folding Six-20 and a Leica III, which was something of a rarity in Britain during the 1930s and '40s and may have been acquired on a trip to Germany. (BS)

During the late 1920s, Gresley became increasingly interested in marine engines and how they might be applied to railway locomotives. In consultation with Yarrows, specialists in this field, the W1 project was initiated and design of a suitable body to take such a boiler began with Spencer very closely involved in the programme. This is one of his early drawings, which sought to adapt the A1/A3 design with rather ill-balanced results. The next design, with 4-6-4 configuration and streamlined body, was accepted and the engine appeared in 1930. (BS)

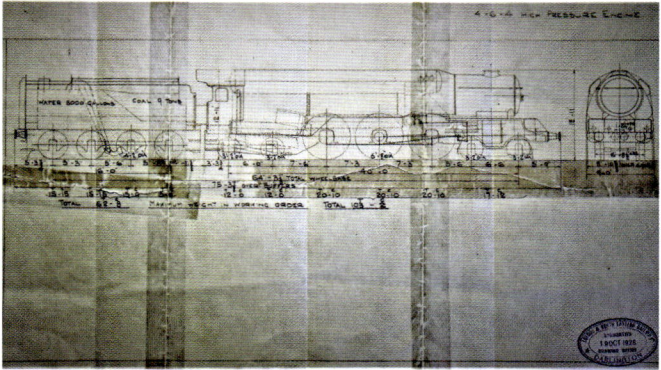

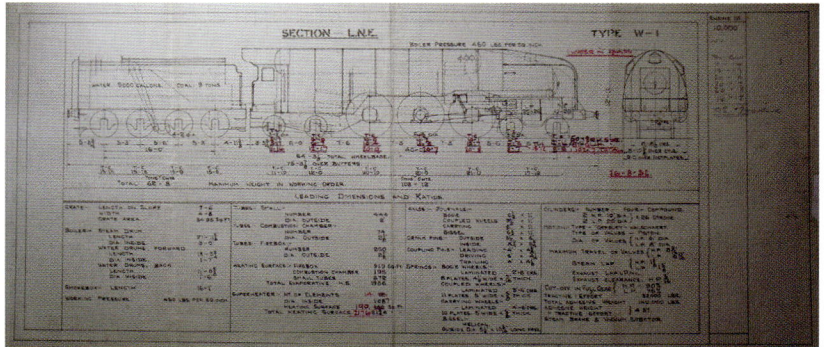 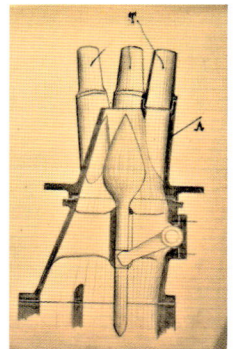

(Above left) Spencer's annotated copy of W1's final design. In the years that followed he was directly involved in testing this engine, which, ultimately, did not offer any significant improvement over more conventional designs. It was rebuilt in 1937 along the lines of the A4s and did sterling service until withdrawn in 1959. (Above right) Tucked into his papers on W1 are several drawings without notes or references attached. It is interesting to speculate what they may be and the thought that went into their preparation. (BS)

Above: Apparently a drawing prepared by Spencer as Gresley considered the shape of the new P2 Class locomotives. (BS)

Below: Spencer's annotated diagram for the first of the P2s. (BS)

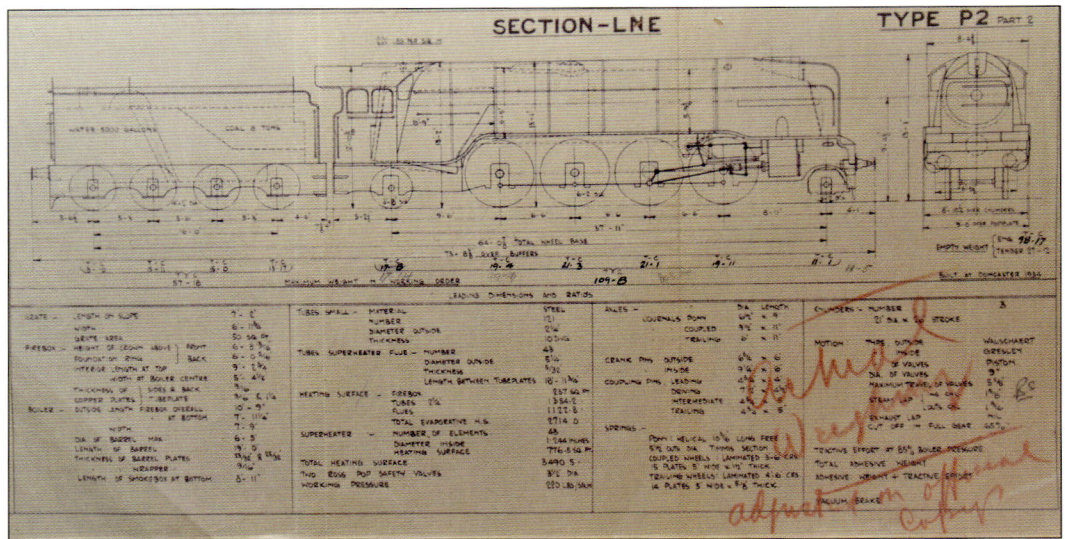

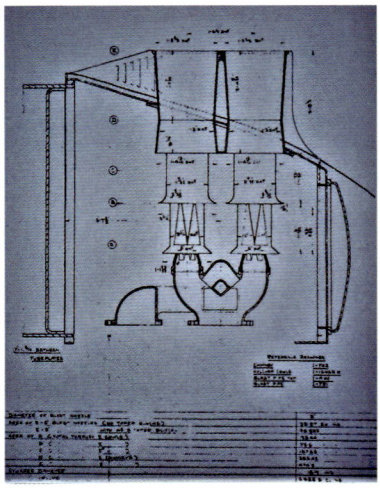

Left and below: Two of many drawings kept of the A4s. During the design process Spencer, by all accounts, spent a considerable amount of time translating Gresley's many sketches into formal drawings and travelling between London and Doncaster to ensure the smooth passage of work. (Left) He was particularly interested in the design of the double blastpipe and Kylchap exhaust system and actively campaigned for its inclusion and eventual extension to the entire class. (BS)

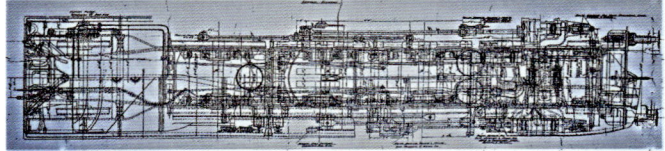

Right: The most important task in 1935 was to design and build the first batch of A4s and the Silver Jubilee rake of carriages. Judging by the papers he retained, Spencer played a central co-ordinating role and produced a number of drawings, including the one here, showing the profile of the engine and carriages. (BS)

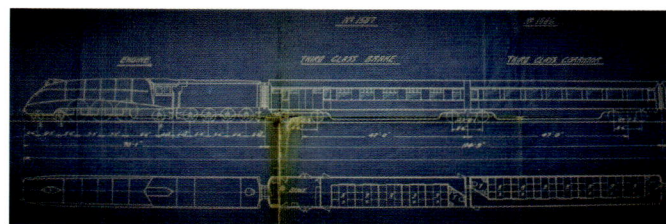

During the 1930s, colour photography was still in its infancy with colour film a rare commodity in Britain with the results being of variable quality. Nevertheless, Spencer acquired a number of negatives during this period and archived them, including the two above. (Left) A badly faded and indistinct photo of 2509 *Silver Link* when new. (Right) 4496 *Golden Shuttle*. (BS)

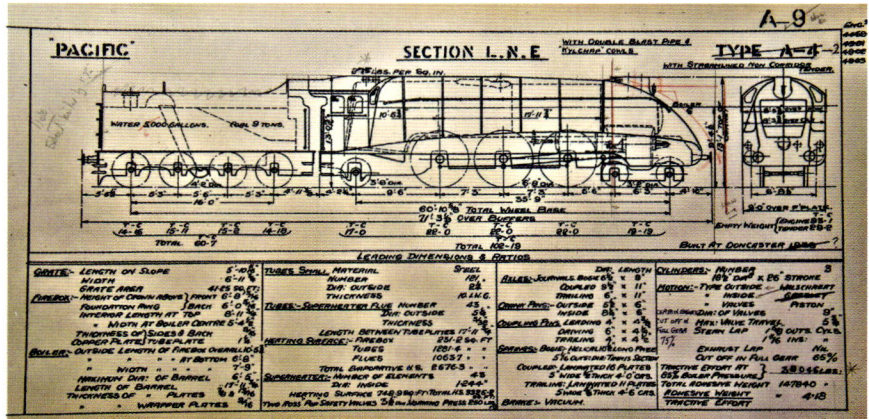

Gresley believed that the A4 could be refined still further. To confirm this, Spencer wrote, 'By 1938 the popularity of the high speed trains was firmly established and it was clear that a demand for longer and heavier trains would eventually arise. A design for a more powerful version of the A4 was therefore prepared having the boiler pressure raised from 250lb to 275lb per sq inch, thus increasing tractive effort from 33,455lb to 39,040lb, but the scheme remained in abeyance'. This resulted in what he later described as a 'Super A4' which he sketched out in a number of drawings. Interestingly, in the diagram above, to which Spencer has added detail in rough form, he has amended A4 to A4-2, then changed this by stencilling in 'A-9'. Although outline work on this proposal continued for a time, the war, then Gresley's death, brought the project to a close. In due course, Edward Thompson would revive plans for extending the Pacific programme, with streamlining one possibility, but the new engines would see a more conventional form adopted with greater emphasis being placed on the cylinders and an alternative arrangement to Gresley's conjugated valve gear. (BS)

In his set of 'mini' diagrams, Spencer captures the arrival of the LNER's last class of Pacific, introduced while Arthur Peppercorn was CME. The first A1 arrived in October 1948 – a project in which Spencer was closely involved as the CME's technical assistant. (BS)

(Above) Before taking the position of Chief Technical Assistant for the Eastern Region at Doncaster, Spencer was assigned to run BR's 1948 Locomotive Interchange Trials, the results of which would feed into the developing Standardisation Plan for steam. In this role he witnessed many of the test runs, recording performances and photographing many of the engines involved, particularly the LNER's A4s. Great things were expected of No. 22 *Mallard*, captured here at Waterloo, but mechanical problems let her down. (Left) With the pace of diesel development speeding up Spencer became closely involved in English Electric's DP 1 programme, of which twenty-two were purchased for use on the Eastern Region shortly after he retired in 1958 (BS)

Two colour slides from Spencer's collection. Above left – an unidentified Peppercorn Pacific in full flow, while the second picture captures a scene only too common to Spencer during a long career. In this case, 60004 *William Whitelaw* is undergoing repair at Doncaster towards the end of her life in 1966. (BS)

Chapter 4

Pressing Home Their Advantage

Life for Gresley's small HQ team was full of interest but was always highly pressured. With such a dynamic leader in charge, a relaxed, more even approach was most unlikely. Each day presented new challenges that demanded great commitment. But there was a downside to this. Family needs would often be relegated to a distant second place. Gresley was not, by all accounts, an unsympathetic or uncaring man, but he drove himself hard and this had consequences for those in his immediate entourage. Elsie Spencer would later write:

> Bert was rarely off-duty, worked very long hours and was always ready when the phone rang to fly off somewhere or other to provide Mr. Gresley with support or deal with some urgent matter that had arisen at King's Cross. He never grumbled, but it did strain our home life quite considerably.

Bert made light of the demands placed on him and never, it seems, grumbled about the extent of the commitment he was asked to make. If anything, he seems to have found deep personal and professional fulfilment in serving Gresley and never seems to have questioned the demands placed on him. Such was the strength of his commitment to his leader and the needs of the railway that he seems to have been ever eager to take on many extra duties. He was not alone in this, though. Gresley seems to have inspired the same level of dedication and loyalty in most people who worked closely with him, no matter what the cost to their personal lives might have been. Eric Bannister caught a flavour of this when he wrote that, 'the effect of that first interview remained with me until the end of my working life. By his patience and willingness to listen to a raw recruit he won my loyalty and respect. He made me want to give him all the help I could – and that unsparingly'. Such a person was worthy of

As the Pacific programme expanded and the fast express services became more firmly established, the level of publicity they attracted increased. This was helped by some very astute 'stunts' that were guaranteed to make headlines. Just such a case occurred in July 1933 when Geoffrey De Havilland, who had recently won the prestigious King's Cup Air Race, travelled on the Flying Scotsman. Here he poses with Driver Bill Sparshatt and Fireman Smith, one of the LNER's Top Link crews, just before departure from Platform 10 at King's Cross. Spencer recalled that 'whenever a VIP was passing through we gathered to watch these events. The most popular was Sir Malcolm Campbell who came to our offices to talk to Gresley on several occasions. Speed, aerodynamics and streamlining were eagerly discussed'. (BS)

this commitment and in Spencer he had a man who would follow him in a most unsparing way, allowing any personal cost to fall where it may.

One compensation Spencer found in working at King's Cross was its close proximity to the City, its museums and galleries and the freedom to walk along streets teeming with all forms of life. He later recalled that:

> Working with Gresley demanded a great deal of effort, but he did not expect us to remain tied to our desks all the time. So when time allowed I would walk to Euston Station or along different streets leading down to the centre of London with my camera to observe life. Gray's Inn Road to Holborn was a particular favourite of mine and then an occasional visit to 'Little Italy' where I had my suits cut and could buy a decent iced cream on a hot day. A walk northwards from my office along York Way was always of great interest because it gave me fine views of the trains storming away from King's Cross and observe how well the engines were performing. Commuting back and forth to New Barnet through London's fast growing suburbs allowed me to do the same. I could have ridden in the cab of those engines, Gresley was always keen for us to do so, but I found sitting comfortably in a carriage allowed me to relax and listen to an engine's beat without getting in the way of the footplate crew.
>
> One of my greatest pleasures was simply to walk along the platforms at King's Cross and across to the sheds to watch engines at work or being prepared for duty. This gave me the opportunity to talk to the crew or anyone else involved in the task at hand. On many occasions I was joined by the CME himself, who never lost his boyhood fascination with locomotives, and was happy to stand and watch them go by or simply talk about ideas then in his mind. He would often seek my opinion and we would discuss possible problems that might occur or likely benefits that might be gained. I formed the view that a lot of this

Above left and right: Spencer's daily life at King's Cross, although very busy, gave him the opportunity to explore London's streets when there was time to do so. From the records he left and the many photos he collected, it is clear that he found these occasional jaunts interesting. For a boy from a smallish town, the hustle and bustle of a big metropolis must have opened his eyes to many different ways of life. These two 1920s pictures, one showing Ludgate Hill leading up to St Paul's Cathedral and the other an overhead view of the Embankment revealing the ever growing influence of road vehicles, reveal the depth of his fascination. (BS)

was simply a way of clearing his mind of extraneous detail to allow a clearer view to form. It also had the benefit of engaging you in a proposal from an early stage and gain a picture of the issues to be considered. His was a remarkable way of working and he achieved a good rapport with all those he met, no matter what position they held, especially footplate crew whose company he greatly enjoyed. He was not unique in this, but he practiced it in an apparently effortless, kindly way with me and others around him. However, he could, when the need arose be sharp if he felt that someone was wasting his time or had not grasped a point he was trying to make.

Another important part of our lives was the occasional trips to the cafes and tea rooms in the station's concourse. A pot of tea and a plate of hot buttered toast or a coffee and 'a fancy' always went down well. Gresley wouldn't join us on these occasions but a small cake appealed to his sweet tooth and so one or two would appear on his afternoon tea tray.

Eric Bannister also left an interesting account of life with Gresley, Bulleid and Spencer at King's Cross, revealing much about the way they worked and their personalities in the process:

As Spencer's assistant I saw a lot of HNG. Bert was very pleasant to work for and first of all sent me out to find lodgings. I was allowed a month's expenses but Bert managed to get me a fortnight's extension ... My first job was to read the monthly technical journals, making a note of any articles that I thought HNG should read ... Of course Bert guided me.

The junior office in which I worked was very airless with one door opening into the office used by Spencer and Norman Newsome [by then Spencer's opposite number on the carriage and wagon side of business] and the back entrance looking out over Platform 11 of the suburban station ... As Senior Technical Assistant, Bert usually dealt with HNG and I usually attended to the requirements of Bulleid who was usually very patient.

My early time at King's Cross was taken up largely with office work and in generally assisting Spencer, Bulleid or Rupert Hart-Davies. On one occasion Hart-Davies and I were on the platform at 11am when we should have been in the office. We met HNG who came up and said, 'I suppose you two are going for coffee. Go and enjoy it but when you return H-D call to see me. There is no immediate hurry and it will wait until you return'. HNG was always considerate to his staff and knew that we would not abuse his trust.

Over sixteen years or so, the smoky portals of King's Cross Station became very familiar to Spencer. Whether it was working in offices with the constant clamour of sounds from the platforms nearby, or searching out a café for tea and toast as a break from work, the station became an important backdrop to his life. As he later wrote 'it was dingy, cramped and poorly ventilated, but never less than fascinating to work there and be at the centre of the CME's professional world'. To commemorate his time there, he kept many photographs, some official, others purely personal, in his archives as shown here. These two pictures capture the somewhat disorganised look of the station in the 1940s on a very quiet day judging by the absence of passengers and activity. (BS)

After a few months came my first outside job for HNG. He had said to BS,'I should like to know why water is getting into the leading axleboxes of the tenders of Pacific locomotives'. BS discussed it at length with me and, as neither of us had any idea as to what was causing the problem I volunteered to go out and see first-hand ... The problem was solved by the insertion of a vertical plate in the mouth of the scoop to split the water, thus avoiding the build-up of pressure that pushed water out forwards. The next day BS was able to give HNG the answer to his 'I should like to know', which was his normal form of inquiry and I had survived my big adventure.

In a letter Banister later added:

HNG was a very pleasant man to work for. He did not like interruptions to his train of thought. Over the years Spencer had established that the best way of supporting the CME was to be patient and wait for him to seek opinions on proposals he was considering. In the meantime, BS would develop ideas that ran parallel to HNG's and feed him information that he had gleaned from many sources on design. In addition, he ensured there was the closest possible relationship with each Chief Draughtsman and his staff. Bill Elwess, until he retired in 1927, then Harry Broughton, Tom Street and Edward Windle were all aware of the closeness of the relationship between HNG and BS and made sure Spencer was given all their support and any relevant papers he needed.

BS was completely open and honest in his dealings with all those around him and always involved himself in what was going on and readily offered his assistance whenever necessary in an open and honest manner. He encouraged me to work in the same way, to think for myself, form my own views, consider all solutions and participate in discussions. He was a good teacher, a very good draughtsman and an exceptional engineer, always capable of thinking up ways of improving locomotives. He may not have been as inventive as HNG and Bulleid, but he was a creative man nonetheless, who was, perhaps, more practical and logical than either of them. The cleverness of his ideas tends to bear this out.

Bulleid was equally close to Gresley but their relationship was in some ways more intellectual in nature. Each found pleasure in the conceptual, occasionally philosophical discussions more common in the world of academia. Henry Bulleid caught a flavour of this when recalling some of the stories his father related to him years later:

Even when taking holidays to the West Country or Scotland, Spencer took the opportunity to observe locomotives of other companies. He seemed intrigued by the big 4-6-0 designs of both the LMS and GWR. His albums contained many photos of both, including these two pictures of Fowler Royal Scots (6107 *Argyll and Sutherland Highlander* and 6136 and *Goliath*, soon to be renamed *The Border Regiment*). (BS)

Pressing Home Their Advantage 109

'This was the type of subject, outside the day's immediate business, which Gresley would discuss with Bulleid after the 5pm rush, the mail gone and now in a more leisurely period before they caught their trains home. It was about this time that their full rapport was achieved, both communicating without notes on general matters and both clearly remembering points made by the other in the most casual discussions, so keen were they on their combined work and hobby. And, of course, there were the entertaining asides giving scope for mock-serious description by Gresley as he stood, back to comfortable fire, sometimes reinforced at Bulleid's suggestion by an additional cup of tea.

Another feature of their rapport was that they never seemed to get in each other's way. No one heard of them both doing the same job, or issuing conflicting instructions, and except at King's Cross and occasional formal events and Continental meetings they were not very often seen together.

In some ways the relationship between Gresley and Bulleid was one of equals, but only one could lead and the other follow. And here there was a problem. Bulleid, unlike Spencer, had a

The 1930s were a golden age in cinema and Bert and Elsie Spencer were frequent visitors to Barnet's Palace Cinema and, later on, the local Art Deco styled Odeon that opened in 1935. His surviving papers suggest an interest in comedy. Top left – a photo signed by Will Hay and (top right) a photograph taken when Laurel and Hardy were entertained by LNER officials. But he was also interested in the way the railways were portrayed in the movies and kept a selection of stills from a number of productions. These included (bottom left) an action sequence being shot for the 1929 feature film entitled *Flying Scotsman* and (bottom right) a sequence being captured for inclusion in the GPO production *Night Mail*, but not used in the film when finally released in 1936 with W.H. Auden's famous poem of the same name providing the sound track. (BS)

burning ambition to be a CME and would never be entirely satisfied with the role of assistant. Simply persuading his leader, by reasoned argument and subtle suggestion, to move in a particular direction was not his natural way of working and doing so appears to have tested his patience to the limit at times. This was especially so when Gresley pursued ideas Bulleid thought irrelevant, such as the W1 or the 'craze for streamlining', as he later called it and even openly criticised the CME for doing so.

Inevitably, this would have created tension in their relationship, with the result that the younger man seems to have been directed towards projects that helped fulfil some of his ambitions, and, as Spencer later recorded, 'kept him out of mischief'. It was here that the continuing development of the Mikado was important. Although clearly overseen by Gresley, it seems more than likely that it became a Bulleid-led project in which he could work with fewer restrictions. At the same time, it allowed his fertile but often erratic imagination freedom to roam and experiment without distracting Gresley from other ideas he wished to pursue. Here Spencer's words are of interest. He wrote:

> Although Sir Nigel supported this work and took a keen interest in the P1's construction, I felt it was a project much closer to Bulleid's heart and in which he played a leading role. He believed that the 2-8-2 wheel configuration held many benefits for freight and fast express services. When becoming the Southern Railway's CME in 1937 he again attempted to take forward the idea, but eventually returned to the Pacific layout with his Merchant Navy's. For the LNER the P2 was probably more of a success than the P1, but neither were great successes.

If this was the case Henry Bulleid's comments about 'never doing the same job', or 'not very often being seen together' may be of great relevance. With so few CME posts to compete for, and with Gresley unlikely to relinquish his position at King's Cross in the foreseeable future, there was nowhere for Bulleid to achieve his ambitions and so such a compromise arrangement may have become necessary

Wherever the truth might lie, it seems that as the 1930s progressed, Bulleid followed, or was being directed along a specific, yet slightly isolated, path, while Gresley and Spencer followed quite another course, with the Pacifics, W1 and much more. And this work increasingly focussed on streamlining, at the time a cutting-edge science made more relevant by the rapid development of metal skinned, monoplane aircraft and high-speed motor vehicles. From the late 1920s, and throughout the 1930s, this passing fashion, as some thought it, dominated the work of many engineers, industrial designers and artists keen to see its influence spread into many different fields. The process was helped by the amount of publicity streamlining seemed to attract, helped by the fact that it reflected a growing desire for better lives in the wake of the sacrifices demanded by the Great War and the rapid growth of consumerism that had resulted. The years of austerity and poverty that followed the conflict demanded much more than a return to an old order where obedience and deference to one's betters, as the language of the time put it, were expected. No longer did the exhortation to be 'satisfied with what you have' carry the weight it once did. So, whilst streamlining had a clear scientific purpose, it came to represent much more and in doing so became a symbol of social change as well as a fashion statement. In the years that followed, critics and supporters would latch on to these different aspects to extoll streamlining's virtues or condemn it as mere frippery.

In some ways, it was a debate that seemed to be dominated by those holding opinions from either side of a wide spectrum. At one end there were traditionalists holding to well-established views seemingly happy to maintain the status quo. Then there were the modernisers eager for change at any price. Luckily, many sat between these two extremes, open-minded and eager to debate an issue then experiment before deciding whether to proceed with a novel and innovative

Above and below: Spencer's interest in streamlining does not seem to have been merely a case of following Gresley's lead but was something he came to believe in quite independently. For example, from the 1920s onwards he was an avid reader of scientific and engineering journals as well as such magazines as *Motor, Motor Sport, Flight* and many others. From these he extracted articles that described new developments that might be applied to the railway business. Amongst them there were many reports that dealt with streamlining of cars and bikes. Just four of these are displayed here with road vehicles of various types being a common theme. The patent for the 1935 version of Cord 810 was placed on the same page as a photo showing one of these cars belonging to the Olympic gold medallist and Hollywood star Sonja Henie. These seem to capture two themes close to Spencer's heart – science and the movies. (BS)

idea or not. Gresley and Spencer fell into this group, each driven by the desire to look beyond known and established solutions. Streamlining fell into this category and in pursuing this new science they were drawn to Frederick Johansen and the world of fluid dynamics and all its possibilities.

Johansen, a graduate of Kings College, London, began working at the National Physical Laboratory in Teddington during 1922. Very quickly he became a key figure in the evolution of aerodynamics, fluid flow research and wind tunnel testing. Much was already known about these issues when he began his work, but the rapid advance of aviation during the Great War,

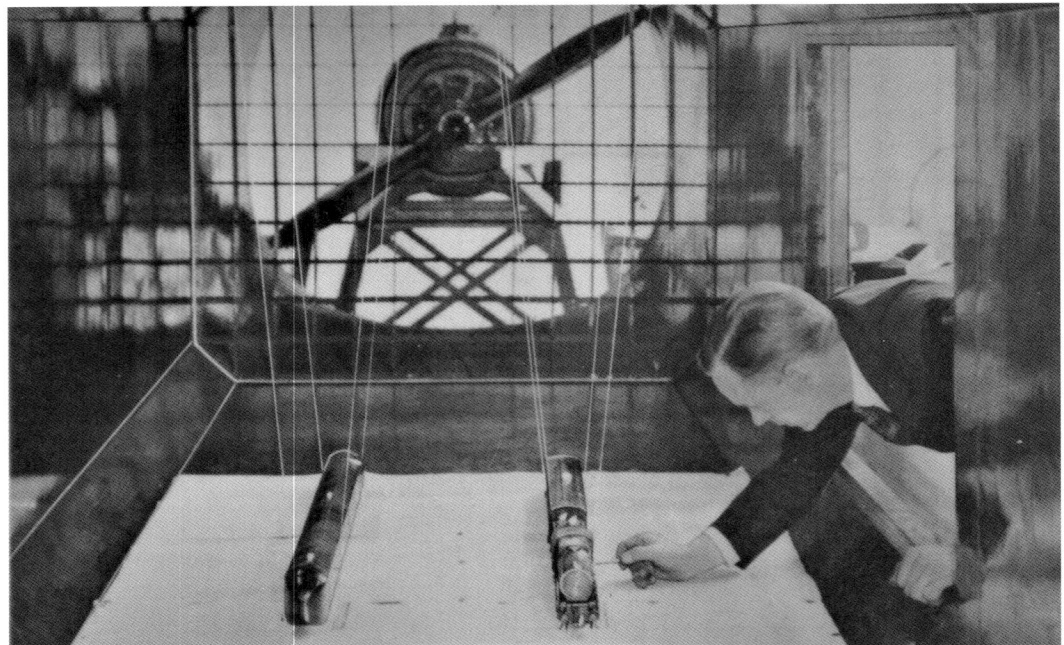

Frederick Johansen wind tunnel testing the aerodynamics of two model locomotives to evaluate the comparative benefits of streamlining. He discovered that a scaled down version of an aeroplane, car or locomotive tended to react in the same way as full scale versions. He first worked for Gresley in 1927 or '28 testing Gresley's experimental W1 and would then be involved in both his P2 2-8-2 and A4 programmes. He also took part in smoke lifting trials with the A3s and then the streamlining of two B17 4-6-0s. In 1932, Johansen became an LMS employee, based part time in Derby, Euston and Teddington, and was directly involved in the creation of Stanier's Pacifics, including the streamlined Princess Coronation Class. All the while he continued advising Gresley. (THG).

where speeds had rapidly increased as well as stress on air frames, called for a much deeper level of research. Johansen became a specialist in this field and was soon advising both military and civilian bodies on streamlining their designs – aircraft, air ships and trains amongst other things. Such was his impact that he would soon number R.J. Mitchell, then in the process of designing his Schneider Trophy seaplanes and then the Spitfire, amongst his clients. Such was his growing influence that he was invited to write a section on aerodynamics for the seminal work *Handbook of Aeronautics*, which appeared in 1931 and soon became a bible for designers and aircrew alike.

He and Gresley appear to have met some time in the latter half of the 1920s through their joint membership of the IMechE. It was a coming together seemingly sponsored by the Superintendent of the Engineering Department at the NPL, Sir Thomas Stanton, William Duncan, a senior figure in a research group there, and Ernest Wilson, Professor of Electrical Engineering at King's College. With such influential backing, coupled to a growing interest in the subject, Gresley invited Johansen to apply these principles to locomotive design beginning with W1 and smoke lifting trials involving the Pacifics during 1927/28. Spencer recalled:

> As far as I can remember the term streamlining, and its application to locomotives and rolling stock, first entered our vocabulary at King's Cross and Doncaster in 1924 when linked to the development of aircraft, most particularly the racing seaplanes. But it also received a great deal of publicity when racing car designs adopted aerodynamic principles. I observed this first

hand when visiting the Brooklands race track in Surrey where the benefits of streamlining were regularly discussed – most particularly, its ability to reduce drag, improve road holding and extend range by improving fuel economy. A little later, Sir Malcolm Campbell's exploits, with his Blue Bird record breakers also drew great attention especially the way their designs adopted hydro and aerodynamic theories when determining their shapes.

Of course, these scientific principles had some currency already, mostly derived from theoretical work undertaken in the 18th Century by Daniel Bernoullie [a Swiss born mathematician and physicist], who I had read about at Doncaster Technical College. Then those such as George Cayley developed these ideas further and saw them applied by ship builders to hull design. The high speed Clipper sailing ships of the mid-19th Century probably brought these theories to a peak and those that followed learnt a lot from their example. It was left to men such as Samuel Calthrop and Frederick Upham Adams to apply these ideas to train design, though neither took them very far beyond the theoretical. Here to I was made aware of their work when studying at college, though the tutors did not press the issue, except to refer to the work undertaken by William McKeen and the Union Pacific Railroad when introducing their 'Windsplitter' railcars before the Great War. These I read about later in railway magazines, but could get no more than very basic information about them. This left me wondering just how successful they were and whether their performance had been evaluated scientifically and compared with more traditional designs. Then when working at Horwich, as John Aspinall reached the end of his long career as CME and General Manager of the Lancashire and Yorkshire railway, I was able to study his work on the subject.

His paper on 'Train Resistance', [No. 3280] presented to members of the Institution of Civil Engineers on 26th November 1901, was so well received that he was awarded the 1902 Watt Medal. It was the first serious attempt at scientifically evaluating and tabulating the effects of wind resistance in laboratory conditions – active testing, using a specially adapted dynamometer car, taking place between June 1899 and January 1900. His work was primarily theoretical in nature, though did reach two interesting conclusions, as well as provide a formula for calculating resistance for trains of different lengths. Firstly, that with a train with five coaches the axle friction, atmospheric and other resistances could be measured at 8 per cent, 42 per cent and 50 per cent respectively of the total train resistance. Secondly, that at 70mph a train of ten bogie carriages weighing 219 tons faced a total resistance of 20.6lb per ton. As a result, he calculated that such a train travelling at an average of 70 mph, on a windless day, would require a 2 ton drawbar pull on a windless day.

From this Aspinall concluded that an engine would require more power if it was to overcome all forms of resistance, but that these resistances could vary each day dependent on such things as weather conditions. As such the unpredictable effects of side winds would render the aerodynamic shaping of debatable value. This was a view not shared by Gresley, who believed that shaping of the entire train could overcome the effects of resistance to some

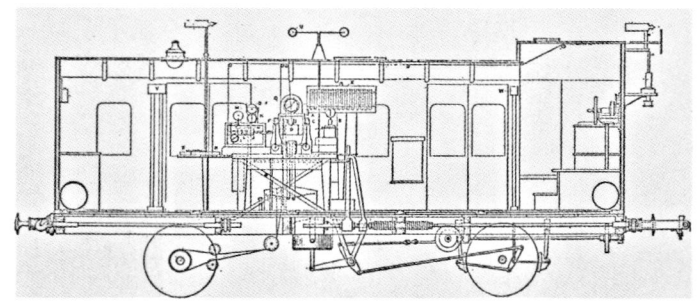

Aspinall's design for a dynamometer car specially for use in his train resistance research during 1899/1900. It included a wind vane attached to a wind direction indicator, an anemometer (an instrument that measures a current of gas) in the centre of the roof coupled to a wind velocity recorder and a wind pressure transducer. (BS)

APPENDIXES.

APPENDIX I.

TABLE I.—TOTAL TRACTIVE RESISTANCE OF TRAINS ONLY. BOGIE-COACHES. OIL AXLE-BOXES.

Number of coaches	5	10	15	20
Weight of train, in tons	115·2	218·7	322·1	429·4
Length of train, in feet	285	542	800	1,057

Speed of train, miles per hour	Resistance in pounds per ton			
10	3·8	3·2	3·1	3·1
20	5·0	4·7	4·5	4·3
30	7·4	6·9	6·5	6·1
40	10·5	9·6	8·9	8·3
50	14·0	12·8	11·8	11·0
60	18·1	16·5	15·1	14·0
70	22·8	20·6	18·8	17·4
80	27·8	25·1	22·8	21·1
90	33·3	29·9	27·2	25·1
100	39·2	35·3	32·0	29·4

TABLE II.—HORSE-POWER REQUIRED TO HAUL TRAINS ON LEVEL. BOGIE-COACHES. OIL AXLE-BOXES.

Number of coaches	5	10	15	20
Weight of train, in tons	115·2	218·7	322·1	429·4
Length of train, in feet	285	542	830	1057

Speed of train, miles per hour	Total horse-power			
10	10·14	18·6	26·6	35·5
20	30·7	54·8	77·4	98·5
30	68·2	120·6	167·4	209·5
40	129·0	224·0	306·0	380·0
50	215·0	373·1	507·0	630·0
60	334·0	577·0	778·0	962·0
70	490·0	841·0	1,130·0	1,395·0
80	683·0	1,171·0	1,567·0	1,933·0
90	921·0	1,569·0	2,102·0	2,587·0
100	1,204·0	2,059·0	2,748·0	3,366·0

Spencer kept a copy of Aspinall's 1901 paper in his archive. It is 'well-thumbed' as though referred to on many occasions. Of particular interest to Spencer, as a man well-versed in testing regimes, would have been data collected during the trials. This particular Appendix was extracted and mounted on card presumably because it was often referred to. The data in Table I records the tractive resistance 'to trains of different lengths and at various speeds up to 100mph'. Table II gives details of 'the horse-power required to haul these trains on the level, on the basis of the resistance indicated in Table I'. In summarizing his findings Aspinall made it clear that these figures, and the formula he deduced from them, were for Summer resistance and 'Winter resistance would probably give rather different results'. (BS)

degree so should not be discarded as an idea. In this he was greatly encouraged by work being undertaken in the United States by the new breed of Industrial Designers there and engineers in Europe, particularly in Germany with their plans for high speed diesel railcars.

With that Aspinall's experiments came to an end and he left it to others to take up this research, which Johansen and others did, quickly followed by Gresley, who had attended the presentation in 1901. According to the record of the event he made no public comment on the day, presumably because he was a junior member. As a result, the question and answer session was taken up by issues raised by those of equal rank and influence as the speaker.

With such rapid advances in aviation and high speed vehicle design in the post war years the potential of streamlining became only too apparent. So, it was hardly surprising when locomotive designers again began to take note, here and overseas. My first practical link to the subject was encouraged by Gresley, who saw in it great potential. It was at this stage that I first met Frederick Johansen and became more closely involved in his theoretical work at Teddington. I visited him there a number of times to view wind tunnel tests in progress and discuss a number of issues with him, on Gresley's behalf. He also became a frequent and welcome visitor to King's Cross, even when working part and then full time for the LMS.

In the years that followed streamlining became a topic much discussed by members of the ILocoE and, I was told by Gresley, the 'Mechanicals', as he called them. This was something he greatly encouraged especially when becoming their President in 1936. As a result, he wasted little time in arranging for Johansen to present his findings at a well-attended meeting in London later that year, quickly followed by a number of regional presentations.

Although not a member then of the IMechE myself, the CME invited me to attend and I sat beside Oliver Bulleid, who found it difficult to suppress his irritation with many of Johansen's conclusions. In doing so he demonstrated a fundamental difference of opinion with Gresley on the subject and one he seemed happy to air in public, much to the CME's

Pressing Home Their Advantage 115

By the time Gresley consulted Johansen during the latter stages of the W1 project, the NPL scientist was already considering ways of counter-acting the effect of air resistance on moving objects other than aircraft. His work on locomotives and carriages was in its infancy but had already thrown up some interesting ideas all of which he wind tunnel tested. (Top – left and right) Some were simply adding different types of deflectors or nose cones of different shapes. Others (lower picture) were more sophisticated attempts to achieve a complete wrap-around effect. In the early 1930s he would refine these ideas considerably and see them influence designs introduced by the LNER and LMS. (FJ)

growing annoyance. This was especially so in the wake of the successful introduction of the streamlined A4s and the Silver Jubilee service in September 1935.

Although to some Gresley seemed to pursue streamlining with all the zest of an evangelist preacher he was not blind to any possible limitations that might exist, as he made clear in his Presidential address to the ILocoE in late 1934:

The air resistance, notwithstanding scientific streamlining, absorbs so much power. Experiments with models of existing types of coaches (pulled by a conventional shaped locomotive) carried out by the NPL show that air resistance of trains average length, say 12 coaches, at 100 mph, is approximately double that of trains travelling at 70 mph. In the case of the Flying Hamburger it is estimated that 85 per cent of the power generated by the diesel engine is absorbed in air resistance when running at 85 mph. Streamlining is essential at high speeds because air resistance of trains increases approximately as the cube of speed, but it is of comparatively negligible value at lower speeds, up to say, 50 mph.

In 1936, with operational experience gained by his A4 streamlined Silver Link in service, Gresley felt free to add more flesh to these bones:

I think I may mention that experiments have been made at the NPL with scale models of the streamlined Pacific and an ordinary Pacific to determine the head-on wind resistance and calculate the horse-power required at various speeds to overcome the air resistance. The results are shown in Table 2 (shown next page).

HORSE-POWER SAVED BY STREAMLINING.									
	Horse-power required to overcome head-on air resistance.								
Speed, m.p.h.	60	70	80	90	100	110	120	130	140	150
Standard "Pacific" type.	97.21	154.26	230.51	328.49	450.92	599.39	778.65	988.95	1235.87	1520.80
Streamlined type.	56.39	89.41	133.61	190.40	261.36	347.41	451.32	573.21	716.32	881.48
Horse-power saved by streamlining.	40.82	64.85	96.90	138.09	189.56	252.98	327.33	415.74	519.55	639.32

To maintain a schedule of 71 mph between London and Darlington with this train entails an average running speed up hill and down dale of 80 to 90 mph, after making allowance for starting, stopping and the various speed restrictions, it will be seen from this table that streamlining results in a saving of over 100 hp continuously at these speeds on a still day. There is, however, generally a wind of greater or lesser intensity, consequently, as the power required to overcome air resistance varies approximately as the cube of the speed, such reduction as may result when running with a favourable wind is not to be compared with the extra power required on the opposite working against a contrary wind. Hence it follows that in the case of this train that probable average saving of power due to streamlining is considerably in excess of 100 hp.

The coal consumption of the engines working this train averages 39lb per mile; if the consumption of coal is proportionate to the power, the saving due to streamlining is about 4lb per mile, or over 20 tons per annum.

To these assessments Bulleid made two telling responses, the first of these in 1934, the second two years later, having listened to Johansen's paper and Gresley's supportive comments:

The thing (streamlining) is no more than a fashion, but as such it cannot be ignored by any self-respecting designer who wishes to be in the swim…Streamlining is a necessity for aeroplanes, as vacuums of air turbulences would mean loss of stability and speed. But with railway trains it is a different matter.

I am quite unable to understand how a theory such as to what happens with a full size train under working conditions could be built from results from small models, obtained under different conditions … a relationship should be established between the results for models and for actual trains … There is a tendency to encourage engineers to think that streamlining would effect savings in trains working which, in practical experience, would not appear possible. I feel, moreover, in view of the LMS's magnificent run from Euston to Glasgow in 6 hours with an ordinary train worked by a Pacific engine not streamlined, that air resistances could not be anything like as high as the figures suggested in the paper. The subject of streamlining is, I think, still very much in the initial stages and requires considerably more investigation.

Coming from his trusted principal assistant these comments must have struck a negative chord in Gresley's mind. So, it is hardly surprising that Spencer would later observe:

With these very public comments a gap between Gresley and Bulleid appeared to develop which became obvious to even the most junior member of staff at Kng's Cross. To me this suggested a malaise in their relationship, possibly caused by Bulleid's frustration at not being CME with the

(Above left) Gresley enjoys a day out on the Romney, Hythe and Dymchurch Railway with the Duke of York and the railway's founder, racing driver Captain Jack Howey. (Above right) Bulleid who seems to have found his last few years with the LNER increasingly frustrating. It seems that as the 1930s progressed a gap between Gresley and Bulleid grew. We shall never know the reason for this, but Spencer suggested thwarted ambitions on the part of Bulleid who was eager to be a CME, as one possible cause, professional differences being another. But with Gresley showing no sign of wanting to retire or move on, the post at King's Cross remained out of reach. And so streamlining became a forum in which they appear to have played out their differences. (THG)

LNER or elsewhere and Gresley's wish to hold on to his post. If they could not reach agreement on such an issue as streamlining, which, in truth, only affected one small part of locomotove and rolling stock develoment on the LNER, albeit of the highest profile, it seemed they must part. It did not surprise me when Bulleid departed for the lesser CME post with the Southern Region, with Gresley's blessing, where he continued in his brilliant but erratic way.

In many ways, Gresley and Bulleid were probably too close to the issue to be truly impartial. Any professional disagreement between influential men or women can quickly become deeply entrenched and very difficult to arbitrate. Certainly, Spencer would have found it almost impossible to mediate between such strong, opinionated men. In any case, his views on streamlining seem to have run along the same lines as Gresley and Johansen, so Bullied would not have seen him as an impartial observer, only a servant of the CME.

In such debates, a message can easily be lost or sublimated into something else, so it is interesting to get a completely impartial view of the streamlining issue from someone at Doncaster with no particular axe to grind. Eric Windle was, at the time, a senior draughtsman at Doncaster, who would rise to become Chief. He later wrote about how these ideas were developed:

It should be recognised that streamlining, so far as the modern locomotive is concerned, had its origins in attempts to reduce smoke which came down on to the front of the cab windows … At first the experiments (to reduce or remove this hazard) were confined to an attempt to control the direction of the air flow around the chimney top…Many schemes in model form were tried, but the completely or almost completely streamlined front gave the most satisfactory results … By this time the principle of more complete streamlining had become popular, its introduction being coincident with the development of the super-high

Although involved in many new projects Spencer still found time to take or collect photographs of the products of his early years with Gresley. (Above left) A3 No. 2752 *Spion Kop*, which entered service in April 1929 and was a Doncaster based engine until 1938, undergoes preparation for another day's service. (Above right) Another A3, the 1928 built No. 2744 *Grand Parade*, makes ready to depart from King's Cross. In neither case has Spencer added any dates to the prints in his collection. (BS)

In an effort to improve the forward visibility of the Pacifics, which was often badly affected by drifting smoke, two Pacifics, Nos. 2747 *Coronach* and 2751 *Humorist*, underwent some front end modifications during 1932 in a series of experiments supported by the NPL and Frederick Johansen. These did not prove particularly successful and in time the two engines reverted to their original condition (Above left and right) Views of 2751 with two forms of chimney and the small deflector plates added in an effort to improve smoke lifting. (Below) 2747 with her unusual cutaway smokebox modification. (BS)

speed trains ... If anyone were inclined to question whether streamlining was effective from a practical point of view, he should travel on the footplate of another engine and let a streamlined train pass him at high speed, and then let an ordinary train pass him at high speed. He would find a vast difference in air disturbance.

Here Windle probably touched upon the nub of the issue and, in so doing revealed an enthusiasm for the project that Bulleid might have done well to copy, or at least feign. Why pick a fight when there was no need to do so, especially in public? Here he might have learnt something from the team playing, diplomatic Spencer. With such a forceful and very clever man as Gresley gentle persuasion and dispassionate debate were likely to pay dividends in an environment where confrontation would, undoubtedly, be counterproductive.

So the path to the streamlined A4s was probably set by the late 1920s and as the project gathered pace, Bullied seems to have become increasingly side lined by the strength of his criticism of the path Gresley had chosen to take. But in doing this the CME moved, as Spencer put it, 'in a measured way, not attempting to take his fences too quickly, learning lessons as he went'. For a man keen on horse racing, this seems an appropriate metaphor to describe his actions and in practice it was an approach that seemed to work.

As Windle stated, the first step in the streamlining programme focussed on an important safety issue. Drifting smoke presented visibility problems for footplate crew. In this, Gresley enlisted the help of the NPL, and through them Johansen, who later described how the work evolved and the issues involved:

While the research was in progress the opportunity was taken to measure the air resistance, at zero yaw, of one-twelfth scale models of the LNE locomotives *Flying Scotsman* No. 4472

Until completely rebuilt in 1937 as a conventional, albeit a streamlined engine, several modifications were made to the W1's front end. In 1935, she was fitted with a double blastpipe and chimney and the following year a 'hood smoke lifter' (seen in the photo above). Neither seemed to improve the engine's performance and it was transferred to Darlington where it resided in the Paint Shop until a decision about her future was made. Spencer wrote, 'I was sad to see the W1 side lined, having been closely involved in all her trials work. It had great potential, but did not show sufficient promise to enable others to be built or for the high pressure engines to replace more conventional classes.' (BS)

and No. 10000 (4-6-4) (the latter already having been wind tunnel tested at Teddington when under development to ascertain the most effective streamline shape to fit around its unique boiler arrangement).

We discovered that with a total air resistance of 38.4 per cent the horse-power absorbed by the unstreamlined Pacific with six coaches would amount to 111 at 60 mph, 262 at 80 mph, 512 at 100 mph and 885 at 120 mph. When we later compared this to LMS's six-hour runs between London and Glasgow we estimated that the horse-power absorbed by air resistance amounted to about 380 hp over the course of the journey (and about 43 per cent of the drawbar horse-power). In both cases, it was concluded that a streamlined locomotive and train would have been considerably more effective.

However, before we grappled more fully with the general principles of streamlining we sought answers to the perennial question of drifting smoke, the dangers this caused and the best way to eradicate or reduce the problem.

According to Spencer:

Gresley was loth to apply the sort of smoke deflectors then coming into use, particularly on the LMS's Royal Scots, to his Pacifics believing that they destroyed their classic lines. Instead we were committed to a number of experiments and began modifying two A3s to test different theories. On one, engine No. 2747 *Coronach*, the smokebox was cut away or had small deflectors added after a Kylchap exhaust and then a double chimney were fitted.

The NPL played a key role in this work, but were too hard pressed with other wind tunnel testing tasks, relating to aircraft and ship development, to do all we required and so agreement was reached with the City and Guilds Engineering College to undertake some of the testing work in their laboratories. This ensured that any proposal that might help steam and smoke to be thrown clear of the cab, particularly when working at early cut-off, might prove effective when matched to a full scale locomotive. To assist in this direction and to

Two institutions that played an active part in Gresley's work and to which Spencer was a frequent visitor as different locomotive projects evolved. (Above) The National Physical Laboratory in Teddington, Middlesex and (Left) the City and Guilds Engineering College in Central London; both as they appeared in the 1920s and '30s. Gresley's seems to have had an ad hoc relationship with each establishment and used their facilities and expertise as and when he needed to. (THG)

provide an improved lookout the cab front was made wedge-shaped – a practice followed in the subsequent A4 programme, the P2s, when engine No. 10000 was rebuilt, the two streamlined B17s and the conventionally shaped V2 2-6-2 tender engines.'

When reading various accounts about this period in the LNER's history, there seems to be some confusion over the institutions and individuals involved in Gresley's work. In some, the NPL looms large, in others it is the City and Guilds College and one account even mentions the Royal Aircraft Establishment at Farnborough, which by the 1930s had begun full scale aerodynamic testing as well as using their smaller wind tunnel for modelling. If there is any confusion in this list of possible contributors, it probably stems from the plethora of contacts Gresley made across the world of science. His open, enquiring mind would have drawn together experts from many related spheres and learned institutions eager to explore new applications for their work or simply offer advice. In this way, Johansen was drawn into Gresley's circle to advise on air resistance and streamlining issues, but so, apparently, was William Dalby, if some accounts are to be believed.

By this stage, Dalby was Professor of Engineering at London University and a Fellow of the Royal Society, having begun his career as an apprentice in the Great Eastern's Stratford Locomotive Works during 1876. Because of this, he retained an interest in the railways and in 1902 produced his text book *The Balancing of Engines*, which soon became a key reference source within the industry. He and Gresley apparently became friends and the Professor acted as advisor during the early stages of the Pacific and W1 programmes. From this it has been assumed that his advice then extended from engine balancing into the specifics of aerodynamic design. According to Spencer this was not so:

Dalby was well-known to both Gresley and Bulleid, but less so to the rest of us at King's Cross. The Professor's work was key to the design of the early Pacifics when it came to achieving the most effective balance between hammer blow on the rails and tractive force. But beyond this he had little direct day to day involvement especially with such things as air flow issues, although he may have discussed some issues with the CME during their many social meetings. Dalby retired in 1931, when severe ill-health overtook him and incapacity

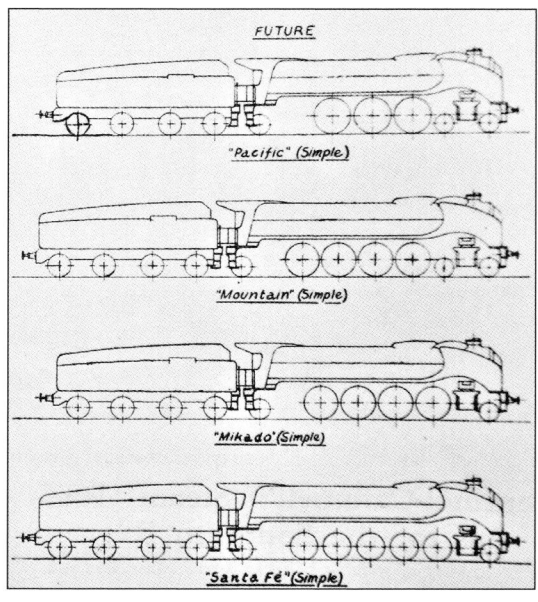

By the time Johansen's work was being taken more seriously by locomotive designers in Britain, the concept of streamlining had begun to take hold in the USA, France and Germany, most notably with emerging high speed diesel railcar developments. In Germany's case it also included the 1929 introduced propeller driven 'Rail Zeppelin' or *Scheinenzeppelin* which is reputed to have achieved 143 mph in trials. Some of these projects were highly successful, but reality, and lack of funds in such austere times, dictated a more frugal approach and so high speed steam locomotives underwent a streamlined makeover instead. This picture highlights how one French company saw the future as the new decade dawned, each design adopting streamlining principles still being formed and tested. (BS)

restricted his movements, and died five years later. After his retirement I do not recollect him being involved directly in any way, least of all on the train resistance and streamlining work.

Over the years it became custom and practice to seek the help of scientists and engineers at the City and Guilds College on many small issues simply because of their location in Central London and their willingness to help. When Johansen, or the wind tunnel at Teddington, was not available some air resistance testing was undertaken by technical staff at the Engineering College. However, the results were, more often than not, passed to Johansen for final analysis and inclusion in his reports to Gresley.

In trying to determine who did what and where there is one further complication to consider. From 1932, Frederick Johansen was employed part-time, then full time by Harold Hartley, the LMS's influential Director of Research. However, his contract did not preclude him from working for other companies on a consultancy basis and so he continued advising Gresley, as well as Supermarine and Hawkers, as they developed their monoplane fighters for the RAF.

In many ways, this was a quite remarkable arrangement. Being allowed to advise the LNER when employed by the LMS, at a time when both companies were in a very public competition for custom seems remarkably generous on the part of Hartley and Josiah Stamp, the company's Chairman. But the reality was that streamlining was a subject in which William Stanier, the CME, seemed to show little interest, preferring to develop more conventional ideas as he built his Princess Royal Pacifics. Without his active support, anything Johansen did would probably have struggled for acceptance no matter how strongly Hartley argued his case. And so it was left to Tom Coleman, who Stanier appointed Chief Draughtsman in 1935, to see the possibilities inherent in Johansen's research and, when given the opportunity, make use of it in the Princess Coronation programme that came to fruition in 1937. So, with little to interest him in Johansen's work, it is perhaps not surprising that Stanier did not try to restrict or curtail Johansen's activities in support of the LNER. So, Gresley had almost constant support from Johansen from the late 1920s to the mid-1930s, although, as we have seen, in later years his efforts were shared with the LMS.

When Johansen left the NPL to work for Hartley it was at Euston; a location undoubtedly chosen so that the young scientist could continue to make use of the facilities at Teddington, but also carry on with his consultancy work. It was not until a wind tunnel was built at Derby in 1936 that pressure was put on Johansen to move northwards, so restricting the extra-curricular support he could give to others such as Gresley.

At Derby, he worked full-time for Tom Herbert, the Head of the LMS's Research Department, and soon found his time taken up by other areas of scientific research, most notably metallurgy and how the effects of metal fatigue might be countered. However, he did not lose his link with the world of aerodynamics and streamlining entirely and continued advising aircraft manufacturers on the principles he had helped establish during the war and well into the 1950s.

If sharing Johansen's research work was unusual in such a competitive business, close friendships also crossed the boundaries often set by competition. Gresley and Stanier, at the very top, became good friends and those lower down followed suit. It was a process helped by the many professional and educational institutions in being, all of which encouraged open debate and a sharing of ideas. However, there was a limit to how far this could go before reputational and commercial considerations came into play. Yet the line could be a fluid one as Spencer later described:

> Tom Coleman and I met for the first time just after the war when he was Chief Draughtsman with the old North Staffordshire Railway and visited Horwich, when I was in the Drawing Office there to discuss some issue or other. He was older than me and married with children, but these differences did not seem to matter. Like Elwess, who Tom also knew, he naturally

Pressing Home Their Advantage 123

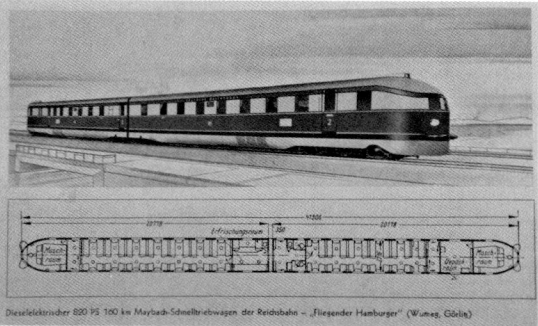

As Gresley's plans took shape, streamlining had become a hot topic around the world with designers seeking to develop the concept as quickly as possible – as a means of improving performance, but also to exploit the publicity this work generated. (Top left) This was none more so than in Germany when the propeller driven high speed *Scheinenzeppelin* appeared in 1929. However, it never advanced beyond being a trials vehicle. (Top right) The streamlined Flying Hamburger diesel railcars, introduced in 1932, proved much more successful. (Bottom picture) Although steam locomotives still dominated American railroads in the 1930s, and would do for many years to come, 1934 saw the introduction of two ultra-modern welded steel streamlined diesel train sets, both of which proved highly successful. The second of these, manufactured by E.G. Budd and Co for the Chicago, Burlington and Quincy Railroad, is shown here beside more conventional rolling stock. (THG)

took young engineers under his wing and offered friendship and encouragement even though they might be employed by another company. When he became Chief Draughtsman at Horwich in 1926 he invited me to the Works to view locomotives being built there and examine plans he had kept of two early, but unsuccessful attempts by George Hughes and Henry Fowler to build Pacifics for the LMS.

He knew of my interest, and that of Gresley, in the next stage of the LNER's Pacific programme and felt we might learn something from the drawings and data he held. At that stage it seemed most unlikely that the LMS would build their own Pacific (and didn't do so for another seven years), so there was a natural desire to share our experiences and knowledge. In return, and with Gresley's permission, Tom rode in the cabs of several A1/A3s and closely observed them on shed, in the Works as well as on the main line. The same thing happened when the P2s and A4s were launched.

Tom was an exceptionally able engineer whose reputation grew each year as he moved to Crewe then Derby as Chief Draughtsman. His growing influence was noted by all, including Gresley. There was a rumour that the CME tried to recruit him when Robert Thom retired as Mechanical Engineer at Doncaster in 1937. If so, it came to nothing and Edward Thompson took the post instead. By this stage Tom and Robert had also become firm friends.

Whenever a new locomotive or service was introduced, its launch would be attended by invited guests or competitors just wishing to see how their rivals were doing. In May 1931, according to this photo and notes left by Spencer, there was a gathering of guests to observe the inauguration of the electrified service on the LMS/LNER jointly owned service between Altringham and Manchester (top picture). (Lower picture) On the back of the second photo, taken on the same day, Spencer has recorded many of the names including 'Myself third from right, Tom (Coleman) second left'. In his collection Spencer has a number of other photos of Coleman plus pictures of his most notable achievements with personal comments from the Chief Draughtsman at Derby attached. This level of detail and the regularity of their contact seems to define the extent of their friendship. They appear to have remained in contact until Tom's death in 1958. (BS)

When it came to streamlining Tom seemed happy to share the results of Johansen's research, but each in their own way adopted different solutions when it came to the aerodynamic shapes applied to their engines. Here Gresley seems to have had first choice with the P2s and then the A4s, while Tom was left with a rather more bulbous solution for his Coronations. To have done otherwise would have resulted in the A4s and the LMS engines being almost identical. 'First come first served' was the way Tom described it and he showed no bitterness at the results.

Amongst all the tasks that crossed his desk both big and small, Spencer chose to record his thoughts and memories of only a few key issues during the later years at King's Cross. This probably comes as no surprise. When looking back one tends to edit out the more mundane experiences and allow the important ones to rise to the surface. After 1932, this was very much the case for Spencer. So for the remaining years of Gresley's life, memories of three projects dominate his writing – the P2,

As early as 1932, Johansen, after four years of careful consideration, had prepared a number of drawings showing how the front end of streamlined locomotives might be shaped. He continued to refine these ideas using scaled down wooden models in the wind tunnel and by studying information gleaned from the W1 experiments. As a result, he had at least four basic designs which seemed to meet Gresley's and then the LMS's purposes. This picture, which he himself prepared in about 1934, is a summary of this work, copies of which were retained by Spencer and Coleman. Although the working numbers refer to possible new LMS locomotives, the shapes can be clearly linked to those used on Stanier's Coronations and Gresley's A4s, P2s (the top right hand drawing shows engines 2001 and 2002 as originally built, then bottom left shows them in streamlined form, which the other four members of the class adopted from new) W1 and the two B17s that were streamlined (BS/TC)

the A4 Pacifics and the V2 2-6-2 tender engines. In his presentation to the ILocoE during 1947, he briefly touched on other tasks, but his more general memoirs gave them little attention. This does make for a slightly unbalanced account of these later years, but hopefully sufficient can be gleaned from his papers to provide as complete a personal history as possible.

The P2 project was one that has generated much controversy. 'To some', as Spencer succinctly put it, 'the class seemed to be unnecessarily experimental, while others thought them too complex, even over engineered for their purpose. Others saw a 2-8-2 design as being unsuited to a route containing so many sharp curves, with wheels, axles and bearings being subjected to excessive stresses and wear, so more likely to fail.'

The need for these engines arose from a requirement identified in 1931/32, for a locomotive that could, as Spencer put it:

> ... pull express passenger trains of up to 550 tons, exclusive of the engine, over the heavily graded route between Edinburgh and Aberdeen at high average speeds. Up to then the maximum unassisted loads worked by the Pacifics over this line were 480 tons northbound and 420 tons southbound. The General Manager Scotland (James Calder) with the Chief General Manager's agreement set out a specification for such an engine, Calder believing, or so I was told, that this would result in a 'Super' Pacific. It was Gresley's wish, urged on by Bulleid, to build a Mikado for the task. Wedgwood bowed to this request and work soon began on sketching out possible options.

> With a 2-8-2 option firmly in mind it was decided to test a P1 on passenger services to see how this wheel configuration and the crew would cope with such an engine on stop/start duties. So during the preliminary design of the P2s, engine No. 2394 was tried on such a train working between King's Cross and Peterborough where it was found that a speed of 65 mph was easily maintained. But the crew found the locomotive very heavy on coal and laboured hard on an engine that did not ride well at such speeds. Its driving wheels at 5ft 2in had no problem on tighter curves, but concerns were soon raised about the 6ft 2in wheels intended for use on the P2s, especially on the difficult line north of Edinburgh. Bulleid felt that this would not present a problem.'

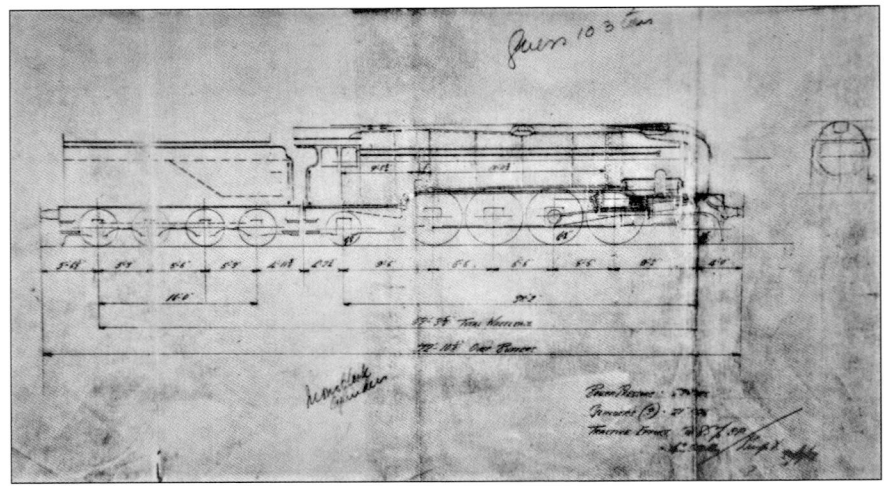

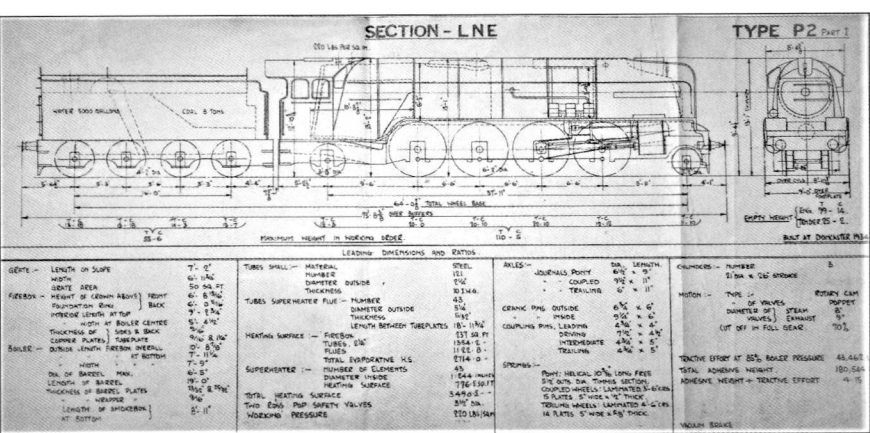

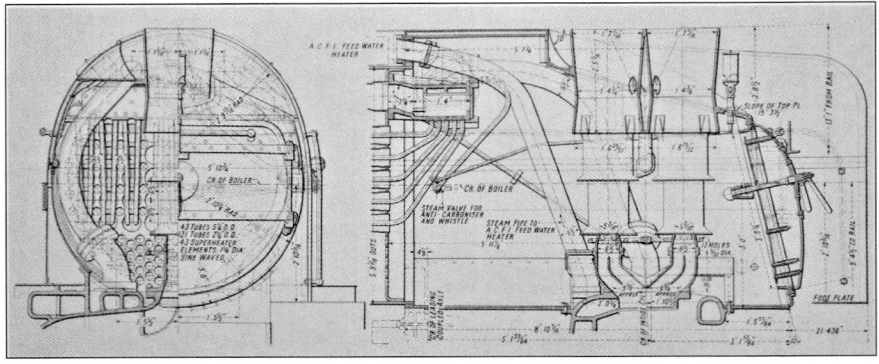

(Top) Though the date is barely legible (February 1932?) and the drawing is badly marked by creases and dirt, this seems to be one of the earliest surviving sketches of the P2 prepared by Bert Spencer. (Middle) Gradually the shape and basic details of the new engine were confirmed by a series of diagrams and from here they evolved into a final and extensive set of drawings all of which were passed through Gresley and Spencer's hands for approval. (Bottom) The final arrangement for engine No. 2001's smokebox showing the superheater and its Kylchap blastpipe and chimney arrangements, plus the Johansen tested front end. (BS)

In late1931, according to Spencer, he was instructed by Gresley to prepare some simple drawings of a 2-8-2 express locomotive. These first efforts strongly resembled his Pacifics – a good model on which to build – but no account was taken of any of the ideas his and Johansen's research had begun to throw up. Then, in early 1932, Spencer took these efforts and quickly revised the layout to produce something strongly resembling the eventual shape of the first P2, No. 2001. However, it took until late 1933 for Gresley, with Bulleid and Spencer's support, to refine his thoughts and begin to engage Robert Thom and Harry Broughton more fully in the design process. The specification issued to them confirmed the requirement for 6ft 2in driving wheels, an adhesive weight of 80 tons 12 cwt, a 6ft 5in diameter boiler producing 220lb sq in of pressure, a 43 element superheater of the Robinson type, 50ft of grate area, three 21in by 26in cylinders, a double Kylchap exhaust system in the smokebox and the ACFI feedwater system. One interesting addition to this was described by Spencer:

> Steam distribution on the first engine (No.2001) was by Lentz rotary cam poppet valve gear, the diameter of steam and exhaust valves being 8in. and 9 in. respectively. Gresley's decision to fit such large diameter valves was influenced by his talks with Chapelon, whose four-cylinder compound Pacifics on the Paris-Orleans Railway were putting up remarkable performances. These engines had poppet valves operated by oscillating cams, the diameters of the steam and exhaust valves on the low pressure cylinders being 8.66 in. and 9.45 in. respectively.'

Many years later he added a brief note to this:

> To test the benefits to be derived from the Lentz rotary cam gear Gresley had, over a number of years, authorised its use on various classes of locomotive – D49s and B12s amongst them. But as work on the P2 gathered pace the gear was installed on two C7 Class Atlantics which were often used for testing items of auxiliary equipment. The results were good and it was decided to go ahead with No. 2001 on this basis.

During February 1933, the Drawing Office were set the task of producing a schedule of material required to construct two P2s. They then began preparing detailed drawings even though Gresley had yet to complete his deliberations on a number of issues. During September, Thom felt he could wait no longer and, worried about the slow progress being made, felt it necessary to prepare and circulate a draft production schedule so that workshops could at least begin to plan their work. But even at this stage the final design was far from complete as a letter he received from Bulleid on the 6th of that month soon confirmed. It contained a description of the CME's developing ideas accompanied by a `sketch` prepared by Spencer showing the locomotive's proposed outline, which seems to be the first time either Thom or Broughton had seen this much detail. Bulleid wrote:

(Right) No. 2001 nears completion. Spencer later wrote that 'Gresley, Bulleid and I were frequent visitors to Doncaster to view the engine and tender under construction. The CME was most concerned about the comfort and safety of the footplate crew (though on a steam engine this was always difficult to achieve. The footplate was a naturally very dangerous place to be). As had become his want he ordered a mock-up of the footplate to be built and tested to make sure it was as good as it could be. He wasted little time when arriving at Doncaster to mount the cab and set to muttering the words 'if someone my size can manage the crew should not have too many difficulties!' as he went. His educated eye soon spotted some things that needed changing and, when revisiting, he made sure the work had been carried out to his satisfaction. (BS)

I enclose pencil sketches showing the proposed side elevation of this engine. As the top of the clothing behind the chimney will require to open for inspection of the feed water heater, it will be necessary for a horizontal line on the bend to show where the lagging plates are hinged, and in view of this Mr Gresley has been considering whether it would be advantageous to do away with the ordinary type of clothing and fit clothing secured by horizontal bands, thereby improving the streamline appearance of the engine.

As a small aside to this, Spencer sent Broughton a short note on 17 September accompanying a ream of rough sketches, on any old piece of paper that came to hand, prepared by Gresley when clarifying his thoughts on the cam gear. Spencer normally took these almost indecipherable drawings and used his draughtsman skills to translate into them something much more legible. But on this occasion time was pressing and he sent the originals with 'Mr H.N. Gresley's sketches re Cam Rollers` written at the top. He didn`t write 'and the best of luck', but it is probably safe to say this is what he thought. These surviving examples tell us much about the way Gresley worked, the level of detail he involved himself in and the value of having someone as talented as Spencer beside him to ensure his thoughts were translated, modified where necessary and conveyed in a cogent way to the men in the field.

With the first locomotive due to be ready by May 1934, Gresley finally approved all the drawings on 17 October, though up to its launch he was still tweaking the design, often focussing on some of the most innocuous items. It was almost as if he thought this locomotive might be the principal achievement of his career and so fussed over every small item. But in the capable hands of Robert Thom, the programme was carefully and effectively managed. Miraculously, to some, he achieved this alongside all the other tasks he had in hand despite the great number of requests for information on the P2 and other tasks he received from King's Cross on almost a daily basis. The few files that remain in public or private hands show the extent of correspondence he received, often beginning with the words 'the CME would like to know what progress is being made on…' or 'see attached the CME's sketch/comment/proposal on..' But the phlegmatic Scot, who was known to stand little nonsense from anyone, was more

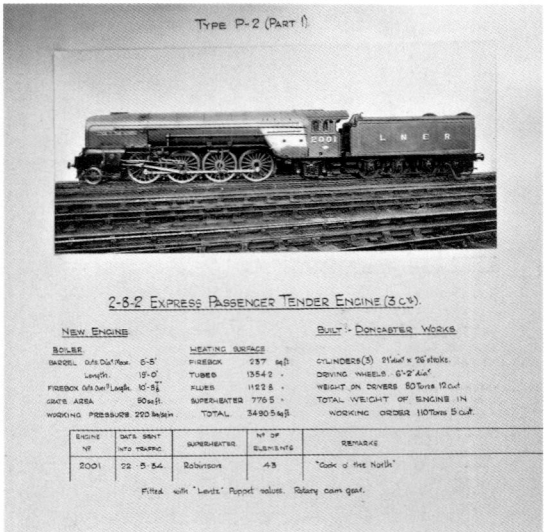

Robert Thom kept an album of all the locomotives, whether new or rebuilds, constructed by the LNER and kept this going until the end of 1935. Sometimes the locomotives were grouped together but in 2001's case the engine warranted a single page, as shown here. Spencer recalled that Thom called this his 'Game Book'. When he retired, he took this album, and several others collated during his career, with him, now all embossed in gold with his name on them. All have survived and together they provide a unique record of locomotive development on the LNER. (THG)

than capable of managing Gresley and Bulleid, together or individually. And in his hands, the P2s were coaxed into life, No. 2001 appearing on 22 May 1934 and No. 2002 on 6 October, the second engine being fitted with piston valves and not the Lentz gear.

The locomotive's launch, then inaugural run from King's Cross took place on 1 June, following an appearance at Doncaster's Open Day on 26 May. And soon the engine was quickly passed to the Running Department, with Gresley, Bulleid and Spencer watching closely to see how she performed. Each of them, it seems, also took the opportunity of riding on the footplate to make their own assessments. Gresley also sought out the crew to gauge their views and reactions to this engine, now named *Cock of the North*. On 13 June, he put some of their thoughts down in a letter to Robert Thom:

> The engine is found to be very hot in the cab, and the enginemen find it necessary to run with the front windows on the first catch. Will you please look into the question of fitting additional ventilators on each side of the cab in the upper portions of the front plate not occupied by the window.
>
> The men are also complaining of the heat from the firehole door, and I should be glad if you would consider fixing a short screen on the fireman's side in addition to the large screen on the driver's side to give extra protection.
>
> Some modification is also required to the large screen, as when opened it interferes with the movements of the fireman.

(Above left) Robert Thom (on the far left) gathers with a group of fellow engineers at Doncaster to launch the first P2. He like Spencer, is someone who has tended to slip from view and yet without his outstanding contribution at Doncaster from 1927 to 1937 it is debatable whether Gresley would have achieved so much. Spencer described him as 'A very astute man, with exceptional engineering skills and a strong sense of authority … He was always polite and had a canny way of remembering a face and the details of a person's life. With his clear Highland accent he could command a room and express himself effectively on many topics … He had an encyclopaedic knowledge of locomotive design, construction and performances, as well as all the functions of the workshops under his control and could work many of the machines as well as their operators did if it came to it … He and the CME worked well together and Thom seemed able to predict many things Gresley wanted and quickly turn ideas into working products … He was his own man, as they used to say, and without him it is likely that all we achieved would not have been possible. No one man makes an organisation and it helps considerably if there is a hard-core of men with the experience and skill of Gresley and Thom who can lead.' (Above right) A successful team enjoying a day out at the races. From left to right they are the LNER's Chairman William Whitelaw, Gresley and Thom. These three talented, determined men seem to have enjoyed a positive and collaborative working relationship devoid of rancour or disagreement. (THG)

1 June 1934, King's Cross and 2001 is launched. It was an event that attracted much attention and publicity. This inevitably raised expectations in some quarters that this impressive looking engine was something very special and would soon warrant all the hard work and expenditure on its development. Sadly, the P2s potential was never realised, some believing that it was unsuited for the purpose for which it was designed. More might have been achieved it they had worked south from Edinburgh, not north to Aberdeen. (Top left) Gresley, just visible on the right, watches 2001 being turned at King's Cross and again in right hand picture.

A group of invited and uninvited guests admire and discuss the new engine. Immediately beside the 2001's nameplate stands a group of four. Spencer has recorded that 'Gresley stands with his back to the camera – hands crossed behind his back. I am the fourth member of the group [in light coloured hat]. Stanier, Bulleid and Thom are nearby'. The man to Gresley's left does, in fact, resemble Stanier (BS)

The enginemen also call attention to the cock fixed on the tender for filling the water bucket. It is too low and difficult to get a bucket under easily. This arrangement should also be modified on the other tenders of this type.

On 19 June, the P2, having completed a few running in turns to iron out any faults, was deemed ready for her first formal trial. She was scheduled to pull a 649 ton load, including a dynamometer car, from King's Cross to Grantham, then on to the Barkston triangle, returning later in the day. With these runs successfully completed, with little recorded in the brief report that might be considered critical or flattering, Gresley took stock of all that had happened so far and authorised more trial runs. On 22 June he wrote to Thom:

As soon as the indicating gear is fitted I want you to take a complete series of cards at slow speed throughout the full range of cut-offs.

As regards the running trials, I have made provisional arrangements with Mr Barrington-Ward that the trials will be carried out on the 11.4 am from Doncaster

Pressing Home Their Advantage 131

(Top left) Gresley's developing ideas are evoked by this photo of 2001 standing beside the 1923 built, Grantham based A1 No. 4479 *Robert the Devil* soon to depart for the North. This engine was rebuilt as an A3 in 1942 and remained in service until 1963 (Top right) Spencer has written on the back of this print 'No. 2001 waiting in the wings at King's Cross'. (Right). 2001 again on 1 June, this time showing Spencer, who can just be seen wearing a light felt Fedora hat at the rear of the group closest to the camera. When researching this book, I found it difficult to find clear photos of Gresley's assistant, perhaps demonstrating his desire to remain in the background and not seek the limelight. (BS)

A few days after her first appearance at King's Cross, 2001 could be found, on 4 June, at Aberdeen Station having brought a special train of twelve carriages up from Waverley Station. The P2 had run 'light engine' to Edinburgh the previous day. Gresley accompanied the train to Aberdeen and is seen here discussing his new engine with the Lord Provost of Aberdeen, Sir Henry Alexander. Spencer later wrote, 'I was invited to attend, but it was then agreed that my time might be better spent attending tests with dynamometer car that would soon follow.' (BS)

and the 4.0 pm from King's Cross beginning on Monday July 2nd. The trials on the 2nd and 3rd July should be carried out with the ordinary load of these trains, but on the 4th and 5th weights of the trains should be made up at Doncaster and King's Cross to just over 600 tons, including the dynamometer car.

The engine is to be indicated and the water consumption taken on each trial. Arrangements should be made to record the superheat at the header, steam chest and exhaust. Smokebox and ashpan vacuum should also be taken.

During the recent runs the ACFI thermometer did not appear to be recording correctly. This should be put in order as I wish the feed temperature to be taken on the trials.'

Spencer kept a number of photographs, documents and press reports in his archive of 2001 and sister engine 2002, *Earl Marischal*. From this is probably safe to assume that his interest was seized by the project. These three pictures come from his extensive collection, but, sadly, come with minimal detail. (Above left) 2001 prepares for another test run, the protective shelter temporarily destroying her beautiful lines. (Above right) On the back, Spencer has simply written 'Down – Aberdeen' and (below) 'Passing Harringay'. (BS)

Whilst 2001 could not be criticised for its power, pulling capacity or ability to maintain a high average speed, there was a note of concern entering Gresley's mind that all might not be well. Over the course of only a few short weeks, some reservations were creeping in about the engine's performance and with them a growing belief that 'on the road' trials would not help resolve them. Something more was needed if problems were to be sorted out. Bearing in mind Gresley's active campaign for a dedicated test facility in Britain, he may have seen this as an ideal opportunity to provide a demonstration of what might

Spencer's personal copy of a report covering a single trip which he made with 2001 on 13th July 1934. It is interesting to note the modifications carried out on the engine, presumably to improve its performance. Any personal comments Spencer then may have passed to the CME and Bulleid appear not to have survived, so were probably delivered verbally (BS)

be achieved if one were built here. For many years, he had been trying to convince the Ministry of Transport of this need and hoped that this department might sponsor construction of a test centre. But his words had fallen on deaf ears, with the recession providing a reason for inaction. Now, perhaps, was an opportunity to push his case even more strongly, with the recently opened test facility at Vitry, near Paris offering an obvious place to undertake more extensive trials. Spencer later recalled:

> The CME was most anxious to get 2001 or 2002 more scientifically tested.
>
> Although we learnt some things about the engine's strength and weaknesses when running on the mainline, with indicator shelter and dynamometer car (many of which I participated in), a more detailed analysis was needed. Gresley considered using the GWR's facility at Swindon, but felt it lacked the capacity to fully evaluate this engine. This left Vitry as the only realistic option, but some baulked at the cost involved and felt it was unnecessary. However, Gresley convinced them that it would be a sound investment of time and money and the go ahead was given, subject to the French authority's agreement. This was quickly confirmed, but dates remained a problem; the facility being heavily booked for the foreseeable future with home built engines. After some careful negotiation the SNCF agreed to defer work on a 241 Class locomotive to allow 2001 to be tested and dates were agreed.
>
> Once this was agreed a lengthy discussion ensued about who should accompany the engine. Bulleid was very keen to go and requested that I accompany him, having been closely involved in the design and with my growing knowledge of testing. Also as part of Gresley's discussions with Monsieur Place [the Engineer in Charge of Vitry] I had visited France to assess the Test Centre to make sure it could meet our needs. However, the CME was not prepared to release me from my other duties for a possibly indeterminate period of time. By this stage the next phase of the Pacific programme was exercising our minds and Gresley made it clear that this is where my priorities lay. It was then agreed with Tom Street at

As trials with 2001 continued engine No. 2002 was accepted into service during October 1934. (Left) Robert Thom's record of the newly built engine designated P2 Part Two (THG). (Right) As built 2002 differed to her sister in a number of ways, most notably in having Walschaerts valve gear rather than the Lentz rotary valve version. Spencer hasn't included any details with this photo except to note that it is '2002 being cleaned between turns'. (BS)

Doncaster that Edward Windle would go in my place and be accompanied by a small team of engineers to make sure the engine remained serviceable. I was disappointed not to go, though did visit Vitry on several occasions to see the work there underway. However, my disappointment was short lived, all my efforts being focussed on the A4s.

When deciding what to do, it probably helped that the Vitry Test Centre came highly recommended by Chapelon. It may also have helped that it was the Frenchman who suggested that the P2 be taken there to be assessed. If so, it was an idea encouraged by an accident on 18 July 1934 when the test shelter, built around the engine's front end to protect technicians working there, was damaged in a collision. The shelter was strengthened, but it brought home to Gresley just how ramshackle and unsafe such a testing regime was. Things moved quickly and on 24 July, the CME discussed 'the proposal to test the P2 type engine on the Locomotive Testing Plant at Vitry with Monsieur Place'. This memo then went on to describe all the items required for the trials, from customs declarations, modifications to the engine and any restrictions in place. All this suggested that Gresley may well have had this in mind for some time and carefully managed the process to achieve his aim. So, with approval given, detailed planning began and a programme agreed with a start date of December 1934; timed to allow the second P2 to enter service.

In the meantime, Gresley kept in regular contact with Chapelon, by letter, phone and occasional meetings, to discuss the P2 but also other projects, including W1 and the Pacifics. Clearly the CME found this of great value, especially as there was no agenda other than to debate their science away from politics and rivalries, both of which are so common in any industry. It was a relationship that both men seemed to find stimulating and refreshing.

(Top left) The French locomotive test centre at Vitry shortly after it opened in 1933. (Above right) Very soon some of France's big engines underwent testing at Vitry, including one of the forty-nine massive 4-8-2 Mountain 241 Class engines built for the Chemin de fe l'Etat Railway between 1931 and 1935. Gresley cast envious eyes at this facility, and a similar one at Altoona in the USA, and redoubled his efforts to get one built in the UK, sadly with limited success until just before the war. (Bottom left) In the meantime, he gained permission to test engine No. 2001 at Vitry – an event that attracted the press and newsreel cameras. (BS)

During a telephone call on 22 October, Gresley appears to have spoken at some length to Chapelon about the P2. As a result, the Frenchman later wrote to him and offered the following assessment:

> I have examined the case of your locomotive No.2001. I am surprised that this engine can produce sufficient steam with blast pipe tops 6 in. in diameter and with the shortest bars 11/16 in. long and 11/16 in. wide. The total sectional area for the steam through the two tops is therefore 327 square cm., whereas from my experience with French locomotives, this section would have to be at most 250/270 square cm. to get perfect evaporation up to the highest rates of firing of 800 kg. per sq metre of grate area per hour.
>
> This difference may be due to the quality of the coal; my experience makes me think it might not be so great, however. I think, therefore, that if 2001 does, in fact, steam often properly up to the highest rates of firing with the present sectional area of 327 square cm. this area ought to be retained without alteration and the thickness of the fire be reduced as a consequence at the lowest rate of firing. Our practice is to run with very thin fires when the working engine allows, and to run with thick fires only when the engine is being forced.

After a great deal more advice he ended with a short, supplementary note, 'the design of the double exhaust for engine No. 10000 is finished and the drawings will be sent at the end of the week'.

Engine No. 2001 was ferried across the Channel during the night of 5 December, arriving at Calais at 8.20 the following morning, being unloaded by 12.30 pm. Steam was raised after lunch and the engine moved under her own power to the local depot escorted, as agreed, by Bulleid, Windle and a small team of engineers. From here she was transferred to Vitry, where testing on the rolling road began shortly afterwards. In the weeks that followed, Gresley and Spencer visited France to observe the tests in progress, together and separately. On one occasion they even brought some spare parts with them.

When visiting Vitry by himself, Spencer kept copious notes of all he saw. These he carefully stored for the CME to digest later, in slower time. He also provided a summary of progress made or any problems that seemed difficult to resolve, adding his own thoughts on possible solutions along the way. Bulleid did much the same on an almost daily basis as well, adopting a very upbeat tone in the process. All this was supplemented by frequent phone calls from his principal assistant, suggesting that Gresley was keeping a very tight rein on what was happening in France. Spencer later recalled:

> Gresley would have liked to spend all his time in France superintending the trials. By training and instinct he was a scientist. For him research and development was second nature and he would quickly immerse himself in the search for new ideas and solutions. I always had the feeling that if he had been given the opportunity to attend university he might have submerged himself in work with a much deeper scientific purpose. The railways offered many opportunities to develop his ideas, but it was a limited field by comparison to such things as aviation, medical science or more esoteric areas of research. He was a truly gifted engineer, businessman and leader, but he seemed to desire much more from the world of science.

By the time testing came to an end, in the first week of February, the engine had run twenty-four times on the rolling road. This was supplemented by trips on the main line between Paris and Orleans. But the whole programme was jeopardised by a series of problems related to the driving wheel axleboxes, which often overheated causing melted metal to spill out. This necessitated removal, replacement or repair. On numerous occasions, the engine's wheels had to be dropped, and this could only be accomplished in the Paris-Orleans works.

As a result, very few of the early tests could be completed and it began to seem that no useful purpose would be served by letting the programme continue. Bulleid's diary described each day's

Engine No 2001

SUMMARY OF TESTS CARRIED OUT ON THE PARIS-ORLEANS RAILWAY WITH A TRAIN CONSISTING OF THE PARIS-ORLEANS DYNAMOMETER CAR & THREE COUNTER PRESSURE ENGINES.

Nº OF TEST.	1637	1638	1639
DATE OF TEST.	4TH FEBRUARY 1935.	5TH FEBRUARY 1935.	6TH FEBRUARY 1935.
SECTION OF LINE	ST PIERRE DES CORPS À ORLÉANS	ORLÉANS À ST PIERRE DES CORPS.	ST PIERRE DES CORPS À ORLÉANS
GRADE OF COAL.	40% BRIQUETTE 60% LARGE CARDIFF	40% BRIQUETTE 60% LARGE CARDIFF	40% BRIQUETTE 60% LARGE CARDIFF
CUT OFF	18%	25%	35%
AVERAGE SPEED	44.7 M.P.H.	55.924 M.P.H.	67.977 M.P.H.
AVERAGE PRESSURE IN BOILER	197.5 LBS PER SQ. IN.	188 LBS PER SQ. IN.	169 LBS PER SQ. IN.
" " " STEAM CHEST.	187 "	174.5 "	150 "
" " TEMPERATURE " HEADER	706.5°F	711.5°F	719°F
WORK IN H.P. HOURS REGISTERED AT DYNAMOMETER	1730	1873	1699
AVERAGE H.P. REGISTERED AT DRAWBAR	1213	1647	1847
TOTAL COAL USED FOR EVAPORATION	5643 LBS	6618 LBS.	6539 LBS.
" " UTILISED.	5588 "	6453 "	6374 "
" " " WITH LIGHTING UP DEDUCTED	4680 "	5800 "	5721 "
COAL PER SQ FT OF GRATE AREA PER HOUR, WHILE REGULATOR WAS OPEN	67 "	106 "	128 "
WATER EVAPORATED PER LB OF COAL	8.52 "	7.58 "	7.1 "
COAL PER DRAWBAR HORSE POWER HOUR	3.26 "	3.53 "	3.86 "
" " " " WITH LIGHTING UP DEDUCTED	2.71 "	3.09 "	3.37 "
WATER " " HORSE POWER.	23.1 "	24.1 "	23.7 "

L.N.E.R DRAWING 35-20 N

Spencer also took part in a number of the trials that took place in France, each of which he reported to the CME. This is one of a number of records he kept, in this case covering three runs over the Paris-Orleans Railway. Whether he was on the footplate, in the dynamometer car or simply a passenger in a carriage is not recorded. (BS)

events, reporting each breakdown, each repair and the downtime this caused. But finally on 10th and 12th January the locomotive completed two full days of testing but it proved to be a false dawn and very soon the axlebox problem returned and two more wheel drops were necessary to allow repairs to be made. On one of these workshop visits, at Gresley and Bulleid's instigation, the method of re-metalling the boxes was changed, helped by a visit from a Mr Murphy of J. Stone of Charlton, following a plea for help. This company, which specialised in marine and railway engineering projects, were also experts in the field of metal casting, quickly considered the

An undated photo collected by Spencer who simply wrote on the back 'at Harwich'. If so, the photo would have been taken on 5 December 1934 as the engine awaited shipment to Calais. (BS)

Pressing Home Their Advantage 137

2001, now in France and well into her testing programme, photographed on this occasion with counter-pressure testing engines behind her. In this photo her status as a new engine is rather overshadowed by the overhead catenary for electric services. Spencer was aware of this dichotomy and wrote that 'it was impossible not to observe the progress the French were making with electric services and diesel railcars and wonder at the parlous state of modernisation plans in Britain, except, perhaps, the Southern with their third rail electric services. Railways on the Continent seemed to be embracing these changes more fully, despite any lack of funds'. (BS)

problem and recommended changes. Murphy's advice was taken, a different method of casting was employed and the trials were allowed to continue.

After so many false starts and such extensive repairs, it was decided, probably on Chapelon's advice, that the engine should be subjected to a period of mainline running to allow the axle boxes, wheels and motion to 'bed in'. So on 26 January, she ran on the Paris-Orleans line, pulling three other engines set in back gear to produce measured resistance. Regular inspections during the day found the boxes to be 'cool' and the problem seemingly resolved. Until 7 February, the trials continued with the section of track between St Pierre des Corps and Orleans becoming her regular haunt. With these runs rapidly eating away the time available, but proving useful in so far as the engine's reliability was concerned, Gresley approved a shortened programme of rolling road

An interested crowd gathers to admire 2001 at Amiens Station. Once again, the date is not given, but Spencer has written on the print 'You can see me in the nearest group my light coloured hat which easily distinguishing me from the others'. This was presumably for his wife or other family member to enjoy. (BS)

tests at Vitry. And on the 8th, 2001 returned to the plant for a successful day's work in which 'the regulator was fully opened and it was found that at 90kph 1,600 horse power was developed'.

More tests were planned for the 9th, 10th, 11th and 12th, but three of these were cancelled due to the engine's inability to maintain steam pressure, a loss of cylinder efficiency due to excessive clearances, failure of the ACFI, severe slipping of the wheels on the rollers and on the 11th the left hand leading axlebox overheating again. So back to the Paris Orlean Works she went for the wheels to be dropped and the box to be re-metalled for the last time.

Once this work was complete, preparations for her return to Britain were put in hand, but first the engine would go on display at the Gare du Nord station in Paris. With this PR work over, she left for Calais and embarked on the 21st, arriving at Harwich the following morning. Very quickly, Bulleid prepared a rather optimistic summary for the CME which highlighted some of the key issues. Gresley then followed this up, a little later, with several memos to Thom and Tom Street, the new Chief Draughtsman, describing changes he wished to make to the engine. Amongst other

Towards the end of 2001's time in France, the engine played a central role in an 'Exposition' held at Paris's Gare du Nord station. On 17 February, she was positioned on Platform 1 with Nord Super Pacific No. 1268 to her rear, separated by a saloon coach. Spencer wrote that 'it was interesting to compare the two locomotives. The French Pacific was deemed by many to be far superior to the Mikado in all ways. I tended to agree, but the A4 was, I believe, far better than than any French or German express engine in service in the 1930s'. (BS)

Engine No. 2002 gets into her stride, but will soon, in April 1935, be fitted with an extra set of smoke deflectors, which Spencer later called 'unsightly'. (Top – left and right) Neither picture is dated, but are presumed to have been taken in the early months of 1935. The only note Spencer has added to either picture, in this case the right-hand one, reads '2002 on an up express near Hitchen'. The lower picture captures this engine with her extra set of deflectors clearly on display. (BS)

things, he wanted to introduce a way of producing lateral play in the leading and trailing wheels, fit a longer combustion chamber, re-design the firebars, develop a more effective axlebox lubrication system and modify the poppet valve gear. But despite all the work put in and improvements made, it seems that the level of success the CME sought was proving hard to achieve.

Spencer, when describing this project in 1947, played down any sense of disappointment they may have felt at King's Cross. But even he, the most diplomatic of souls, eventually let his professional mask slip a little bit:

> As originally turned into traffic, No. 2001 had continuous cams, but after approximately 10,000 miles service trouble was experienced owing to the point of contact of the follower rollers breaking down the casehardened surface of the inlet cams. Stepped cams were fitted, but the valve events were consequently restricted to six ranges of cut-off in fore gear. On an engine of such high tractive effort the large difference in power between cut-off positions proved inconvenient and was not conducive to economical working.
>
> The second P2 was fitted with 9 in. diameter piston valves and had outside Walschaert gear with Gresley gear for the inside cylinder in order that a direct comparison could be made with the poppet gear on No. 2001.
>
> At early cut-offs No. 2002 would not clear the smoke and it was necessary to modify the front end arrangement. As a result of further wind tunnel experiments (overseen by Frederick Johansen and, apparently conducted at the City and Guilds College) a second set of deflector plates, positioned about 18 in. from the inner plates, were fitted and shaped internally to deflect air upwards to the rear of the chimney. This unsightly arrangement proved successful.
>
> With smaller clearance volumes and an infinitely variable cut-off No. 2002 proved lighter on coal than No. 2001. Numbers 2003 to 2006 were therefore fitted with piston valves as was 2001 in April 1938.

It seems that Spencer was following the old adage 'if you can't think of anything good to say, say nothing', when describing the P2s. Nevertheless, later on he did make a pertinent point:

> These engines would have performed better if they had been allowed to operate in the south where their great power could have been harnessed without fear of doing damage to the track or the driving wheels. But overall they proved costly to run and were difficult to maintain in good running order. I recall it being said that for every day spent out of service by the A3s and V2s the P2s had 3.

In contrast, Bulleid's undoubted pride and commitment to the P2 programme, came over very clearly when he commented on Spencer's paper to the ILocoE and presented a strong argument to counter any criticism:

One of the LNER's classic publicity photos that appeared widely in the press at the time. The title could simply be 'Progress' each engine marking another step forward in locomotive design, albeit steam and not a more modern form of motive power. Left to right – 2002, then the 1924 built A1 No. 2552 *Sansovino*, which did not become an A3 until 1943, and Ivatt C1 Atlantic No. 3288 which entered service in August 1904. (BS)

Cock of the North had a lesson for everyone. She was not extravagant at all, but was in fact extremely efficient on the testing plant, and compared favourably with the French engines in her coal consumption per rail.h.p., and better still, per d.b.h.p. When tested on the open road between Orleans and Tours she developed a very high horse-power, of the order 2,800, and again showed herself to be an efficient engine from the point of coal consumer, per d.b.h.p. In service, however, she was an extravagant engine. The fundamental reason for this was that she was not put to the use for which she was designed. Instead of working trains well within her capacity over long runs, she was employed on a service such as Edinburgh to Dundee, went to Aberdeen and hung about there, and did a very poor mileage per day, with the result that she showed a heavy coal consumption most of the coal being burnt through misuse rather than working trains.

Although not responding to Bulleid's advocacy on behalf of the P2s at the time, Spencer later added an interesting footnote, revealing much about the dynamics of life at King's Cross during these enthralling years:

Bulleid and Gresley had many lively discussions about the comparative potential of the Pacifics and Mikados. The former often expressed frustration that the LNER did not make more of the 2-8-2 and seemed thwarted by this lack of interest or commitment.

Even all those years later (in 1947) his strength of feeling on the subject was only too apparent. So, it didn't surprise me to read, much later on, that he had proposed building a Mikado for express services on the Southern when becoming their CME. Here, I believe, he was thwarted by the coming of war and, perhaps, a degree of realism on the part of their General Manager. Nevertheless, he did manage to build his eccentric Pacifics. Like him they were both brilliant and frustrating at the same time.

When Gresley decided to build the last four P2s as streamliners in 1936, at the same time as 2002 was rebuilt in this form, Bulleid was clearly displeased. Perhaps to appease his assistant Gresley agreed to leave No.2001 in largely original condition. If so, Bulleid's departure in 1937 to the Southern made this unnecessary and Gresley ordered the rebuilding of 2001 within days of his going as the engine entered a period of General Repair. This may have been one reason that Bulleid argued so strongly that the P2s as built were effective engines.'

As the P2 programme moved slowly forward, an even more important project was waiting in the wings. It was one that would test Gresley and his team to the very limit and leave a legacy that still resonates with us today.

The LNER were very keen on displaying their latest locomotives and carriages and used open days to assist in this process. Here 2001 and 4472 *Flying Scotsman* are the focus of attention at Ilford. (BS)

Chapter 5

To Greater Glory

In 1960 Spencer wrote of the mid-1930s:

> By then our lives were becoming increasingly dominated by events in Germany and the rise of Hitler. At first the general reaction was relaxed, many believing that a sturdy Germany would be good for Britain. And, of course, he had many supporters in this country believing that we needed such a strong leader to take us out of the economic doldrums. It took a long time for them to realise the risk the Nazis posed, by which time it was almost too late to do anything. In the meantime, we could do little but carry on as though nothing was happening, the powers that be deciding matters on our behalf without any true insight into the consequences.

After many years of struggling financially, the outlook for many seemed to be improving as the events triggered by the 1929 crash began to recede into history. Unemployment, though still high, had come down from a peak of more than 3 million, industry was picking up and, in some quarters, consumer confidence was returning. So, by 1935 there was a growing belief that the worst was behind them and now was the time to enjoy the fruits of their labour. In many ways, this was an illusion. Many parts of the country, particularly those reliant on mining, were still mired in poverty with any signs of recovery still hard to spot. Even this late in the day, the damage caused by recession, and the abhorrent behaviour of mine owners in cutting wages, was still inflicting extreme poverty on many. The divide was huge and while some prospered, many faced great hardship.

On a personal level, the 1930s were a good time for Spencer and the challenges he faced were primarily professional ones directed by the LNER's Board. If he had any sense of impending doom because of the situation in Germany this may have been fed by Gresley's occasional visits to that country as Hitler's power increased. He went there to view developments in motive power, particularly the new high speed diesel railcars, but the subjugation of opposition and persecution of the Jews would have been only too obvious to him and Spencer, who went with him on two occasions.

Spencer, leaning forward in a self-assured way perhaps reflecting his growing confidence in his role as Gresley's assistant. By this stage he had become a recognisable figure in his profession, a contributor to the work of the ILocoE and attended many important functions, as demonstrated here in the early 1930s by a 'white tie' dinner at which Gresley, Stanier and many other leading lights in the railway industry were present. (BS)

Salisbury Hall near St Albans, once the home of Winston Churchill's mother, which Gresley and his daughter occupied in the 1930s. It became custom and practice for Spencer and Harold Harper to regularly visit him here – one to discuss technical matters, the other administrative tasks. As the CME's health continued to decline, Spencer found himself journeying there ever more frequently from his home in New Barnet. It is likely that this meant acting as Gresley's eyes and ears and increased his level of influence over day to day business. It was a role this honourable man was unlikely to have abused. (THG)

Meanwhile, life at King's Cross continued on much as before, but for one subtle change. By 1935 Gresley had begun to work from home on a more regular basis. Spencer had first noted such a change to the CME's working practices before his wife's death in 1929:

'Occasionally there was a pressing need to discuss new plans and projects or the performance of different offices or workshops. This could best be carried out at Camlet House in Sir Nigel's study where we could work undisturbed. It came to be a regular practice especially when the W1 and then P2 were in planning.

Social and sporting events continued to play an important part in the life of the LNER, as the difficult days of the 1920s gave way to slightly better times in the '30s. Athletic competitions were encouraged and directors and senior managers made every effort to attend as witnessed at a Works sports day held at Doncaster. On this occasion Gresley (back row third from the left) is accompanied by Robert Thom (left of the CME), Douglas Edge (to the right and soon to replace Bulleid at King's Cross), and Thomas Henry Turner (far right) Gresley's Chief Chemist and Metallurgist (who Spencer described as 'very tall, reserved with a dry sense of humour and exceptionally intelligent') (THG)

By 1935, the advances being made by the DRG in Germany were only too apparent, most notably with (above left) the arrival of the first two streamlined Class 05 express engines (002 shown here). Perhaps, of greater long term interest (above right) were the high-speed diesel/electric record breaking SVT 877 and the SVT 137s which appeared in 1933 and 1935 respectively. 1935 would see Gresley respond with his own high speed streamlined A4s. (THG)

It was a pattern of work that continued and deepened when Gresley moved from Camlet House to live near St Albans, in Salisbury Hall, with his daughter Violet as companion. With a longer journey time to King's Cross it became, as Spencer recalled:

> His habit in working from home became more frequent with myself and Harry Harper visiting him to discuss many current issues and future plans. I would drive from New Barnet, my back seat covered with drawings and reports, and return each evening with reams of notes and orders to issue the following morning. The CME, whose health had waned considerably, seems to have preferred this way of working. This allowed him to build up his energy for the more strenuous days he would spend in London. However, his increasingly poor health meant that his time at home gradually increased as the decade came to an end.

It would seem that as his health slowly declined, Spencer and Harper, in particular, increasingly became his eyes and ears at work, acting on his behalf when necessary. Both men seem to have been ideally suited to such a task and neither seem to have let him down, remaining trusted confidants until the end. Meanwhile, there was still the dominating presence of Bulleid to help ideas, information and orders flow through the organisation. But as Spencer later wrote:

> He seemed to grow more frustrated with each passing year. He was a man who seemed destined to lead, but was denied the opportunity to do so. Whilst he clearly admired Gresley his presence, though positive in many ways, restricted the younger man's ambitions. It probably did not help that in 1933, when Stamer retired, Bullied was not promoted to be Deputy CME as the Mechanical Engineer at Darlington had once been. It must have come as a blow to Bulleid who must have harboured ambitions to succeed Gresley and this would have been another step towards achieving this ambition. I do not know why Gresley chose this course of action, but did wonder if it denoted an underlying reservation in their relationship. Yet they were clearly very close personally and professionally.

1935 saw the Spencers take a summer holiday in the Lake District, travelling from Euston along the West Coast Mainline. He recorded that 'we returned to London pulled by Princess Royal number 6203. A good run with no slack'. Again, his professional curiosity must have been teased by travelling with the opposition and he must have, naturally, drawn comparisons with the LNER's Pacifics. In fact, 6203, *Princess Margaret Rose*, only entered service in July that year so was barely run in when the Spencer's travelled behind her. This photo of 6203 was collected by Spencer at some stage, but does not appear to relate to his holiday. (BS)

Perhaps of greater interest to Spencer than the Princess Royals in 1935 was the appearance of Stanier's 4-6-2 turbine powered locomotive in June that year. In many ways this project adopted the novel approach to developing steam motive power familiar to Gresley with W1 and Fowler with his 4-6-0 Fury. Unlike these two well-meaning experiments, though, the results were much more promising. However, despite its success, No. 6202, *Turbomotive* did not offer sufficient advantages over conventional engines to justify the cost of development and in 1952 she was rebuilt. In his papers, Spencer kept a number of reports which described the design in some detail, as well as many photographs such as the picture above showing the engine in full flight. (BS)

As 1935 dawned, and the first two P2s gradually made their way through test and modification programmes, there was much else to engage Gresley and his team. Various long running locomotive programmes were still in being. These included the J39 0-6-0s, which would continue being built until the last 18 of 289 appeared in 1941 and the B17 4-6-0s which in 1937 would reach the end of their production run of 73, if not their development; two being streamlined in late 1937 in an attempt to spice up the express services from Norwich to Liverpool Street. Then there were the last ten D49 4-4-0s which left the workshops at Darlington in 1935 at the same time as the last nine A3s were rolled out at Doncaster. Last but not least there was the 2-6-2 V1/V3 tank engine programme which began in 1930 and ran on until 1939, by which time 92 had been built at Doncaster.

There was also an active modification programme to consider, though one element of this was slow to move forward. The conversion of the A1s to A3 standard virtually came to a halt after four underwent rebuilding in 1927/28. Perhaps the lack of movement was motivated by an 'as and when' attitude suggesting that the A1s were deemed good enough by Gresley to function as they were. Spencer remained largely mute on this issue, but did later observe:

While work on the A4 programme dominated life at King's Cross and Doncaster and headlines in 1935/36 there was much else happening at the time in terms of locomotove development. In particular there was the continuing B17 4-6-0 programme with naming ceremonies being captured in newsreels and in the press. Here we see No. 2848 *Arsenal* at King's Cross on 5 March being named by club officials with both William Whitelaw and a smiling Gresley in attendance. Spencer later wrote that 'the Chief relished these occasions and thoroughly enjoyed the pomp and ceremony'. (DN)

The A1s as built were important to the CME. They were his first major design and he was loth to rebuild them too quickly. There were, of course, some interim modifications carried out to do with the long lap issue, but during Gresley's lifetime their complete conversion to A3 standard remained a dormant programme apart from one in 1939 [No. 2566 *Ladas*, which apparently experienced a serious failure that year]. When Thompson became CME the programme began in earnest and was then completed by Peppercorn in 1948 when the last two were rebuilt.

However, with twenty-seven new A3s 'Super Pacifics' by 1935 there was probably no immediate need to upgrade the remaining A1s too quickly. And that year the Pacific fleet would be greatly enhanced by the arrival of the first A4s, which for twelve months or so had dominated the minds and muscles of many skilled workers at Doncaster and King's Cross.

When Spencer came to record his memories of these projects, he was quite selective in his words. He chose to focus on particular elements of the work and then describe how Gresley and his team sought

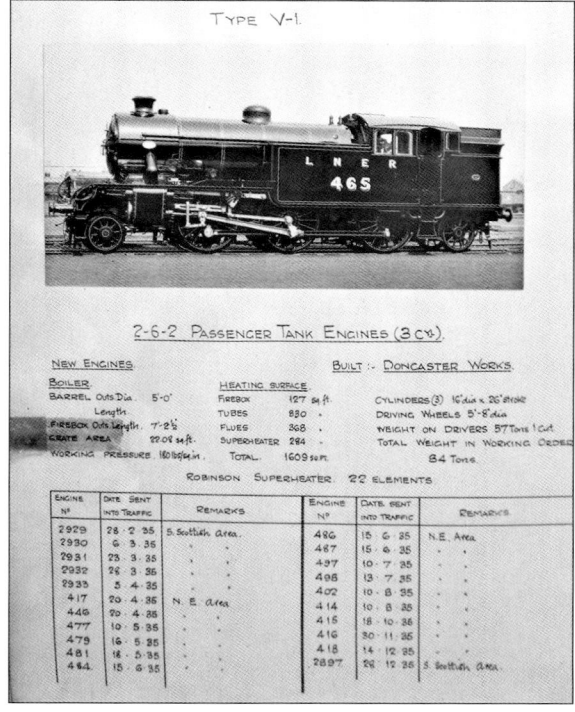

Another of Robert Thom's personal records, this time showing the 1935 phase of the V1 2-6-2 tank engine programme. When production ended in 1939, the V1/V3s had expanded to ninety-two. Of these, eighty-two were constructed as V1s, of which sixty-three were later rebuilt as V3s. They were described as 'excellent performers', with many lasting in service until 1964. (THG)

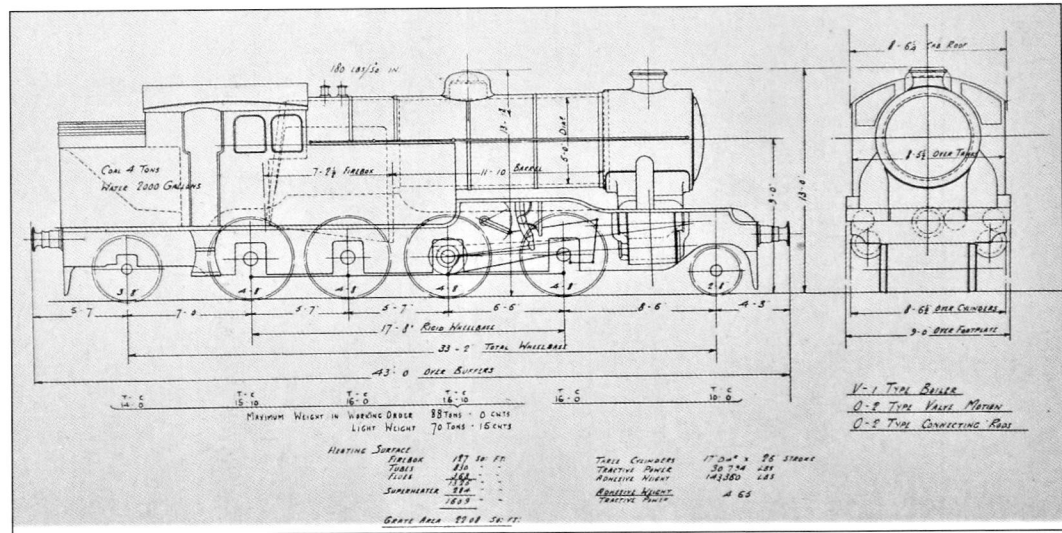

The development of a concept as demonstrated by Spencer during his 1947 presentation to the ILocoE, in this case evolving ideas, considered and rejected, for large tank engines on the way to producing the V1/V3 2-6-2 classes. (Top picture) The 1928 design for a large tank engine to pull heavy coal trains in Leicestershire. (Bottom) A bigger, heavier refinement of the 2-8-2 design which was described by A.F. Cook in 1947, as 'based on the standard O2 and estimated to weigh 100 tons and would probably have been the largest tank engine in the country for other than purely shunting duties'. (BS)

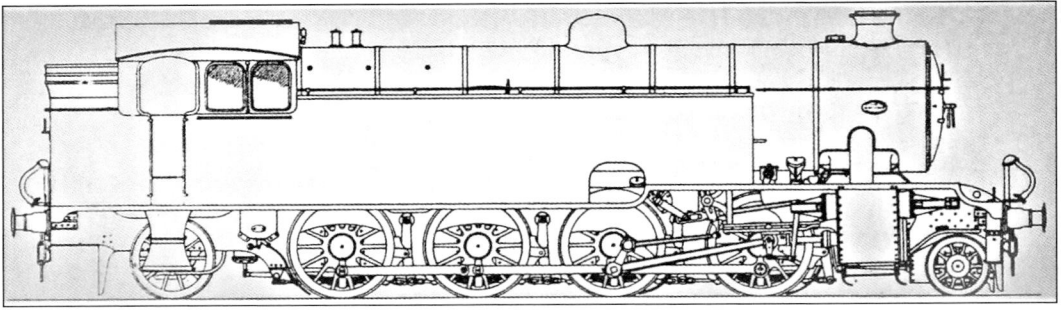

to develop a concept, sometimes as an academic exercise to demonstrate the evolving nature of design and a 'mix and match' engineering methodology. This was particularly so when it came to the V1/V3s and here his descriptions help provide a clear insight into the way Gresley worked in relationship to tank engines for suburban services and other duties. In 1947, Spencer wrote:

> The first of the V1s had 5ft 8in coupled wheels, three 16in x 26in cylinders and a 5ft diameter boiler carrying a pressure of 180lb per square inch. A later series of 10 (the V3) had the boiler pressure increased to 200lb., thus raising the tractive effort from 22,464lb. to 24,960lb. Whilst this is the only new design of tank engine built during the Gresley regime, other types were contemplated but not developed.
>
> A design for a 2-8-2 type three-cylinder tank engine with 4ft 8in diameter coupled wheels and 17 ½ in x 26in cylinders was prepared in 1930 to replace the R1 class 0-8-2 type two-cylinder Ivatt side tank engines employed on local colliery working in the Colwick district. The proposed engine was to have the 5ft diameter boiler of the V1 class and

the valve gear and connecting rods of the O2 class 2-8-0 type, mineral engines. It was subsequently decided to cover the duties of the R1 class by tender engines having the advantage of greater coal and water capacity and the proposal to use 2-8-2 type tank engines was therefore dropped.

This constant search for better locomotive designs reflects Gresley and Bulleid's active, creative minds. It was Spencer's duty to see that each idea was developed to a point at which there was a practical design to consider and then provide an assessment of its advantages/disadvantages, plus alternative solutions if there were any. In this he was supported by the Chief Draughtsman and his team. But essentially it was his duty to pull many threads together, possibly bring some reality to bear and support these creative men through the decision making process to reach practical and cost effective solutions. Spencer confirmed this when he wrote:

> It was the role of a good assistant to guide very busy, often overloaded leaders through the practicalities of what was possible. With such creative men as Gresley and Bulleid this was even more important. They often did not have the time or, on occasions, the inclination to get involved in the nitty, gritty of design. As a consequence, they needed to be assisted, if not guided, through the process. One of my key roles, and that of the small team of draughtsmen in the headquarters, was to see that anything emanating from King's Cross and passed to the drawing offices was unambiguous, gave clear instructions and kept flights of fancy to a minimum. I was not necessarily successful in this all the time. On these occasions the Chief Draughtsman or the Mechanical Engineers at Doncaster, Darlington and Stratford would often apply a restraining hand. When all else failed an impractical idea might well be lost or held up in administration. The difficulty was in filtering out the unrealistic from the ideas that held real merit. The A4 project was one of these and, such was its nature, it passed through the system with remarkable ease and a minimum of fuss, although the schedule we faced was a very tough one indeed.

It is difficult to pinpoint the exact moment when the idea for a streamlined, high speed Pacific gripped Gresley's mind and it is an issue on which Spencer wrote little. Was it a eureka moment or a slowly evolving scheme drawing inspiration from a number of sources, in Britain and from overseas? From the available evidence it seems to have been the latter, with a key business need at its root. However, in harmony with a commercial requirement there was, undoubtedly, a strong professional ambition to push back scientific boundaries and test what was possible with the technology available to them at the time.

When collecting photographs, Spencer remained quite eclectic in his tastes, gathering in subjects that interested him day by day. A professional interest dominated but not to the exclusion of other things. He seems to have been fascinated by the occasional passage of celebrities or VIPs, major or minor, through the LNER's hands. Here this is best exemplified by a photo of Peregrine Cust, Baron Brownlow, Mayor of Grantham and equerry to the Prince of Wales, and his daughter Caroline on the footplate of 2557 in 1934. (BS)

By the 1920s and '30s, providing high speed non-stops rail services had become a key part of business here and in France and Germany. Whether profitable or not, they attracted headlines. This was particularly so of the GWR's Cheltenham Flyer service, which began running in 1923, since when its timings had gradually been reduced. In 1932, 5006 *Tregenna Castle* very publicly cut the time of the 77.3 mile journey to Paddington to a remarkable 57 minutes, attaining an average speed of 81.7 mph in the process. Then, in 1935 they went one step further when introducing the much publicised high speed, non-stop service from Paddington to Bristol, with a booked time of 105 minutes for the Down journey.

In 1933, the first of the LMS's new Princess Royal Pacifics appeared, under Stanier's guiding hand, suggesting that the LNER's chief business rival would soon begin high speed, high profile non-stop services as well. The fact that this did not happen until 1936 did not diminish the level of intent implied by their actions. Gresley was also probably aware, through contact with Johansen, that the LMS were also showing an interest in streamlining their Pacifics as early as 1934, so might claim a lead in work that had engaged him for many years. Who comes first can be an issue that trumps other more practical considerations and may easily have encouraged hard-headed directors and experienced engineers to act.

Whether in response to all this is unclear, but in early 1934, Gresley instructed Spencer and his team to prepare outline drawings of a new Pacific and in May the first diagrams began appearing. Visually, the A4, as it was called, owed much to the P2s then being developed. There was a degree of streamlining, but perhaps of greater interest was the use of two bogies on the tender rather than six or eight fixed wheels in some designs. It was a layout favoured by Churchward when building his only Pacific, the Great Bear, and Robert Urie with his 4-6-0 H15 and N15s for the LSWR, and later, the Southern Railway.

At the same time, Gresley was looking eastwards, observing and admiring what was happening in Germany, as he later recalled in 1936 during his Presidential Address to the IMechE:

After prolonged trials the Flying Hamburger was put into regular service - its average speed is 77.4 mph. It consists of two coaches only, articulated, and carried on three bogies. The motive power is two Maybach 410 hp diesel engines mounted on the outer bogies and directly coupled to electric generators. Since then many new services with two and three coaches have been inaugurated in Germany.

The success and popularity which has followed the introduction of the various extra-high speed trains (both steam and diesel) is such that their running has become firmly established and is bound to be extended. (In addition) the demand for trains of greater carrying capacity has led to the development of steam locomotives capable of hauling much heavier trains.

As Spencer kept a number of negatives, it may be assumed he took these pictures. If so, he seemed to have a preference for views such as this undated picture – an engine, in this case No. 4475 *Flying Fox*, at speed at an unspecified location (undoubtedly Welwyn Garden City Station) on the East Coast Mainline. (BS)

To Greater Glory   149

I visited Germany in the latter part of 1934 [thought to be September or October] and travelled in the Flying Hamburger from Berlin to Hamburg and back. I was much impressed with the smooth running of the train at a speed of 100 mph, which was maintained for long distances, that I thought it advisable to explore the possibilities of extra high speeds travel by having such a train for experimental purposes.

I approached the makers of the train and furnished them with particulars as to the gradients, curves and speed restrictions on the line between King's Cross and Newcastle. With the thoroughness characteristic of German engineers, they made an exhaustive investigation and prepared a complete schedule showing the shortest possible running times under favourable conditions. They then added 10 per cent, which they regarded as adequate to meet varying weather conditions and to have sufficient time in reserve to make up for such decelerations or delays as might normally be expected.'

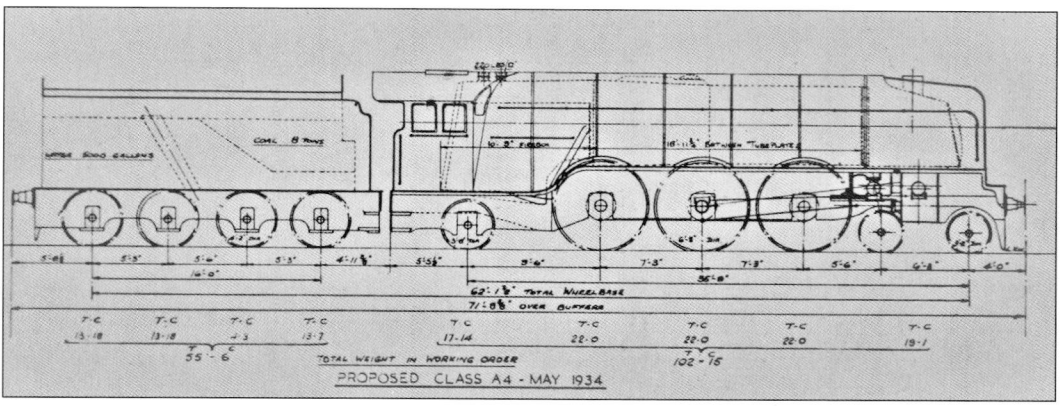

As early as 1934, Gresley had demonstrated the way his thoughts were going as he contemplated his next generation of Pacifics. The top diagram, which appeared in May, was one of a number produced and shows how shape was again being influenced by Johansen's streamlining research and the experiments carried out with the first two P2s. The lower drawing, dated March 1935, shows how the design continued to evolve as Gresley considered how best to present his case to his Chairman, General Manager and the Locomotive Committee for approval to proceed. In this version, the extent of the streamlining is becoming more pronounced and the shape bears a strong resemblance to the solution eventually adopted by the LMS for their Coronation Pacifics. However, this option and that eventually applied to the A4s both used solutions suggested by Johansen's research and wind tunnel testing. Of greater interest is the tender with its double bogie rather than four sets of fixed wheels. It was an idea Churchward adopted for his single Pacific, the Great Bear, and Robert Urie for his H15s and N15s. (BS)

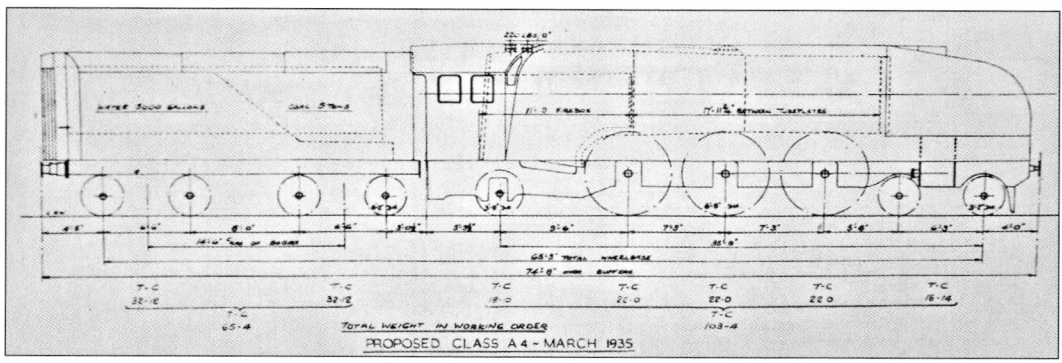

Whether Gresley was seriously contemplating procuring such a rail car from Germany or building his own version is unclear. But on his return to Britain, he actively engaged Wedgwood in a debate over the best way to go forward and reported, 'My Chief General Manager suggested that with an ordinary Pacific engine faster overall speed could be maintained with a train of much greater weight, capacity, and comfort (than the German railcars).'

So to test the viability of such a service using steam, Gresley proposed that a trial run be undertaken on Friday, 30 November from King's Cross to Leeds and back the same day with a train weighing only 147 tons containing restaurant and dynamometer cars. For such a special run, 4472 *Flying Scotsman* was chosen and spent several days undergoing maintenance and preparation for this important task.

The locomotive was crewed by the hugely experienced team of William Sparshatt and Fireman Robert Webster and 'a fast run was expected', as Spencer later wrote. After a speedy start they did not let up for the rest of the day as a report in the LNER's *Journal* made clear:

> The outstanding features of the outward trip were the 94.7 mph at Three Counties and the most wonderful uphill climb from Tallington to Stoke tunnel at an average of 82½ mph, the overall timing from King's Cross to Leeds being 151 min 56 sec., 13 min .04 sec. under schedule.

> In view of the more satisfactory results achieved, it was decided to add two extra vehicles to the train, bringing the load up to 208 tons. The return journey was not uneventful and the outstanding excitement was the run between Stoke tunnel and Essendine. It was quite obvious to those on board that history was being rapidly made, and mile posts of 97½ mph and 100 mph were reported – the dynamometer car reading subsequently confirming the latter. The sensation of timing these speeds was even more exciting than watching a closely run race, and the thrill as the quarter-mile posts were passed at an ever reducing number of fifths of seconds is indescribable. King's Cross was reached in 157 min 17 sec., again under schedule despite a serious permanent way slack near Sandy, and the second run was over.

To prove his point, and flesh out his plans, a second high speed trial was held on 5th March 1935. The question of boiler capacity was crucial and Gresley wished to explore this issue a little further. In the November trial, 4472 could only muster 180psi and the CME wished to see how an A3 with 220psi boiler might perform under the same conditions, and chose engine No. 2750 *Papyrus* for the occasion. As things turned out, the results were more impressive than expected.

Engine No. 2750, *Papyrus*, was chosen to pull the second high speed trial train in March 1935 because Gresley wished to use an engine with a boiler producing 220lb of pressure as a comparison. But, as Spencer later wrote, 2750 was also chosen because it had a good reputation amongst footplate crew. This was born out by her performance on the 15th, which was exceptional by any standard' (BS)

The day's events were recorded first-hand by Charles M. Stedman, Chairman of the LNER's Locomotive Running Superintendent's Committee:

On Tuesday 5th March the engine travelled from King's Cross to Newcastle and back, a distance of 536 miles, in 570 minutes. On the return journey a world's record speed for a steam locomotive was attained. The train passed Grantham at 68 ½ mph and this speed was maintained for five miles up the gradient of 1 in 198, the speed at the top of the hill being 70 mph. From this point the speed steadily increased on the downward gradients of 1 in 178 and 1 in 200 to a maximum of 108 mph. For a distance of 12.3 miles between Corby and Tallington the time taken was 7 minutes 20 seconds, which was equal to an average speed of 100.6 mph.

On the run from King's Cross no attempt was made to improve upon the schedule timing. On approaching Doncaster, the brake was applied on account of a signal check, and after passing through the station at reduced speed the train was stopped for 24 seconds about a quarter of a mile of Arksey Station. The delay was due to some derailed wagons on the up line, and the train was in consequence 1¼ minutes late passing York. Darlington was, however, passed 3 minutes ahead of time, and Newcastle was reached 2 minutes 22 seconds before the booked arrival time. The average speed from King's Cross to Newcastle was 68 mph.

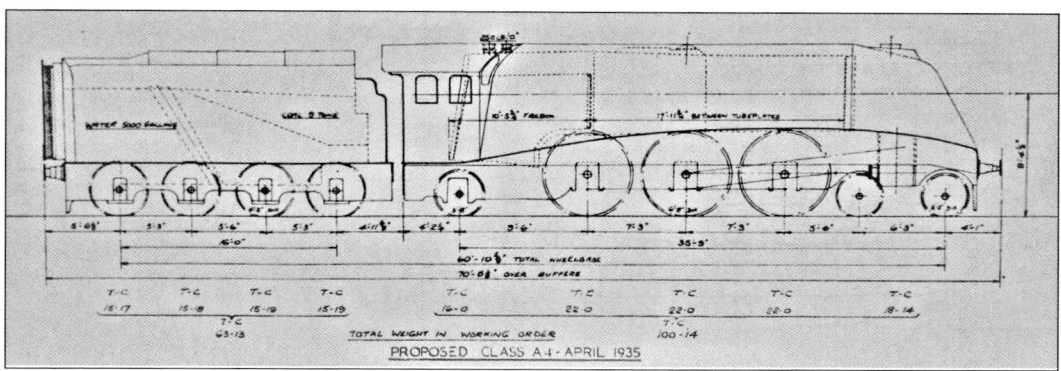

The early months of 1935 were crucial to the A4 programme. If there had been any delay in finalising plans or gaining approval to proceed, then a September in service date would have been impossible. But as shown in these two diagrams, the engine's outline continued to be modified month by month. In six months it went from the rather angular shape in the upper picture to the more aerodynamic shape we all know so well today, and expounded by Johansen in his research earlier in the decade. (BS)

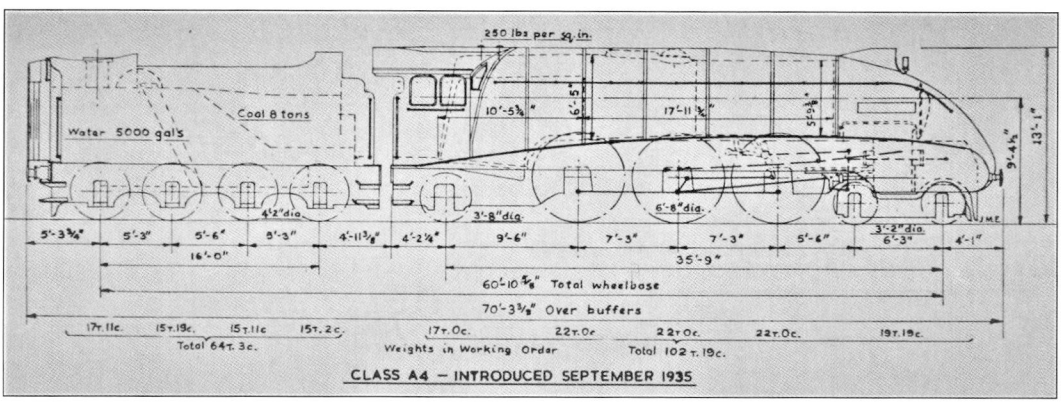

The return trip was worked by the same engine but with a fresh set of crew. On the section from Grantham to Peterborough Sparshatt was given the opportunity of showing what the engine could do, and the booked times were considerably improved upon.

From all this Gresley concluded that:

> The trial with a train of seven bogies demonstrated that the run could be accomplished with reliability in less than four hours under normal conditions. I felt that to secure a sufficient margin of power it would be essential to streamline the engine and train as effectively as possible, and at the same time to make sundry alterations to the design of cylinders and boiler which could conduce to freer running and to securing an ample reserve of power for fast uphill running.

And with this, the long-considered issue of streamlining entered into its most active phase for Gresley, with a clearly stated scientific principle riding on the coat tails of a pressing business need. There seems to have been no detailed declaration by the CME of the benefits to be derived from such a development, though, if he had wished, he could have pointed to a summary produced by Johansen in which he underlined the advantages to be gained by having a streamlined train:

> The air resistance can be reduced by 50 per cent without drastic departure from conventional design, and by 75 per cent by ideal streamlining.
> Air resistance is augmented by side winds, the increase being due to frontal pressure on exposed surfaces. The lateral wind force is large, but the consequent increase of forward resistance due to flange and bearing friction is relatively small, except for highly streamlined trains.
> Streamlining measures are, on the whole, more effectual in side winds than in direct winds or in still air.
> A surprisingly large proportion of the air resistance of a coach is contributed by the bogies and undercarriage structure. Consequently, it is advantageous to use articulated stock, to include the undercarriages in streamlining measures, and to extend the fairings to the end of the coaches leaving no exposed gaps between them.
> The air resistance of a conventional locomotive, amounting to 20-40 per cent of that of a complete six-coach train, can be reduced to 25 per cent by rounding the smokebox front and covering the tender to the general contour of the train.
> The streamlining of steam locomotives calls for aerodynamic study of the machine as a whole, attention being paid simultaneously to air resistance, the deflection of the exhaust away from the driver's vision, access of air to the fire grate and bearings, and the design from the standpoint of accessibility and operating convenience.
> The full benefit of measures to reduce air resistance can be realised only if the locomotive and the coaches are all streamlined.
> The ideal streamlined train is a continuous cylindrical body, with well-rounded ends, having a polished surface free from external fittings and irregularities.

Over the months, the A4's design was refined, with its outline only changing marginally, and in March 1935 Gresley felt sufficiently confident to present his ideas to Whitelaw and Wedgwood in a bid to seek their approval to build the first four members of the new class. He was successful and on the 28th the CME was able to set his signature to Order No. 338 (work numbers 1818, 1819, 1821 to 1823) authorising construction of these engines at Doncaster.

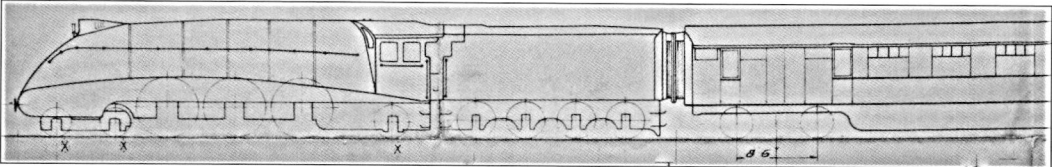

Spencer kept many drawings and sketches he prepared during 1935 as the A4 programme progressed. A lot of these, as above, focussed on the outline of loco and streamlined coach set. The depth of his involvement may be gauged by the sheer volume of his drawings, his correspondence with the Chief Draughtsman and Robert Thom and his frequent visits to Doncaster during construction. On one level, he was a progress chaser, on another a facilitator for Gresley and to these he contributed a creative edge, adding his own thoughts on design to the collective mass. (BS)

Timing was everything. It was King George V's Silver Jubilee that year and it was important to celebrate such an occasion, take advantage of the publicity surrounding the event and, in doing so, exploit the arrival of a new, high profile express service. As a result, the design team and workshops were challenged to produce the first two engines and a streamlined, articulated coach set by September, so that the LNER's Silver Jubilee service could begin.

During his 1947 presentation Spencer described this programme in very simplistic, undramatic terms, making no mention of the part he played:

The train trials hauled by a standard A3 Pacific demonstrated that the run could be accomplished in less than four hours under normal conditions. It was felt, however, that an economy in working and a greater margin of power would be secured if a form of streamlining could be embodied in the design of the engine and the train.

As far as the engine was concerned it was of vital importance that any modifications made to reduce air resistance should not prevent steam and smoke being lifted clear of the cab front windows when working at high speed and early cut-offs. For this reason, it was decided to adopt the horizontal wedge form of front end.

Various forms of chimney were tried during wind tunnel experiments carried out at the City and Guild Engineering College (an institution affiliated with Imperial College and based at Finsbury within walking distance of King's Cross) in connection with smoke lifting, before the design of the outer casing now fitted, which also houses the anti-vacuum valve, was evolved (sometime in 1934).

It was originally intended to carry the casing back to the level of the boiler to form a straight line from the chimney top to the cab roof, but, whilst such an arrangement was satisfactory in a head wind, a wind other than head-on caused an increase in air pressure

Although his health was in decline in the latter part of the 1930s, Gresley still led his department with strength and vigour. His reputation as a public figure also continued to grow and he was increasingly in demand, none more so than to boost the LNER's public relations. His attendance at a model railway exhibition in the 1930s underlines this, but also captures a continuing boyhood fascination with steam locomotion. Spencer recorded that 'the CME liked nothing better than jumping on a footplate and taking the controls'. (BS)

on the windward side of the boiler and a reduced air pressure on the lee side which tended to draw down the smoke and obscure the look-out. The difficulty was overcome by cutting down the casing at the rear of the chimney and this permitted a flow of air below the level of the chimney top.

Experiments were carried out at the NPL with scale models of the streamlined Pacific engine and an ordinary Pacific engine to determine the comparative head-on wind resistance and to calculate the horsepower required at various speeds to overcome the air resistance.

Several modifications were made in the basic three-cylinder Pacific design to ensure freer running and an ample reserve of power for fast uphill working. The boiler pressure was increased from 220lb. to 250lb.per sq in., and a distance between the tube-plates was reduced from 19ft. to 17 ft/8in., the combustion chamber length being increased accordingly.

The three 18½ in. by 26 in. cylinders were provided with valves increased from 8 in. to 9in. diameter and particular attention was paid to the size and shape of steam and exhaust passages. In the actual castings the passages were carefully examined and all roughness removed. Standard Pacific valve gear, with full gear cut-off restricted to 65 per cent was fitted.

In order to reduce stopping distances the brake power on the engine was increased from 66 per cent to 93 per cent of the adhesive weight, as compared with the A3 class, and on the tender from 53 per cent to 62 per cent of the weight in working order. The centres of the laminated springs on the coupled wheels were increased from 3ft. 6in. to 4ft. and the flexibility was increased from .135in. to .27in. per ton to ensure good riding qualities and to limit the unloading effect in the event of the engine rolling at high speed. Forty percent of the reciprocating weight was balanced.

As originally built the A4 class had bogie control springs giving initial loading of 2 tons and a maximum loading of 4.55 tons at 4in. throw over. It is apparent that more wear was taking place on the flanges of the leading coupled wheels than on the driving or trailing wheels and the initial loading on the bogie control was subsequently increased by 4 tons with a maximum loading of 7 tons. At the same time, the control on the trailing carrying wheels was reduced by altering the inclination of the Cartazzi slides from 1 in 7 to 1 in 10.66.

To this brief, purely academic statement Spencer added a much more personal note in 1962. Once again, there is no claim for personal credit, but it is possible to read between the lines and see how great his contribution had been:

Most of 1935 was taken up with the A4's design. At the same time Norman Newsome spent considerable effort on the inner workings of the streamlined carriage set, their external profiling being considered by me as part of the trains overall outline. For this purpose, I liaised with Frederick Johansen on a number of occasions and gathered his thoughts on these issues, modifying the design where necessary.

For much of the year Bulleid was present but his continuing involvement with the P2s meant that he was little involved with the new trains. With the emphasis on streamlining, and his obvious disagreement with these ideas being so apparent, this was understandable.

As planning proceeded and his orders were given Gresley stood back from the task and allowed his managers to manage. During other locomotive projects he had chased and harried his Mechanical Engineers, but on this occasion chose not to. Nevertheless, he still continued to produce rough sketches highlighting some design issue for me to expand upon before passing those I thought appropriate to the Chief Draughtsman. By this stage there was a noticeable slowing down in his daily routine; the dynamic, constantly busy man we had known for many years stepping back due to ill-health. To my knowledge he was

To Greater Glory 155

The construction process fascinated Spencer and during the development of the A4s, he often visited Doncaster to view the work in progress and collect photos, of which these are but a small sample. Sadly, he kept no notes of dates or engines involved, but by the process of elimination and notes kept by others it seems that photos 1,2 and 3 show No. 2509 under construction in mid-1935 (mould for inside cylinder, cylinder completed and placed within frames, frames ready for wheels and boiler to be fitted). 4. Engine No. 4490 nears completion in 1937. 5 and 6. Thought to be 2509 but not confirmed. The framing of the engine's streamlined front end and cut down smokebox are of note. 7 and 8. 2509 in both cases although 7. may have been taken at a later date when the engine was undergoing periodic maintenance. 8. Shows the newly completed locomotive at Doncaster. (BS)

increasingly affected by bronchial and circulatory problems and was being regularly treated by his old friend Sir Maurice Cassidy at St Thomas's.

The main planning effort fell on Tom Street and his team at Doncaster who ensured that all drawings were completed on time, material estimated and ordered and specialist items procured from suppliers. But it was Edward Windle who managed the locomotive's design each day and Frank Day who did the same for the carriages. It was they who liaised with Robert Thom to make sure that the work was scheduled and construction tasks planned and executed on time. Throughout this programme Newsome and I visited Doncaster frequently to discuss progress and agree any changes the CME made to the design. This was all achieved with the minimum of fuss, mostly through the good offices of Thom, who moved mountains to make sure the first two locomotives and carriage set were completed and tested on time.

During 1935, Eric Bannister, then a newly trained draughstman, found himself in the enviable position of working on the A4's design at Doncaster, before transferring to King's Cross to be Spencer's assistant there. He would later write:

This was an exciting time to be at Doncaster. The detailed design work was being started on the A4 Pacific by Mr Windle, mainly on the cylinders. The design of 250psi boiler was begun by the boiler draughtsman, Mr Hibberling. Mr Street was working with some ideas of measuring the overflow of the Gresley 2:1 valve gear on the centre cylinder in response to a letter from King's Cross.

There was much visiting between King's Cross and Doncaster in connection with the design of the A4. I met Bert Spencer and got to know him. One day he told me to go at once to the National Physical Laboratory at Teddington and take with me a wooden model of the A4 to test in the wind tunnel. I was to observe the action of the chalk dust.

The chalk dust took the expected way along the higher part of the part of the boiler and to the cab windows. The fairing at the back of the chimney was shaped level with the top of the boiler and we could think of no other way of deflecting the smoke other than by providing some deflectors at the side of the smokebox. William Dalby [in fact Johansen according to NPL records, Dalby having retired due to ill health four years earlier] had some stiff card available for trials so at first we tried the model just as it had been supplied from Doncaster and then lifted it out.

When it was on the table, we noticed a depression in the plasticine fairing behind the chimney, apparently made by one of us when we lifted the model from the wind tunnel. Dalby said, 'Let's put the wind on and see what happens'. To our surprise the chalk 'smoke' passed along the boiler, but lifted well above the cab windows. We tried it a second time, with the same result.

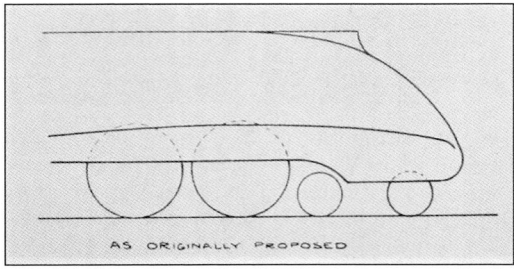 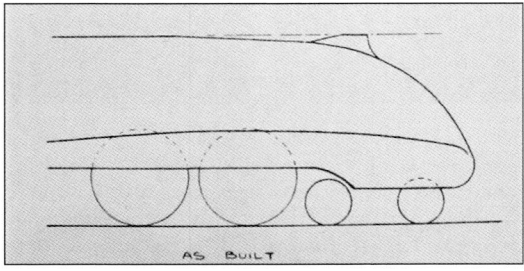

To illustrate the changes made to A4's strealined shape to improve smoke lifting, Bert Spencer prepared very basic before and after drawings, showing the slight indentation Eric Bannister ascribed to his thumb when handling plasticine on a wind tunnel model of the engine. (BS/RH)

Our conclusion was that the slight depression seemingly caused a vortex which caused the chalk to be lifted clear. This dip in the fairing was at once made in the fairing of all A4 engines as instructed by Mr Gresley.

In September 1941, Spencer added a slightly more prosaic note to this account:

During the wind tunnel experiments the top of the engine and cab on the original model were in one straight line. This was satisfactory in a head wind, but in a side wind a pressure was set up on one side of the boiler and a partial vacuum created on the other, as a result of which smoke drifted down on the lee side in spite of the streamlining. The difficulty was overcome and the smoke lifted by cutting back the chimney casing to allow air to pass from the windward to the lee side.

With this careful analysis of the A4's design absorbing much of Spencer's time and effort, the months passed quickly, but this did not exclude him from other important work. Having gained extensive knowledge of accident investigation and become Gresley's eyes and ears when major incidents occurred in the process, he had to drop everything on 15 June that year and race to Welwyn on the outskirts of London where two trains had collided. Of these events he later wrote:

These were a terrible few days and not easily forgotten. In the very early hours of the morning Gresley received a 'flash' report that there had been an accident with two engines and there had been many fatalities. When the CME rang me at home he had very few details and asked me to get to the crash site, twenty or so miles away, as quickly as possible and assess whether the condition of the locomotives had played a part in the accident. One never knew what to expect in situations such as this and so there was a degree of apprehension in my mind. On these occasions you simply had to put these thoughts to one side and concentrate on the job at hand. This was something that four years later, followed by the 'Blitz', became our daily routine. And yet, nothing I saw during the war years could compare to this accident at Welwyn station.

When I arrived it was still dark, though the sky was lightening in the East. Bodies were still strewn everywhere and the injured had barely begun to be removed or treated. Instinctively, you want to set to and help, but there were already many firemen, policemen and medical

(Left) Dawn on 15 June soon revealed the extent of the damage caused to the 10.53 pm departure from King's Cross not long into its journey to Newcastle when hit from behind by the 10.58 pm to Leeds. (Right) Considering the force of the high speed collision, the Class K3 2-6-0, No. 4009, appears to have suffered only minor damage. The same could not be said of the rear carriages of the train which, as Spencer recalled,'simply exploded when hit, killing and maiming many in the process and leaving body parts all over the track'. (BS)

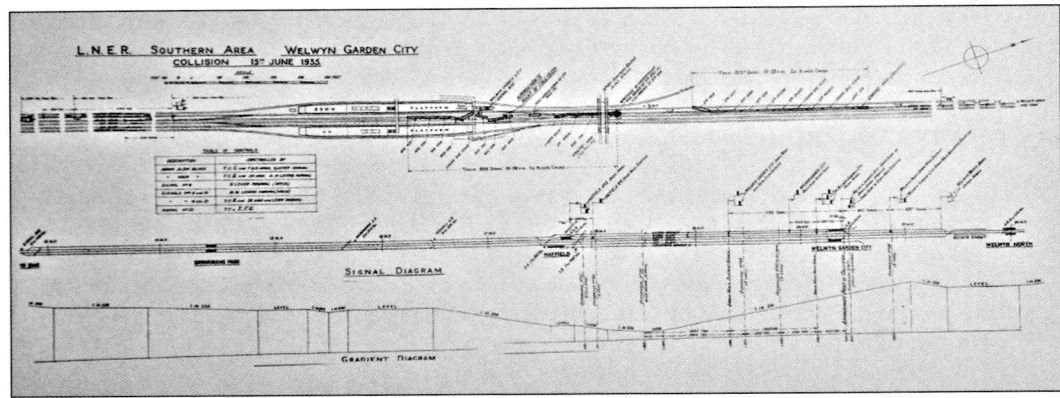

The crash scene at Welwyn on 15 June as recorded by Ministry of Transport officials. The simplicity of this drawing belies the scene of devastation, confusion and horror that greeted rescue parties when they arrived on site in the middle of the night. (BS)

staff on hand and I was advised to stand to one side. So I made my way along the track to observe the two trains involved. I remained at the scene until the Ministry of Transport team, headed by the familiar figure of Lt Colonel Mount, arrived and made my report to them, as well as Victor Barrington-Ward, the Superintendent of the Western Section.

In describing the scene, I can do no better than quote the words used in the MoT report, a draft of which came to the CME in late July. I reviewed it and suggested some amendments. A copy of my notes and the final report I have before me as I write:

'The accident occurred at about 11.27 pm on Saturday 15th June at Welwyn Garden City Station on the Western Section, Southern Area, of the LNER.

'In this case, a down express passenger, parcels and mail train, No. 826, which left King's Cross at 10.53 pm for Leeds, overtook and came into violent collision with the rear of an express passenger train, No.825A, which left King's Cross at 10.53 pm for Newcastle....No. 825A had been incorrectly checked by signals when approaching the station, and was apparently travelling at about 15 mph, whilst No. 826 is assumed to have struck it at not less than 65 mph.

'I regret to report that 13 passengers (including three children and a railway servant) and Guard J McIntosh of train 825A, lost their lives. In addition, 29 passengers were seriously injured and detained in hospital, while 52 others received treatment for minor injuries and shock.

'Train No. 825A was hauled by a two-cylinder engine No. 4441, an Atlantic type (4-4-2) with a six-wheeled tender weighing, in working order 112 tons 14 cwt, and comprised 11 bogie carriages, weighing 350 tons 12 cwt ... Train No. 826 also consisted of 11 bogie vehicles, weighing 271 tons 8 cwt unloaded and was drawn by a three-cylinder engine No. 4009, K3 type (2-6-0) [built at Doncaster in 1921].'

Brief and to the point, but in the early hours of the morning this was all far from clear and confusion reigned, with insufficient light available to see clearly what had happened and needed to be done.

I had a flashlight with me and, having parked some way away from the station, so as not to get in the way of the emergency services, I made my way along the platform confirming with police officers who I was and why I was there. One of them accompanied me to the 2-6-0

rounded corners – despite the ingress of water and, consequently rotting timbers. These were issues on which he and Edward Thompson, who probably had wider experience of coach design, fundamentally disagreed. Thompson preferred to use metal throughout and pointed to successful safety trials carried out in the States with such vehicles. The CME was not unsympathetic to these arguments, but did move closer to Thompson's position after the accident at Welwyn in the design of the new streamlined Silver Jubilee set.

It must have been with some relief that Spencer returned to his normal duties a day or two later and quickly allowed the A4 programme and several other new locomotive projects to re-absorb him, while Bulleid continued to focus on the P2 trials and carriage design.

These may have been difficult days for the Principal Assistant. A fundamental difference of opinion with Gresley over the benefits of streamlining, an ever-growing ambition to become CME and living with the frustration these issues may have caused would have taken their toll. He still had Gresley's ear, but his influence was growing less with each passing year. Observing all this from close quarters, Spencer simply recorded, 'though still close there was a loosening of the bonds that had tied them together for two decades. As this happened so Bulleid's dissatisfaction increased, as did his level of criticism of the direction in which the CME was taking the department, and the

Being the first of the streamliners meant that 2509, *Silver Link*, quickly acquired a special status within the LNER and the wider world. It may have been just another steam locomotive, but it sat at the pinnacle of what this form of locomotion could offer. And so it was often photographed, as shown here, and visitors in small or large groups sought to be photographed on its footplate or in front of the engine. The lower picture captures just such an event with Gresley, William Stanier and Robert Thom amongst the group, which included many wives. On the back of this print Spencer has written, 'Stanier stands behind Gresley, his old friend, with Thom to his right. I managed to grab a spot on the footplate leaning out of the rear window with Thompson just below me'. (BS)

two men increasingly worked apart'. With the more accommodating Spencer appearing to occupy an ever more influential role at King's Cross, Bulleid may have thought himself side-lined; a not unreasonable conclusion in the circumstances.

By this stage, all the planning work for the first A4s and their carriages was all but complete, only subject to minor changes or those forced on the team by the practical realities of construction. As Spencer later recalled:

> It was like completing a jigsaw when many pieces had rough edges and would not fit together. These could only be dealt with as and when they occurred on the shop floor often by rough and ready methods. This ensured that no engines were entirely the same and each would perform slightly differently in identical circumstances. As a result, it was an often heard joke that scientists worked to 1/10,000th of an inch, carpenters to 1/10th and fitters to the nearest locomotive. But it seemed to work.

So to Thom and his workers fell the arduous, compelling and pressured task of forging, shaping and then fettling a small mountain of metal to make it all fit together in only six months. And during September, like a conjuror pulling a rabbit out of a hat, Thom produced his miracle and engine No. 2509 was towed out of the works ready for service. But first the engine was tested and 'run-in' on the mainline around Doncaster then down to London, which, as Spencer related:

> Involved the CME and myself on occasions. While this was happening Bulleid oversaw the preparation of the carriage set. No. 2509 returned to Doncaster on the 19th for trial running with the new streamlined carriages, which allowed brake tests to be conducted and didn't return to King's Cross until, the 25th. On one of these runs the locomotive easily reached 101 mph near Tallington and 100 mph going down Stoke Bank, thus showing her strength and potential.

Although proving to be a sound design, in a very short time there was one significant problem to be overcome if a fast schedule was to be achieved with adequate safety margins. Spencer wrote:

> When the engine was tested with its new carriages before returning to London for the 27th, the opportunity was taken for brake tests, to make sure the train could stop safely in an emergency from high speed. To ensure this could be achieved it was decided to use the standard Westinghouse vacuum brake variety, but with 24in cylinders, the largest the company made. In addition, the standard brake pipe vacuum of 21in of mercury gauge was used. This was thought to be sufficient. This proved not to be the case, a problem not helped by the articulated stock which had fewer wheels and so fewer brake blocks than more conventional carriages. It was a problem which taxed our minds for some time and involved engineers from Westinghouse.

Patrick Remnant, who in 1935 was a junior engineer working for Aloysius Brackenbury at Westinghouse, and became a close associate and friend of Spencer, took up this story:

> It was a shortcoming that could have had serious consequences. When operating the A4s with articulated stock they would often face checks and slacks caused by slower running trains ahead or track maintenance. So it became necessary to use the engines very considerable acceleration to keep the trains on time … It was not at all uncommon when making up time after a check or slack for locomotives to run up to 95 mph or more, at which speed it could prove impossible to stop the train between distant and home signals safely and in time… As a result, instructions were issued that two signalling blocks, instead

In his archive, Spencer kept many photographs of the first few weeks of the Silver Jubilee service and took the opportunity to ride on the loco and train to assess its performance. These are just five from his extensive collection, the upper and middle photos he dated as being 27 September and captured the train's departure from King's Cross. The lower picture he left undated, but the slightly grimy state of the engine suggests it was taken a little later. (BS)

after passing this important junction that the maximum speed was attained, twice – once near Arlesey and again between Biggleswade and Sandy.

At least four world records were established on this trip, and these were the running between mile-posts 30 and 55 at an average speed of 107.5 mph; the running from Hatfield to Huntingdon, a distance of 41 miles 15 chains, at an average of 100.6 mph; an entire distance of 43 miles in one run covered at an average 100 mph (these are applicable to either diesel or steam propulsion), and the running from Wood Green to Fletton Junction, 70 miles in 45 mins 44 sec, at an average of 91.8 mph. This last is a world record for steam traction.

In the face of this and many other adjective-strewn accounts, Spencer remained ever practical, no matter how stirred he may have been about this great success. It was, after all, just the beginning of the A4's active life and much remained to be done to make sure the entire class were built and ran well in service all the time. In the meantime, Gresley and his team had to ensure that the success of the inaugural run was repeated the following week, as Spencer recalled later:

> No. 2509 remained in light steam over the weekend ready for the Monday run, while maintenance staff examined the engine from end to end looking for the slightest fault. They were joined by two fitters from Doncaster to assist them in this work. With such a new engine arrangements had been made for the 27th to get her to Darlington or Doncaster for repair if required. Suitable stand in Pacifics had also been arranged to keep the service going should 2509 have failed.
>
> Luckily neither of these measures proved necessary, but had to be repeated for the week ahead. The inspections revealed that the left pony truck circle box had been running a little hot, though not dangerously so. The carriage set was also inspected very closely, as well as being thoroughly cleaned. However, nothing could be done about a certain roughness experienced in the train's riding quality. For the moment though it was considered to be a minor problem that could wait for a more detailed investigation. The brake issue was another matter and it was hoped that two block signalling solution would be sufficient for safe running until Westinghouse came up with an improved vacuum brake.'

In a letter he later added:

> When the opportunity arose the first two A4s were stripped down to see how all the moving parts were coping with the stress of high speed running. There were very few signs of excessive wear and Gresley's 2 in 1 valve gear, in particular, appeared to be standing up well as most expected it would. By this stage shed staff were well versed in the maintenance techniques necessary to keep the gear in good shape. The only incident of note involved No. 2512. During a Heavy Repair at Doncaster in late August 1936 it was found necessary to replace the centre cylinder and piston head due to damage after a very fast run that month. A year later fitting a new centre motion bar also became necessary.
>
> Apart from this there were periodic concerns about overheating when the locomotives were working at high speed. This seemed to affect the connecting rods, coupling rods and the pony truck circle box on several engines. As a result, improvements were made to the mechanical lubricators to ensure a free flow of oil to the affected parts. It was thought that under the influence of centripetal forces generated at high speeds that oil in the reservoirs became static, restricting flow until a critical moment had passed. Despite the remedial measures some footplate crew continued to report their concerns, though I do not remember many failures due to overheating.

By the time this photograph was taken, the success of the Silver Jubilee service was assured and this led to an increase in the train's length with the addition of an eighth carriage as shown here. (BS)

In due course, as experience of the class grew, other modifications were made. The first four engines had been built with short buffers, which did not provide sufficient protection and were replaced with longer buffers. Then in 1937/38 the coal capacity of ten tenders was increased from 8 to 9 tons in response to concerns expressed by the Regional Managers about safety margins on the long non-stop routes.

Undoubtedly, Spencer would have shared the excitement of seeing these new engines and streamlined carriages enter service so dramatically, but his job was to stay calm and analytical at all times. And this is what he did so well, heavily underlining his importance to Gresley along the way. Post-1936 this would increase exponentially as the CME's health continued to decline and staff changes took place at senior level. In the meantime, as the number of A4s continued to

Production of the A4s ran from 1935 to '38, the last emerging as Robert Thom's career came to an end and Edward Thompson took his place at Doncaster. During these early years the A4s were painted in different colour schemes. The first four appeared in shades of silver/grey to reflect the Silver Jubilee celebrations, but after that the LNER decided to paint the next nine in LNER green, with black and white lining. The first of these, No. 4482 *Golden Eagle*, is captured here by Spencer when new. However, the green paint scheme did not last long and all members of the class were turned out in Garter Blue, with red and white lining, by October 1938. (BS)

grow towards an eventual thirty-five, the LNER's Board felt able to sanction other streamlined, high-speed, non-stop services, with London to Edinburgh being top of their list.

To establish the viability of such a service using the A4s, a test run was arranged for Saturday, 26 September 1936. In this case, it was simply a matter of taking the Silver Jubilee set, which spent the weekend at Newcastle, on a special run to Waverley. On this occasion, it would have a dynamometer car attached and be pulled by the third member of the class, No. 2511 *Silver King*, and be in the hands of the very experienced Gateshead driver, Tom Dron. To give the occasion some added frisson, Gresley and Eric Trask, the 42-year-old District Running Superintendent at Gateshead, were on the footplate. Meanwhile, Edward Thompson, who had become something of a fixture on many of these 'specials', and Spencer were in the dynamometer car. He later remarked:

> With the success of the A4s and the Silver Jubilee service assured, the two runs on the 26th had the air of an excursion to the seaside. There was much banter and an unmistakeable sense of gaiety about the day. The chief was in excellent spirits all day.
>
> The intention was to see if the A4 could equal or better the booked time of 130 minutes for the 124.5 miles from Newcastle to Edinburgh. For comparison purposes No. 2511 followed the A1 [2582 *Sir Hugo*] pulled Queen of Scots Pullman, which performed exceptionally well that day and covered the journey in 119 minutes. 2509 with a slightly lighter load managed 118 minutes northbound and 114 minutes southbound, even though the conditions were very poor and the track slippery especially in the tunnels and on the Cockburnspath bank. But the engine held up well and did not struggle or lose its grip at any point. It was later calculated that the IHP [Indicated Horse Power] produced during these runs was in the order of 2,500.

Armed with this information, Whitelaw and his board were swift to approve the introduction of two more streamlined services – one from London to Edinburgh and the other from King's Cross to Leeds, to begin in July and September 1937 respectively. Whilst this was happening, the long expected departure of Bulleid took place, with the Southern Railway confirming his appointment as their CME. In his place came Douglas Ross Edge, who could not have been more different to the ebullient, challenging Bulleid, suggesting that Gresley may have grown tired of such dynamism so close to home.

Ross was born on 19 April 1885 in Altrincham, the third and youngest child of William, a railway clerk, and Marianne. During 1902, he become an apprenticeship fitter at the Great Central's Gorton Works and when qualified. proved to be a talented engineer, rising quickly through the ranks, becoming a carriage and wagon specialist in the process. When the LNER was formed in 1923, he was appointed C & W Works Manager at Dukenfield, and remained there until 1934 when Gresley posted him to the Carriage and Wagon Works at Doncaster. Why, in 1937, the CME chose him to replace Bulleid and not another locomotive man, is unclear. One can only assume that he had impressed his leader in some way with his skill and ideas and could offer a fresh perspective on the rolling stock side of business. However, there may also have been a more personal reason. Perhaps Gresley wished to have an assistant happy to assist and not tax his patience and authority in ways that Bulleid appears to have done. Wherever the truth might lie, it was certainly an interesting appointment which gave Bert Spencer a great deal more authority in the locomotive field than he had before.

In the few years left to him Gresley and Bulleid remained friends, the older man often visiting the Bulleid family at their home on Box Hill in Surrey. Here, he took a great delight playing with Bulleid's children and joining in their fun and games. But, as Bert Spencer recalled, these moments of light relief from the demands of his life with the LNER proved be a double edge sword. 'Bulleid's young son Hugh was tragically killed in 1938, when his bike was hit by a car. Sir Nigel

In July 1937, the second of the A4-pulled streamlined services commenced with the inaugural run of the Coronation from King's Cross. A few days earlier, on 30 June, the LNER ran a highly publicised 'press run' of the new train from King's Cross to Barkston pulled by engine No. 4489 *Dominion of Canada*, when only a few weeks old. Spencer collected many photographs and reports of the day's event of which these are but a small selection. (BS)

The 'Up' Coronation, with A4 No. 4490 *Empire of India* which only entered service on 25 June in charge, leaves Waverley Station in July 1937 to great fanfare, being received at King's Cross in a similar vein. (BS)

Very quickly the Coronation and the West Riding, the new non-stop service to Leeds, proved popular and became a regular feature of life on the LNER. But after only a few few days they began to attract far less attention (as the picture on the left, of engine No. 4497 *Golden Plover* in slightly grimy garter blue livery, demonstrates). (Above right) An unidentifie A4 heads north with its new set of streamlined carriages in gleaming condition – a perfect advertisement for the LNER. (BS)

The A4 programme continues but at a fairly leisurely pace – thirty-five locomotives in nearly three years was not a demanding programme for such a large company. Here in May 1937 the fifteenth of the class, No. 4491 and soon to be named *Commonwealth of Australia*, nears completion and will enter traffic on 22 June. She will pull the first Down Coronation service a few days later on 5 July. (BS)

was profoundly saddened by his death and remained so for some considerable time. Hugh held a particular place in Gresley's heart.'

In the months before and after Bulleid's departure, the team at King's Cross were kept busy with many other projects beside the A4s. It was in the way of a final flourish before peace gave way to war, which by 1936/37 seemed unavoidable to a growing number of people, as Spencer recalled:

> Many people turned a blind eye to what was happening in Germany and saw in Hitler a leader to be admired. Many also expressed a wish for such a man to take Britain out of the doldrums and crush the Trades Unions, who were seen as disruptive to daily lives in their bid to achieve equality through better pay and working conditions. Too late did they realise that Hitler's ambitions were so very dangerous.
>
> Gresley visited Germany a number of times in the mid-1930s to view some of the DRG's steam and diesel projects. During two of these tours I saw for myself the 'Jew baiting' by Nazi officials that went on, unchecked by the civil police. Stories of the first concentration camps were also widely circulating and the Nazi rallies were well publicised in our newspapers and seen in newsreels at our cinemas.

To Greater Glory

Julius Dorpmuller (second from the right), head of the DRG as it prepared for war, the future Nazi Transport Minister and Gresley's one time associate and professional rival in the 1930s, enjoying a day out with his master. Spencer met him on a number of occasions and wrote 'he greeted us with a Nazi salute, which was not well received. It did not surprise me to read that Dorpmuller rose to high rank in the Nazi party'. (THG)

As things deteriorated Gresley told us to limit our contact with our German opposite numbers with whom relations had, up to then, been good. This included Dr Julius Dorpmuller and Dr Wagner of the DRG who were both became well known to us at King's Cross and were fairly regular visitors to our offices at King's Cross from the late 1920s up to 1935.

There was one final visit in June 1938 when both men dropped in to see Gresley, quite separately, while visiting Britain on a tour hosted by Stanier and the ILocoE. The CME and Dorpmuller then travelled to Edinburgh behind an A4, with Gresley's son Roger in attendance. Roger later described the journey to me as being 'frosty', both men being polite but clearly aware that their countries might soon be at war. It did not help that Dorpmuller was by then a senior official in the Nazi Party and likely to be gathering information on Britain's preparedness for war while being chaperoned by Stanier.

If this is so, the Germans would have found much to observe on the LNER. Other than the A4s, the late 1930s saw the continuation of a number of existing programmes – the V1/V3s, D49s, B17s, J39s and P2s – and the development of a number of others, including the heavy mixed traffic V2 2-6-2s and a resurrection of electrification projects. While simple economics dictated that steam would dominate for many years to come, electric trains were clearly the long term goal of Britain's railway companies. But progress, since the cancellation of Raven's projects in 1923, had been painfully slow, as Spencer recalled:

I believe that Gresley was loth to mothball the electrification projects begun by Raven before amalgamation, but, as he told me later, the political will to continue was absent, as were the funds. Coal was the mainstay of the country and was cheap and plentiful. There was also the issue of providing sufficient power to meet electrifications needs. Put simply, these were the days before a national grid had been created and there were not enough power stations in existence to meet the burgeoning demand. So, with many misgivings the LNER chose to halt electrification and focus on steam until the Government took action to produce a power generation system across Britain of sufficient strength and reliability. It was different around London where adequate generation to meet the need of electric trains on the Southern Railway and the underground system could be guaranteed.

The key to change was the Weir Committee which was set up in the 1920s to consider how the power industry was managed and might be developed over the coming decades. Ralph Wedgwood was one of the railway's representatives and Gresley acted as an advisor. After much deliberation a number of recommendations were made which led to

By 1937, the number of A4s available was nearing thirty, though the A1/A3s outnumbered them by quite a large margin. Their modernistic shape continued to attract press attention and producers of films and newsreels. As a result, many photos regularly appeared in newspapers and journals. Most famously *Silver Link* had a starring role in the early scenes of Will Hay's 1937 film '*Oh! Mr Porter*'. In the picture above, taken that year, engines Nos. 4489, Dominion of Canada (ex-Woodcock), 2512, Silver Fox, still in her silver/grey colour scheme, and 4490, Empire of India, apparently in a cold state, are lined up for the photographer (BS)

the 1926 Electricity Supply Act. As the number of power stations gradually increased, industry, most notably the railways, were encouraged to make use of the ever-expanding national grid. But following the Great Crash of 1929 this proved difficult. Nevertheless, by 1935 Government funding allowed the LNER to begin developing electrification plans a long time in gestation, which pleased Gresley immensely. Having recruited Henry Richards and a small team of specialist electrical engineers to manage these programmes in 1924, the CME could finally begin turning ideas into firm proposals and seek the funds to begin work.

He and Richards had many schemes in Britain and overseas to consider when developing the LNER's services. For example, the Southern Railway had chosen to use a third rail system to supply power to its trains. However, after much thought, Gresley plumped for an overhead catenary power supply. Here development work undertaken by Metropolitan-Vickers in South Africa was of particular interest to Gresley. Although a narrower gauge the locomotives built for this system became the basis for the LNER's designs.

By 1936 Richards had identified two schemes that might be developed quickly without disrupting existing services to any great extent. The first of these proposed electrifying the heavily graded line from Woodhead Line, via Sheffield to Manchester and Wath across the Pennines. This had become a major route for carrying coal, with passenger numbers increasing also. The second focussed on commuter routes from Liverpool Street and Fenchurch Stations to Shenfield and Stratford.

The cost of developing the Shenfield lines was estimated at £3.4m, with this outlay spread over a four or five year period. But it was predicted that this investment would increase traffic from 1.4 million loaded train miles per annum to at least 2.0m or more and reduce operating costs by a third. The Pennine link produced similar figures making both projects capable of a return on the company's investment in a 10 to 12 year period, even without the offsetting effect of any work needed to keep steam running on these routes.

When developing his plans for electrification, Gresley had a fairly solid bank of information to consider, in Britain and overseas. There was, of course, Raven's work for the NER before amalgamation and recession put paid to these plans. By this stage, Metropolitan-Vickers had made considerable advances in designing electric locomotives and Gresley forged a close working relationship with the company and carefully observed what they were doing, particularly in South Africa for the State railway there. During 1938, he and his son, Roger, visited the country to view their system in operation, coming away much impressed by what they had seen and by the narrow gauge locomotives built by Metro-Vick (above) for service there. (BS)

When it came to developing the multiple units and locomotives to work these services Gresley chose to involve Tom Street and myself very closely in the work. We had both shown considerable interest in these projects and saw them, plus an electrified East Coast Mainline, as the future of Britain's raiways and wished to be part of this work from the very start.

From very early in the project Gresley was determined to build examples of locomotive and multiple unit to populate these lines, so that they might be evaluated. Past experience shaped his thoughts and such a crucial project couldn't be allowed to fail simply because testing had not been undertaken properly. It was here that Metropolitan-Vickers experience proved crucial in designing the new units. King's Cross and Donaster planned and built the trains, but the impetus for this work came from the Lancashire company. They and their suppliers were also responsible for manufacturing many parts, such as the electrical equipment.

The first batch of seventy engines for the Woodhead line were ordered in 1939, but it wasn't until September 1941 that the prototype locomotive, No. 6701, was completed, the coming or war and problems with the design causing many delays. However, by this time work on the line had also been deferred, partially due to the hostilities, but also the need to complete expensive civil engineering work on a new double-track tunnel at Woodhead. Despite the war 6701 continued to be tested for a while, but was then placed in store 'for the duration'. It would be many more years before the line was complete, which was far too long for such an important project.

Progress on the Shenfield line was slow by comparison, with the result that the LNER only signed contracts allowing construction to begin in 1939. With war only a few months away, further

The coming of war placed electrification on the back-burner for the duration. But there had been progress on designing and building a prototype Bo Bo Class locomotive, No. 6701, for the Woodhead line (above left) and multiple units for the Shenfield commuter line (above right as they appeared in 1949 when the line was finally open). Some testing took place, but the war and threat of invasion curtailed this work. (BS)

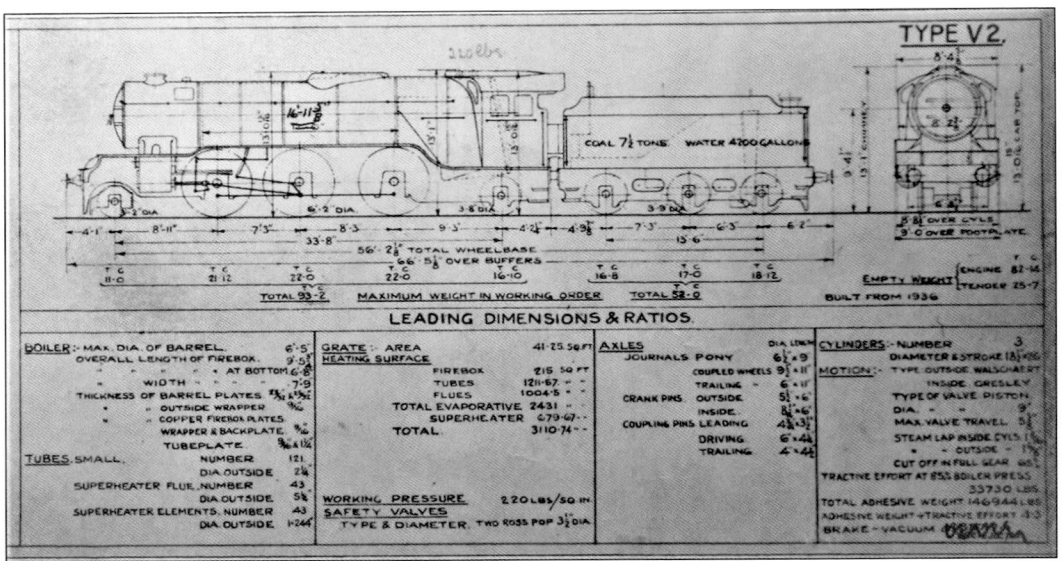

Spencer's personal copy of the V2's diagram with some brief notes attached. (BS)

delays were inevitable and little infrastructure work had been completed before Germany invaded Poland and war came to Britain. Meanwhile, development of new Electric Multiple Units to work this line continued and a few, rumoured to be six in number, had been built when the project was halted. These were then the placed in store. It would be ten years before the line was completed and the EMU's potential could be fully explored.

Meanwhile, steam projects continued to be developed the most noteworthy being the V2. In 1947 Spencer described the background and course of this important project in simplistic terms, giving no hint of his own contribution:

> For some time (since at least 1932) a need had been felt for an engine more suited than the 4-6-0 type K3 class for express goods and passenger services. In response, during 1936, a new series of 2-6-2 type class, three-cylinder engines were put into service.

The first V2, No. 4771 *Green Arrow*, captured in photograph form by Spencer and kept in one of his albums. He has added in a brief note 'travelled on the footplate several times in July/September 1936. Found the engine of good quality and worth the effort. Reported back to the CME accordingly'. (BS)

Prior to the preparation of this design Gresley had given consideration to the possibility of building a three-cylinder 2-6-4-4 type articulated engine and tender having 6ft 2in diameter coupled wheels and incorporating the K3 class boiler, valve gear, connecting rods, pony truck, axles and axleboxes. The proposal, however, was abandoned in favour of the more powerful V2 engine, the first of which, No. 4771, *Green Arrow*, left Doncaster works in June 1936.

Much of the design work was completed by Clifford Cocks [who joined Bulleid on the Southern in 1937 and was involved in the design of both his heavy and light Pacifics, plus the controversial 'Leader' Class, then, in 1949, replaced Tom Coleman at Derby], a senior draughtsman in the Doncaster Drawing Office, who seemed to have had a particular liking for 2-6-2 engines. These engines have 6ft. 2in. diameter coupled wheels and 18½ in. by 26 in. cylinders, with 9in. diameter valves. The 6ft. 5in. diameter boiler carries a working pressure of 220lb/sq in., and follows the design of the A3 class boiler, with the distance between the tubeplates being reduced from 18ft. 11¾ in., to 17 ft (and a 'banjo' steam collector replacing the A3 type traditional dome). Gresley valve gear is arranged in front of the cylinders, which drive on the second coupled axle.

When discussions were taking place regarding the maximum traffic availability of the V2 class there was some criticism because of the engine being too long for certain outlying turntables at that time used by the K3 class engines. The suggestion that the K3 should be retained as the highest powered engine on the routes affected was not acceptable as it was considered that they were not really suitable for the high speeds required. A scheme was therefore put forward for a 4-6-0 engine with 6ft 8in diameter coupled wheels and a 220lb per sq inch boiler pressure as an improvement not only on the K3 class, but also on the B17 ... The proposed engine had a 6ft diameter boiler tapering to 5ft 9in diameter to permit the use of the Pacific cylinders and front engine arrangement. As conditions on some of the routes affected had changed by the time the first V2 engines were actually in service, it was decided not to proceed with the proposed 4-6-0.

There were also several other interesting features in the V2's design where some originality of thought was needed as well as an ability to adapt ideas used successfully in other engines. These included wider spacing of the coupled wheels than the A3s, and a slightly longer wheelbase. The cylinders were contained in a Monobloc casting which incorporated the smokebox saddle, outside steam pipes and steam chest. There was a simple blastpipe

By the time V2 No. 4799 appeared in March 1938, another twenty-eight of the class were in service and establishing a good reputation on the routes over which these mixed traffic engines were allowed to travel with their 22 ton axle loading. Here 4799 gives a clear demonstration of what she is capable of doing and appears to be making light work of a freight turn. (BS)

arrangement and the cab was wedged like the A4s. In addition, a standard 7½ ton, 4,200 gallon capacity, six wheeled tender was attached. This was adequate for most needs, but when the engines began substituting for Pacifics on the longer routes and took on particular arduous duties during the war this proved to be something of a disadvantage.

With a 22 ton axle loading their ability to run over all LNER lines was limited, as it was for A3s, A4s, P2s and others. With this restriction in mind, and with a perceived need for a more powerful mixed traffic engine to work over the rest of the network, the possibility of building a lighter version to achieve this wider route availability began to be explored and resulted in the three-cylinder V4 2-6-0s, of which only two were built before Gresley died and the project came to an end. It was not until Thompson led in producing the B1 4-6-0s that that the need for a true mixed traffic engine with wide route availability was met. In this he and I had closely observed the success of Stanier and Coleman's mixed traffic Black Fives.

In the short time available to him, Spencer was limited in what he could say in his paper about the V2s. However, he could have added that, at one stage, streamlining was seriously considered. In the event, this idea was not developed even to a modelling or wind tunnel testing stage, let alone to the final design. One can only speculate on why this was so, especially with the A4s being produced in such numbers at that time and the P2s, the W1 and two B17s to follow a streamlined route shortly. Perhaps it was simply a case of the Drawing Office lacking the time or inclination to design and test the effects of the casing. Or it may simply have been that an engine being produced for fast freight and occasional passenger duties was unlikely to travel at speeds where streamlining would prove beneficial, though the issue of smoke lifting remained a constant.

The V2s were later described as 'engines that helped win the war'. True or not, 184 were built between 1936 and 1944 and their sheer number would have made them a force to be reckoned with especially during the conflict. But they were not without their faults and limitations as Spencer later explained:

Under the conditions that prevailed between 1939 and '45 they, like Gresley's other three cylinder engines with conjugated valve gear, suffered more severely than other types of locomotives. Greatly reduced maintenance standards, due to staff shortages, coupled to very heavy wartime use gradually took their toll. This increased their time under repair and reduced their efficiency quite severely at times. However, when in good working order they were strong and efficient performers and on occasions were recorded as pulling quite

With war only a few weeks away, the great and the good gathered at King's Cross to witness the naming of V2 No.4844. With re-armament slowly gathering pace, after a ponderous start, it is perhaps not surprising that this new engine was named *Coldstreamer* on 20 June by Major-General Sir Cecil Pereira with company Chairman, Ronald Matthews and Nigel Gresley standing together in front of the engine's cab beside him. Edward Thompson and Spencer were also in attendance standing together. Spencer recalled later that 'we gloomily discussed the future as the Coldream band played and wondered where we would be one or two years hence'. (BS)

prodigious loads. The most impressive of these was observed in March 1940. A V2 [No. 4800] took on a 850 ton express train, made up of twenty-six carriages, heading south from Newcastle to London at Peterborough when another engine failed. It handled this great load with apparent ease and only slightly behind timings allowed for a Pacific pulling a much lighter load.,

However, heavy wartime use and reduced maintenance did expose a problem with the V2s lead pony truck. These were designed with Gresley's patented double swing link suspension fitted and were found to suffer from excessive wear in their pins and lubrication was not as good as it could be. This may have been a contributory factor in a number of derailments at this time, though the dilapidated state of the track was considered by myself and Thompson to be a more likely cause.

The Monobloc cylinder casting was prone to cracking and this led, early in the war, to several modifications to the design – relocating the upper flanges to make them more accessible during servicing and improvements to the oil-feed system to make it more effective. This did not entirely resolve the problem and later on the opportunity was taken to remove the Monobloc casting and fit three separate cylinder castings when engines were undergoing periods of General Repair [it was a slow programme that had seen only 71 engines so modified before stream disappeared from Britain's railways in the 1960s].

Nevertheless, they proved to be stalwart performers and worthy of the title 'a Gresley engine'. They certainly played a key part in the LNER's contribution to the war effort.

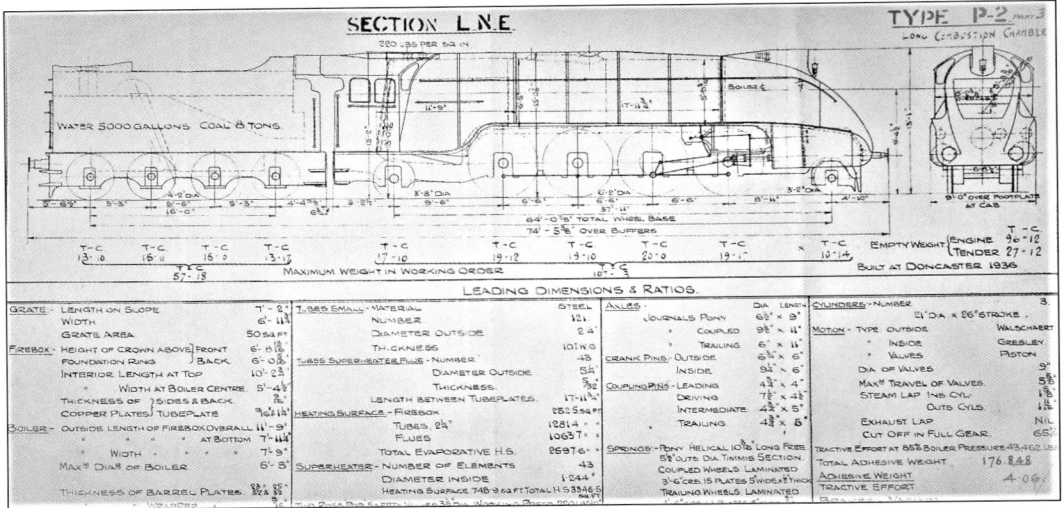

Spencer's copy of the diagram covering the P2s as streamliners, in this case called Part Three suggesting it may well cover the rebuilding of engines 2001 and 2002 in 1938 and 1936 respectively. (BS)

By the time the V2s began appearing, the P2 programme had run its course. Four more appeared during 1936, in a A4 like streamlined form but without side valances over the driving wheels, with the first two being similarly modified in 1936 (No. 2002) and 1938 (No. 2001). All were then employed north of Edinburgh as planned, despite growing concerns over their suitability for this line, as Spencer later related:

> Overall they proved costly to run and were difficult to maintain in good running order. During the war this became something of an embarrassment and, under pressure from the Regional Manager and the General Manager, Thompson decided to rebuild them as Pacifics. This was a sad outcome, considering the significant part they had played in Gresley's career, but he would probably have done the same himself when faced with the operational problems they caused and the safety issues concerned [highlighted by incidents of fractured crank axles]. In many ways it was Bulleid, not Gresley, who pursued the development of the 2-8-2s and when he departed to the Southern the CME's interest in them appeared to wane.
> And despite Bulleid's impassioned arguments in their favour, the issue of economy could not be ignored and these were expensive engines to operate, even when giving them full credit for their considerable pulling power.

So it probably came as no surprise when Thompson took the decision to rebuild them in 1943/44, although his motives in doing so have been interpreted as malicious ones by some. But as Spencer later wrote:

> Something had to be done to make them more efficient and of greater use. However, they were magnificent engines and would probably have reached their full potential if able to operate on a railway system such as that found in France and Germany where Mikadoes seemed to find their feet much better. I was sad to see them go, but I did not dispute the need for their rebuilding. After all, you cannot live in the past, but continue to strive for better solutions when one avenue has been explored to its limit. By the time this work was being planned and carried out I was working directly for Thompson preparing his standardisation plans, so had some involvement in the P2 to A2 project, assisting Edward Windle in the process.

As streamliners, the P2s again adopted the aerodynamic principles set out by Frederick Johansen some years earlier and wind tunnel tested, except for the side valences to the rear of the outer cylinders. These, Spencer related, were 'dismissed for reason of access while the locos underwent maintenance on shed, but also to ensure the eight coupled wheels did not meet any obstructions when negotiating the tight curves on the line between Edinburgh and Aberdeen'. His interest in their construction is probably reflected in the number of photos he kept in his archive of which these are just six. (Top – left to right) Engine No. 2006 *Wolf of Badenoch* with frames and cylinders in place. Boiler installed on No. 2003 *Lord President* and framing for her streamlined nose being constructed. (Middle) Nos. 2004 *Mons Meg* and 2005 *Thane of Fife* nearing completion. (Lower) Nos 2001 *Cock of the North* and 2004 in service in all their glory. (BS)

Meanwhile, the fate of the W1 was sealed by Gresley himself. Despite his best endeavours, the engine had stumbled along making some headway but never quite achieving its hoped for potential. Perhaps if she had offered clear cost and efficiency savings over existing locomotives things might have been different, but she fell far short of doing this and gradually the engine spent more time in the sidings or in the workshop and not out on the road. According to Spencer:

> [Gresley was] greatly disappointed by the results, but it was a worthy experiment which sought to improve steam locomotion and make it more efficient while reducing running

costs. Sadly, it was not to be and Gresley, with some regret, finally agreed to rebuild her in a more trditional, well proven guise. It is true to say that this was a great disappointment to him as Turbomotive was to Stanier, though in this case the engine did meet all expectations.

So, in 1937 W1 entered the workshops at Doncaster to emerge in rebuilt, streamlined form. The high pressure water-tubed boiler and four-cylinder compound drive had been stripped away, to be replaced by three-cylinders and a boiler similar to the type fitted to P2 No. 2006, with its pressure raised to 250psi, plus a firegrate measuring 50 sq ft. Her 6ft 8in driving wheels were retained as were both trucks and she remained a 4-6-4. In 1947, Spencer added a few words to describe the remaining elements of this work:

> The conversion, which utilised the existing design of 20 in x 26 in cylinders with 8 in diameter piston valves as fitted to the A1 Pacifics, increased the tractive effort at 85 per cent boiler pressure to 41,437 lbs that made it the most powerful engine with 6 ft 8 in wheels in Britain'.

Once completed, W1 was assigned to King's Cross to work alongside the Pacific fleet and remained there for fifteen years, easily holding her own beside the A4s, in particular. In October 1953, she was transferred to Doncaster, from where she was withdrawn from service on 1 June 1959 and cut up, remaining a streamliner until the end. But she was not the last Gresley engine to draw upon Frederick Johansen's work and the B17 class provided one last flourish.

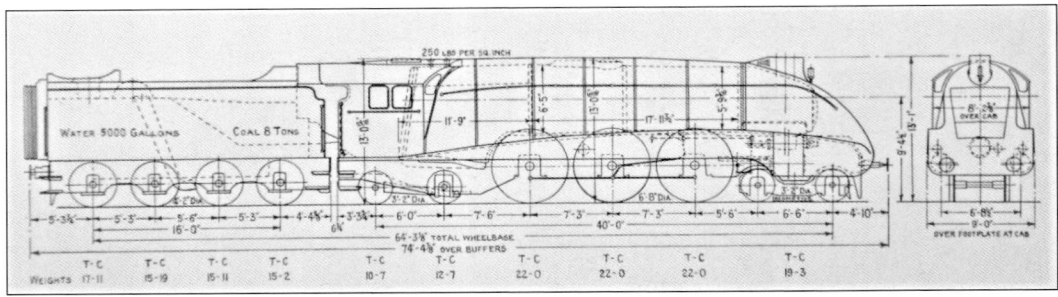

If W1 could have been saved in its original condition Spencer would have been greatly pleased.'It was' he wrote 'a worthy experiment which sought to improve steam locomotion and make it more efficient while reducing running costs'. It was not to be, but in her new form W1 impressed Spencer and, according to several accounts, the crews who took her out on the road. Her transition left the 4-6-4 configuration intact and the streamlinined casing ran very close to the A4s outline,as the above pictures of No. 10000 confirm. (BS)

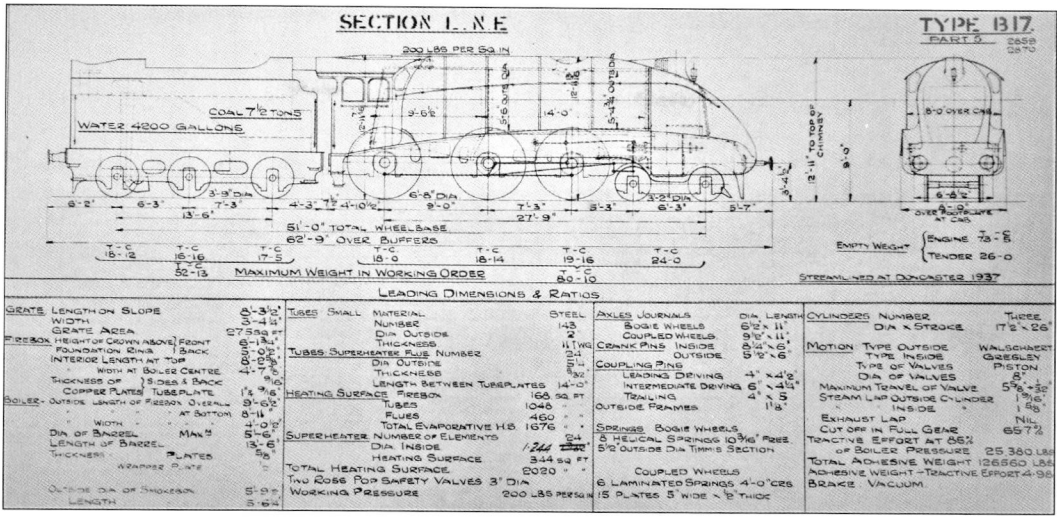

In 1937, two of the seventy-three B17s built were rebuilt as streamliners to take advantage of the publicity value of express services pulled by such locomotives. Nos. 2859 and 2870 were given an A4 style makeover and in September ran for the first time on the East Anglian service from Norwich to Liverpool Street Station and back. They remained streamliners until 1951. (Top) Spencer's diagram of the B17/4s. (Lower left) 2859 *East Anglian* (ex-*Norwich City*) awaits her next turn of duty. (Lower right) 2870 *City of London* (ex-*Tottenham Hotspur*) when new in green livery. (BS)

By 1937, production of the B17s was coming to an end. Since 1928, seventy-three of these impressive locomotives had been built and were doing unglamorous but sterling service on secondary routes, primarily from London into East Anglia. As such they were not the usual candidates for streamlining, but this was all to change following the commercial success of A4 pulled services. Spencer recalled:

> The PR Department could not resist one last bight of the apple, even though the justification for streamlining engines used on routes where high average speeds were insufficient to take full advantage of these theories was minimal. However, the A4 look did improve smoke lifting on the two B17s modified, though the side valancing did increase servicing times slightly. As I prepared some outline drawings Gresley showed great interest in what I was doing and was open minded about the benefits to be gained and felt that there was some justification for proceeding on scientific grounds alone. However, he could not deny that publicity would be well served by such a move and this appeared to be the case with the

'East Anglian' proving to be a great success, though denied a streamlined carriage set on cost grounds.

When two B17s, Nos. 2859 and 2870, were modified, there were probably some raised eyebrows, but there was no denying that their sleek, modern outline would attract publicity and customers. This proved to be the case, but the experiment was not extended to any other engines and remained firmly rooted in the design of A4s, P2s and the singleton W1. But here Spencer added an interesting footnote, 'given time and money Gresley would have streamlined the A1s and A3s as well, and continued to work these principles into other speculative designs being considered at the time'. In 1947, he described one of these after first dealing with the issue of an upgraded A4:

> By 1938 the popularity of the high speed trains was firmly established and it was clear that a demand for longer and heavier trains would eventually arise. A design for a more powerful version of the A4 was therefore prepared having the boiler pressure raised from 250lb to 275lb per sq inch, thus increasing tractive effort from 33,455lb to 39,040lb, but the scheme remained in abeyance.
>
> Whilst the provision of an engine capable of working such trains at the required speeds presented no insuperable difficulty, the arrangement of a clear path through the dense general traffic to enable these speeds to be maintained was a most difficult problem for the Operating Department.
>
> Any appreciable increase in the average speed of the heavy passenger express trains, averaging 50-55 mph, could only be secured by faster uphill running and, to effect this improvement in timing, designs for a three-cylinder 4-8-2 type engine were considered. The proposed engine had 21 in x 26 in cylinders and 6ft 8in diameter coupled wheels, the tractive effort at 85 per cent boiler pressure being 47,700lb. The 6ft 5in diameter boiler carried a working pressure of 250lb and a grate area of 50 sq ft.
>
> There was every prospect of this engine and the modified A4 being proceeded with when the war intervened.

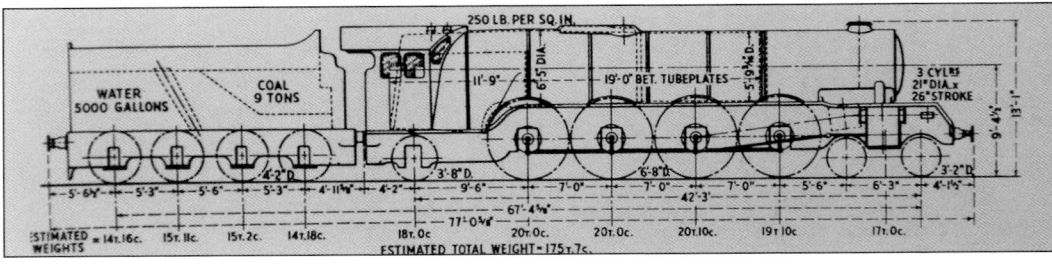

Gresley's evolving design for a powerful 4-8-2 locomotive. As war took hold, development of this type of engine, and an even larger streamlined 4-8-4, provided a distraction as the world appeared to be collapsing around him. (BS)

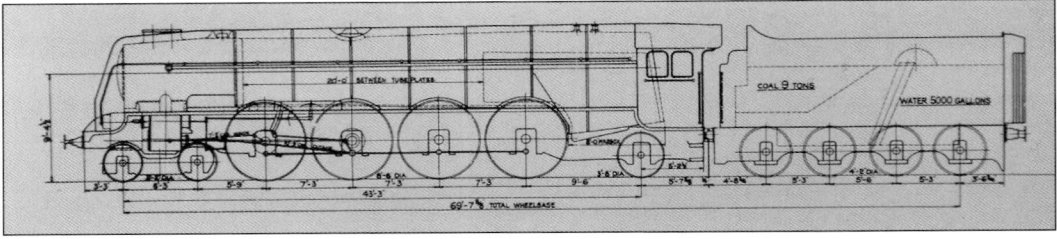

To this he later added that:

> These were not our busiest years at King's Cross although new ideas or adaptions of old ones still crossed my desk on a regular basis. Gresley was gripped by the electrification programme and this took up a great deal of his, Tom Street and my time as locomotives and multiple units were developed. Although Gresley's interest in steam did not waver there was a slackening of the pace here. Later on I wondered whether this was caused by the CME's worsening health, which had begun to cause some concern by 1938/39. For this reason, he had begun to spend more time working from home and when on official visits was accompanied more and more by his son Roger or his daughter Violet.
>
> Other than a 4-8-2 and a more powerful A4 we became engrossed for a time in designing a 4-8-4 streamlined engine. It was by way of a simple exercise to test the theory and, in many ways, replicated the work of Wagner in Germany, with his two 1939 built Class 06 three-cylinder engines, and Chapelon in France, with his single 242A1, that appeared in 1943. Gresley and Chapelon kept in contact until France capitulated to Germany in June 1940. An exchange of ideas continued until near the end, though by that stage we were at war and more goods engines became the order of the day.
>
> Such a large engine was unlikely to have been built and so the drawings and specifications we prepared remained in a simple form for that reason. Nevertheless, it was an interesting idea that Gresley and I discussed and developed at various times during the last two years of his life. However, it was resurrected later when Thompson was CME.
>
> In addition to this there were a number of other proposals under consideration, but like the modified A4 these tended to be developments of existing types. Apart from the K4 and V4 nothing came of them, partly because of the coming of war, but also a lack of support from the business; the engines in the fleet by then meeting most requirements effectively, in type and quality. Some of these ideas are worthy of note, though, because they not only demonstrate the way Gresley's mind was working, but also the evolutionary process being applied by staff in a good design office. This, I feel sure, is something common to all areas of scientific research; a constant search for a better way of doing things.
>
> One of the last of these arose from the need for a more powerful engine for the West Highland route from Glasgow to Fort William and Mallaig to cope with increasing loads and the severe climbs and curves found on this line. The requirement was for an engine having a tractive effort approximately 50 per cent greater than that of the K2 class then

The first of six K4 engines (No. 3441 *Loch Long*) as it appeared when introduced to the Highland Line in March 1937 and on which Spencer rode a few weeks later. (THG)

used on the line and to keep weight and hammer blow effect within the bridge loading limits imposed by the engineer. The first scheme considered was for a 2-8-0 type three-cylinder engine using the O2 class cylinders, 5ft 2in diameter coupled wheels, and a 5ft 6in boiler tapering to a 5ft diameter at the smokebox. After much work this idea was dropped and during 1936 another 2-6-0 design was substituted. In this case it was decided to have a three 18½ in by 26 in-cylinders and a K3 class valve gear and coupling rods with 5ft 2in diameter coupled wheels and a 5ft 6in diameter boiler based on those fitted to the B17s. The tractive effort at 85 per cent boiler pressure was 32,939lb, an increase of 40 per cent over that of the K2 class.

The first engine of the K4 class, No. 3441, *Loch Long*, went into service in March 1937, and proved to be capable of successfully handling 300 ton trains – something I witnessed first-hand in the summer of that year, during a tour of LNER facilities in Scotland. As a result of this visit I suggested that the boiler pressure could be raised from 180lb to 200lb per sq inch, to take advantage of the boiler's designed capacity and so raise the tractive effort of the engine to 36,598lb, an advance of 56 per cent over that of the K2 class. This, it was calculated, would facilitate faster uphill working and increase the engines overall efficiency. This proved to be the case in service when five more of the class were constructed at Darlington between 1938 and '39.

While the ever fertile minds at King's Cross and Doncaster continued to pursue these new challenges, they did not forget to review performances and undertake modifications to the well-established locomotives in the fleet. Even though the A4s were still new and performing well, this did not mean that they were hidden from the CME's critical gaze. It was here that a report about 'their propensity to nose and roll at speed' caught his eye, as Spencer recalled later:

> Word got back to the Chief that footplate crew were increasingly concerned about rolling that took place on the Pacifics, particularly the A4 where the problem seemed much worse. There were also concerns that the front bogies may not have been guiding the front coupled wheels as effectively as they might into curves. As a result, Roland Bond was consulted, but could offer little in the way of solutions. A rolling road might have established the cause quite quickly, but there was little or no chance of taking a locomotive to Vitry for trials. So I was tasked with studying the problem having observed the rolling effect first hand from the footplate of 4495 on a number of occasions, and for comparison purposes two

One of many photos Spencer collected in his travels – for business and pleasure. Here it shows his continuing interest in the A1s in this case No. 4476 *Royal Lancer* on a date and at a place unrecorded. This engine was converted to A3 form until 1946. However, in 1935 her cab was altered when longer vertical handrails were fitted and cut outs to the rear of the side windows were made smaller. (BS)

A3s –Nos. 2743 and 2751. It seemed clear to me that the balance of the engines needed adjustment or the problem lay in the leading or trailing trucks. We decided that there was a need for much closer observation.

In the circumstances it was natural that he should involve Eric Bannister, who later wrote:

I discussed the matter with BS who instructed me to examine the drawings for possible cause. As I couldn't find anything I suggested that it might be the Cartazzi axlebox used on the trailing truck and he sent me out to ride again until I found the reason! The Cartazzi axlebox wedge slides were intended to centre the engine again following a curve but I noticed a jerk as the centring action took place.

BS and I discussed the fact that the Cartazzi slides were designed to have an angle of 1:7 and he asked me to calculate how the engine weight would be shifted if the angle of the slides was altered. Calculations showed that an angle of 1:11 would be suitable. BS spoke to HNG who discussed what I believed I had discovered.'

At Spencer's bidding, Gresley agreed to the change and issued an instruction for the slides to be altered in this way as soon as possible. He also told Bannister to 'continue riding on the footplates of the Pacifics' to gauge the effect of this change and in due course he found an 'appreciable improvement', but not a complete solution because 'the jerking may have stopped, but the nosing continued!'. In due course, he found that 'the thickness of the plates of the carrying wheel springs needed a slight adjustment'. While this was happening, Edward Windle's drawing office team were considering other solutions and this resulted in an alteration to the number and thickness of the laminated springs on both driving and carrying wheels. More observation followed and Bannister judged that the final link in the chain might be established by a 'T shaped bracket with a slot extending between two frames of the bogie, the slot bearing a vertical and renewable strip of lead about 1/8th thick which would be marked by the proximity of the main frame when the engine rolled.'

One was fitted and then tested on a run to Edinburgh where at each station Bannister descended from the cab and 'drew round the lead profile'. Then:

After examination by HNG, Doncaster Works were instructed to make and fit brass brackets on both the main and bogie frames with a space between them [as established by the marks

Even though locomotives filled his working days it seems as though Spencer would also take any opportunity he could to visit exhibitions as a paying member of the public, as many of his photos reveal. (Left) The 1933 built D49 No. 292 *The Southwold* is ready for inspection at an unidentified location, in the background sits the 1924 built A1 No. 2568 *Sceptre*. (Right) Walthamstow May 1937 and it is A4 No. 4482 *Golden Eagle*'s turn to attract a crowd. At this time, the engine is still painted LNER green, but will, in January 1938, be turned out in garter blue. (BS)

Considering how close their relationship was it is difficult to find photographs of Gresley and Spencer together. There is an indistinct picture taken at an ILocoE dinner in the md-1930s and then we have a group shot taken when A4 No. 4498 *Sir Nigel Gresley* was being named. On this occasion past and present members of his team gathered together on 26 November 1937 to honour the great man. These photographs of the two men were taken a few days apart that year. According to friends and relatives, these pictures capture the character of both men very well at this time, not master and servant but two gifted men working together for the greater good. (BS)

made on the lead strips]. The faces of the brackets were lubricated to slide together when the rolled. When this was bolted on position, I rode on the footplate and found the alteration prevented undue rolling.

Spencer, who had been carefully monitoring the progress being made by his young assistant, was obviously pleased by his commitment to the task and the solution found in this case, and may have had this in mind when he wrote:

> There were always niggling problems to sort out. Often they were time consuming and impossible to resolve without a complete re-design, which was impractical. But by close examination and careful analysis it was often possible to do something. To achieve this, it was important to have clever men around you who were prepared to roll up their sleeves and get their hands dirty in establishing cause and effect. The A4s tendency to role at speed was just such a case and it took some months of trial and error to find a solution, albeit only a partial one.

As the 1930s moved to a close, this level of support was becoming ever more important. Gresley's health continued to decline, imperceptibly at first but ever increasing, and this began to place a heavier burden on his assistants and their staff. Spencer alluded to this when writing about the highly publicised celebrations that took place on 30 June 1938 to commemorate the 50th anniversary of the Flying Scotsman service. It was an occasion made special by the choice of A4 Pacific to pull this train – 4498 *Sir Nigel Gresley*:

> The Chief was clearly moved by this recognition and thoroughly enjoyed the day. When at Stevenage he was one of the first to walk down the track to photograph both engines

[the A4 and a Stirling Single] and then mingle with the crowd, answering many questions. But by the end of the day he was very tired and clearly struggling with exhaustion, a more frequent occurrence at this time.

Despite this, Gresley continued to keep in close touch with the way his engines were performing. Since mid-1937, his team had been carefully monitoring the performance of a number of A4s to see if they were performing at peak efficiency. They did this by collecting and analysing the output of the Flaman recorders after each run, then adding reports produced by the footplate crew, inspectors and shed staff. Occasionally an opportunity arose to attach a dynamometer car to a train, and this created a wealth of additional information to aid analysis. But according to Spencer:

> As the months passed and the A4s continued to perform outstandingly, unofficial reports were reaching us that the drivers were taking liberties and going very fast when the opportunity arose. Certainly the Flaman rolls often recorded speeds of 115 mph and over or appeared not to have been working on other trips south where high speeds were possible. With the German world record for speed of May 1936 by their Class 05 locomotive, still rankling, spurred on by what was happening in that country with Hitler, it little surprised us that an A4 might be given its head. This proved to be the case and happened shortly after a party of German engineers, led by Dorpmuller and Wagner in 1938, had visited Britain, the former having ridden with Gresley behind an A4 pulling the Coronation set a few days earlier. There was also Stanier's British speed record, with his 6220 *Coronation* on 1st June 1937, to consider.
>
> So permission was given for a run to take place on the coming Sunday (3rd July) knowing that the track would be clear of heavy traffic, apparently without consulting Wedgwood or the powers that be. Gresley also approved the use of 4468, part of the Coronation set and a dynamometer car. By this stage this A4 was four months old, well run in, and described by the footplate crew as being a 'good un'.

By July 1938 A4 No. 4468 *Mallard* had been in traffic for only four months but would have been well run-in and proven in service by then. Performance wise, she would have been helped by having a Kylchap double blastpipe and chimney fitted. This made her a good choice for the special run on 3 July. Spencer has written on the back of this print, '*Mallard* getting into her stride'. (BS)

The CME made it clear to Douglas Edge, Norman Newsome and myself, that he expected to see the engine let go if the conditions were suitable, but gave no other instructions. However, his intentions were clear to all three of us and Edge then briefed Bernard Adkinson, Assistant Motive Power Superintendent at King's Cross, Inspector Jenkins, Driver Duddington and Fireman Bray. The CME instructed me to remain at King's Cross and oversee the collection of data when the train returned to London and report the results to him.

Eric Bannister who travelled in Spencer's place, later recalled the build up to this event:

'By this time, the test runs for the quick acting brake valves [being overseen by representatives of Westinghouse] were almost finished and HNG told Norman Newsome that he could 'have a go'. In great secrecy a speed run was arranged in conjunction with one of the Sunday brake tests.

On 3rd July, I was present on the train when the Doncaster A4 No. 4468 *Mallard* headed out of King's Cross with the Coronation set of coaches [in fact only three of the twin articulated carriages] and the LNER dynamometer car.

The Westinghouse people were surprised to see the dynamometer car added to the articulated Coronation coaches as this would mean that the day's run would not be comparable with previous tests. However, we proceeded to Barkston, where we turned on the triangle. Douglas Edge, the senior LNER representative, told the Westinghouse team what was proposed and offered them a taxi if they did not wish to return with us. They declined!

While this was happening, Gresley was travelling north to Scotland for the launch of the new Flying Scotsman service on the 4th, staying with his son Roger at the North British Hotel above Waverley Station overnight. He must have been sorely tempted to join his team with *Mallard*, but his visit to Scotland was undoubtedly pre-arranged. In any case, remaining in London may have drawn too much attention to what was happening and perhaps a restraining hand might have been applied by the General Manager.

If so, news of the run was kept so secret that the Civil Engineering Department were not even informed, which was something of an oversight. There was some planned maintenance underway in the Grantham area that weekend, so a speed restriction was in place at this crucial point just when the train needed to pick up speed quickly if it were to stand any chance of a record. If, as has been suggested, Gresley wanted his engine to reach 130 mph or more, this probably made that impossible.

The 3rd began quietly with the engine collecting her carriages, dynamometer car, plus her passengers before *Mallard* set out from Wood Green waterworks sidings and headed towards Barkston for turning. During a brief pause before launching the train southwards, the crew built up the fire. At the same time, Sam Jenkins and Eric Bannister crawled underneath the engine where they proceeded to cover the middle big-end with superheater oil 'as a precaution against possible overheating' and then inspected the rest of the engine. With these checks complete, they were given the signal to proceed and pulled away from Barkston South Junction at 1615hrs. As they did so, the driver turned his cap back to front in true racing style, eliciting the comment from Bannister that 'he was that sort'.

As the engine got into her stride, it was hit by the 'unexpected' permanent way check as it approached Grantham and slowed to 24 mph. But after this brief pause the engine quickly picked up speed and breasted Stoke summit at 74½ mph, then with gravity in its favour the driver gave the engine its head and, as he famously recalled when interviewed by the BBC six years later:

Spencer has written on the back of these prints 'various photos taken on the 3rd as the engine is readied for her record breaking run. Neither I or the CME could attend'. To which he might well have added the word 'sadly'. (BS)

She just jumped to it like a living thing. After three miles the speedometer in my cab showed 107 mph, 108, 109, 110 and before I knew it the needle was at 116 mph and we'd got the record. They told me afterwards that there was a great deal of excitement in the dynamometer car. 'Go on old girl' I thought,' she can do better than this', so I nursed her through Little Bytham at 123 and in the next 1¼ miles the needle crept up further, 123½, 124, 125 and then for a quarter of a mile, while they told me the folks in the car held their breath – 126 mph.'

Despite Bannister and Jenkins's best endeavours in adding superheater oil to the middle big end, the smell emanating from a crushed stink bomb inserted in its hollow crankpin, as a warning measure, spoke of overheating. This odour was soon picked up by those leaning out of vestibule windows behind the dynamometer car and Adkinson signalled to Jenkins on the footplate to 'steady up', fearing the big end might fail completely.

Mallard again on the 3rd, the dynamometer car soon to record a new record for steam. (BS)

Duddington allowed the train to decelerate and coast through Tallington. While this happened Douglas Edge considered what to do next. The severity of any damage to the engine could not be assessed whilst *Mallard* was moving and the poor PR value of a failed engine, no matter how fast she had run, had to be taken into account. In the event, caution guided his actions and at Peterborough the engine was disconnected from the train and 'went to the slip points and on to New England Shed'. Meanwhile, a standby engine had been requested and an old GNR Atlantic was soon coupled up for the final part of the journey to King's Cross. Bannister recalled:

> On arrival, as the youngest and most agile member of the team, I dropped off the train, ran over the central bridge to my office [to brief Spencer, who was waiting there] where I had a number of photographs of the A4 and returned to the platform. Meanwhile, Mr Edge had invited the Press into the dynamometer car to look at the record charts. They did not realise that this was done to divert their attention from the Atlantic, which was taken to the slip road to Top Shed while they were occupied. The plan worked.

Spencer, who must have been awaiting the train's arrival with great interest and, perhaps, some excitement, then took steps to gather all the relevant information and a prepare a more detailed report for the CME to consider:

> Bannister came rushing into my office with the good news, before dashing off with photographs and other souvenirs for the waiting journalists. Shortly afterwards he returned, with Douglas Edge holding the rolls and charts from the dynamometer car. Once I was certain that the record had been broken I telephoned the CME at the North British Hotel and gave him the good news. Douglas Edge had called him earlier while at Peterborough, but the Chief wanted confirmation that the records had been verified. He was returning on the Flying Scotsman the next day and asked that traced copies, with Silver Jubilee's record run included for comparison, be ready for him to examine.

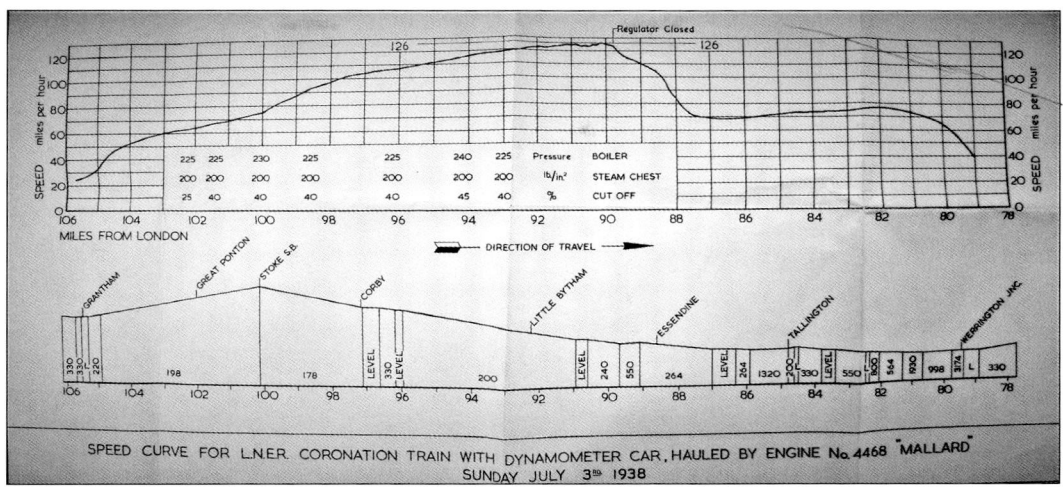

Spencer's personal copy of a chart tracking *Mallard's* record run on 3 July. This was found tucked inside a number of old newspapers covered with reports of the day's events. (*BS*)

No. 4468 remained at New England where examination showed that any damage caused by this fast run was thought to be minimal, though I was told that the white metal in the bearing had been renewed, perhaps as a precautionary measure. The engine moved to Doncaster under her own steam on the 5th where Bernard Adkinson later examined her. He inspected the engine very closely, accompanied by Edward Thompson, who had just replaced Robert Thom as Mechanical Engineer. On the 6th he reported personally to Gresley and confirmed that the damage to the axle and bearing were no worse than would occur with any other hot-box. Nevertheless, and to be on the safe side, the CME ordered that the axle be replaced, although Adkinson thought this unnecessary.

Successes such as this have to be savoured and remembered, but while Gresley and his team celebrated, events in Europe were deteriorating rapidly. The Munich agreement was signed only two months later, but the eurphoria that accompanied this historic event soon turned to dismay. Within months it was realised that Hitler had no intention of keeping his side of the bargain and in September 1939 Britain would again be at war. Spencer recorded:

It was clear to many, including Gresley, that war was inevitable from late 1937. It was just a matter of time before the Nazi domination of Germany spread outwards. And so it proved to be, but befor it happened my wife and I enjoyed a final holiday to Scotland in 1939, travelling up from Euston on the Royal Scot behind a Stanier Coronation Pacific. We returned via-Edinburgh and a brief stay in Doncaster to see my family, a week later, by which time gas masks had been distributed and Anderson Shelters were being supplied and the evacuation of children was well underway. These brought home the seriousness of the situation we faced and increased talk of bombing and invasion.

It was generally thought that London would quickly fall victim to the Luftwaffe, as had happened during the Spanish Civil War, with vast areas laid waste and casualties running into 100s of thousands. My wife was very concerned about this and we considered, as many did, how best to reduce the risk bombing presented to us. With my job remaining at King's Cross there was no other option but to stay where we were for the time being.

Inevitably Spencer showed great interest in the A4s principal rival in Britain – the Stanier/Coleman Coronations and rode behind them on a number of occasions, including a holiday to Scotland in 1939. His archives contain many pictures of these engines of which this is just one example (date, location and engine number not recorded). He later wrote that 'it would have been interesting to let one of these beasts loose on Stoke Bank and see what it could really do. The West Coast mainline was not conducive to very high bursts of speed'. (BS)

All anyone could do at this time was wait and see what might happen and react accordingly. While this happened, life went on much as usual at King's Cross, with Gresley's idea for a new 2-6-2 reaching fruition; a 'swan song' project that followed on from the V2 programme, then well into its stride with five more years to run. Once again Spencer described the background of the V4's development in his 1947 presentation, using it to conclude his impressive review of his leader's many achievements:

> The three-cylinder 2-6-2 type V4 class engines were destined to to be the last of the many classes built to Gresley's design. Prior to the construction of these engines it had been the policy on the LNER to relegate to secondary main line trains and branch lines engines which had been supplanted by the large new express and mixed traffic engines. It was felt that considerable economies could be realised by the introduction of a modern engine of medium power for such services and the preparation of a design for a light 2-6-2 type engine incorporating the outstanding features of Gresley successful express and mixed traffic engines was taken in hand during the early part of 1939. The first engine, N0. 3401 *Bantam Cock*, was completed at Doncaster works in February 1941.
>
> In order to conform to the limitations imposed on secondary lines by the Engineer, various methods were adopted to reduce weight, such as the use of a 2 per cent, nickel steel for the boiler barrel and the extensive substitution of fabricated construction in place of steel castings. The boiler, which carries a working pressure of 250lb per sq inch, follows the same design as those fitted to the Pacifics and V2 class engines but is of smaller proportions, the maximum diameter of the barrel being 5ft 4in, tapering to 4ft 8in at the parallel front end course. The three 15 in x 26 in cylinders have 7 in piston valves and drive on the second pair of 5ft 8in diameter coupled wheels.
>
> The second V4 class engine, No. 3402, completed at Doncaster in March 1941, differed from the first in having an all-steel welded firebox with a single Nicholson thermic syphon, but this was replaced by a copper firebox in 1945.

To Greater Glory 193

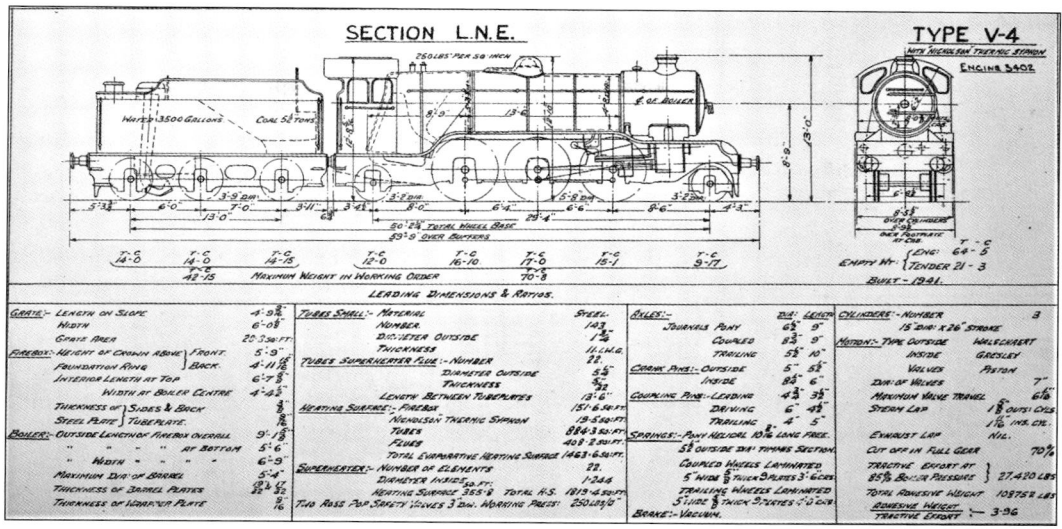

Gresley and Spencer's final design – the 2-6-2 V4 of which only two were built before the programme was cancelled. In describing these engines, Spencer showed a strong proprietary interest in the design and bemoaned the fact that it did not achieve wider acceptance with many more being built. The first of the two built, No. 3401 *Bantam Cock*, is displayed here in diagram form, under construction at Doncaster and when entering service early in 1941. (THG)

The V4 class with their maximum axle loading of 17 tons have a high route availability. Out of a total LNER route mileage of 6,114 miles these engines are permitted to run over no less than 5,000 miles as compared with the 2,752 miles of the Pacifics and V2 class engines. These engines proved themselves capable of handling widely varying types of traffic. During its early trials No. 3401 successfully timed a 495 ton Leeds to King's Cross express on a test between Leeds and Doncaster, and on later tests in the Scottish Area the same engine was found to be capable of hauling freight trains equivalent to those worked by the J38 class two-cylinder engines which have a greater tractive effort.'

Throughout his presentation, Spencer simply described Gresley's work in a balanced and reasoned way, offering evidence to back up his precis and avoiding controversy as far as possible. Even when answering questions, some of which were critical, he maintained an even handed approach. However, it is interesting to note that in describing the V4 programme, a certain edginess is evident. It is as though the project had faced criticism or been condemned as unnecessary by some and he felt there was a need to validate the work more fully in a public way.

There seems to be a genuine pride in the performance of the two V4s built before the programme was cancelled after Gresley's death. Does this suggest a strong proprietary interest in them because he played a leading role in their development? With the CME's health in sharp decline during 1940, this may well be so, in which case a sense of disappointment in the outcome is understandable. Nevertheless, it had been an interesting experiment which, if nothing else, acted as a distraction as war took hold and defeat followed defeat until Britain stood alone, facing invasion and subjugation. Spencer captured a sense of the time when he wrote:

> The undeniable feeling was one of gloom. Everyone hoped that the 'war to end all wars' had been just that. There was certainly no immediate rush to join up as there had been in 1914 and conscription soon began. Most had fathers and relatives who had served with many dying or suffering appalling injuries, so were reticent about committing themselves too soon. Though once Hitler invaded the low countries and invasion seemed likely this quickly changed.
>
> Confusion reigned at King's Cross for a time. Very quickly instructions were issued to mothball the Silver Jubilee, Coronation and West Riding sets. It was believed that there was no place for their glamour in such austere times. There was even talk of withdrawing the A4s for the same reason and for a short while this came about for a number of them. But the Chief's reaction was a simple and practical one. He made it clear that the Pacifics were just locomotives and were capable of pulling huge loads of any type. His arguments prevailed and the threat of mothballing soon passed. It was to his credit that throughout the war A4s did sterling service with minimal maintenance and attention.

The war comes to Barnet. Although not bombed as heavily as Central London or the docks, this outer suburban area came under attack from the Luftwaffe and was badly damaged in parts, such as seen here in this view of Bells Hill. Spencer's home in Longmore Avenue came close to destruction on several occasions, greatly increasing concern for his wife's safety. (THG)

The CME's health continued to decline during this period and he spent most of his time at Watton where we continued to visit him almost on a daily basis. All new schemes [except the V4 which ran on until both engines were in service by March 1941 and conceptual work on such things as 4-8-2 and 4-8-4 designs] had been shelved and the main effort was directed towards keeping locomotives and rolling stock running.

Meanwhile there was the evacuation of Dunkirk, then the Battle of Britain followed by the Blitz to contend with. We quickly grew accustomed to seeing the enemy overhead and living a dangerous and troubling existence wondering when invasion would come or our loved ones be killed by bombs. Even Barnet was not spared and during 1940 sticks of bombs fell either end of the road in which we lived causing much damage, plus many deaths and injuries. All we could do was carry on and for a time my wife moved away from London to stay with relatives in the country.

During these difficult months Gresley's influence grew less with each passing month. As this happened the main centre of activity shifted from King's Cross to Doncaster or the LNER's new Headquarters near Welwyn [in Lord Hamden's country house which had been taken over for 'the duration']. The CME had not chosen another deputy following the departure of Arthur Stamer, but, nominally, Edward Thompson began to fill in for Gresley in a quiet, unassuming way, presumably with the General Managers agreement. By late 1940 I had begun to report to him on locomotive matters and he agreed that I should go on supporting the ailing Gresley for the time being in whatever way I could.

Unfortunately, this involved attendance at the scene of another rail crash, this time between Harold Wood and Brentwood in Essex on 10 February 1941. With so much death and destruction going on all around him, it was a sharp reminder, if one were needed, that accidents could still just happen, often with devastating consequences. The Ministry of War Transport report, written by Major Wilson, captured the salient details:

The 10 am express service from Liverpool Street to Norwich (thirteen carriages pulled by B17 4-6-0 No. 2828 *Harewood House*) came to a stand on the down through line some two miles beyond Harold Wood Station, owing to shortage of steam when ascending Brentwood Bank. It had been standing for about eight minutes when it was run into from the rear by the 10.6 am stopping train [ten non-corridor carriages pulled by B12 4-6-0 No. 8556] from Liverpool Street to Southend, which had passed the proceeding automatic colour-light signal at danger.

The collision, (at 10.46 am) which occurred at about 30 mph was violent and I regret to report that that five passengers were killed outright and two company servants died from their injuries later. In addition, 17 passengers and the two enginemen on the Southend train were taken to hospital with serious injuries.

In his report to Thompson, Spencer avoided any detailed description of the scene, though arriving two to three hours after it had happened meant that he would have witnessed many disturbing sights and sounds. Perhaps to disguise his own feelings, he concentrated on practical issues and simply described the state of the engines involved, reaching the conclusion that driver error was the primary cause, a summary with which the crash inspectors agreed. Later on, he wrote an additional note:

Although both locomotives were in good working order it was noticeable that after nearly seventeen months of war how far their overall condition had deteriorated. By this stage many experienced men had joined the forces – conscripted or volunteered – and many tasks that were standard practice in 1939 were no longer undertaken. I concluded, from this accident, and more general observations of locomotives on shed, that things would only get worse and

The crash scene near Brentwood on 10 February 1941 as witnessed by Spencer, who attended on behalf of the CME to inspect the damage to the engines and rolling stock concerned. In this case, though, the driver of a D49 Class locomotive, No. 8556, (shown above) was deemed to be at fault for not keeping a proper look out which resulted in the collision. (BS)

accidents become more frequent. I also reached the conclusion that accidents such as this might well be avoided if some type of Automatic Train Control could be installed. I discussed this with Major Wilson who did not agree, but included the point I made in his report.

I personally briefed Thompson on the issues raised by the accident and he agreed with my conclusions. He asked me to write down my thoughts on how we might arrest the deterioration, which I did.

With his health now rapidly deteriorating it would have come as no surprise when on 5 April 1941, as Britain suffered the worst of the Blitz, years of bronchial and heart problems finally claimed Gresley's life and he died at home in Watton. He was buried near his birthplace in Netherseal, beside his wife and parents. A memorial service followed on the 9th, in London at Chelsea Old Church, which Spencer attended. Sometime later, after years of considering the impact his greatly admired leader had made, he wrote a very personal obituary:

I admired Sir Nigel tremendously and never found him inconsiderate or too busy to listen and discuss my ideas. He had the ability to think broadly and absorb a great deal of information before reaching conclusions. He sought the advice of those he respected and would always consider other possibilities, modifying his own plans accordingly if the arguments put forward held value. But once a decision was made he pursued a course of action with great determination, taking stock and reviewing progress all the time.

When a job was complete he insisted on a programme of testing to make sure the locomotive was as good as it could be and used whatever information he collected to modify the design. It was a constant frustration to him that the authorities were so tardy in building a test centre where better solutions might have been developed. He believed that Churchward achieved greater success because the GWR invested in such a facility and the LNER struggled to match their achievements because we had none.

He inspired confidence and led us all with a sure touch, often in very difficult circumstances. He was a great man and it was a privilege to work for him. At the end of my presentation in 1947 I summarised all his new locomotive designs for the GNR and LNER in a single table. Although not everything he did was included, I felt that this would speak for itself in describing his greatest achievements. I don't think there was another designer except, perhaps, Churchward, who accomplished so much.

To Greater Glory 197

I was lucky enough to see the CME's ideas on electrification finally come to fruition after the war and see his influence continue to spread. Whilst his steam locomotives clearly pleased him I have no doubt that he would have been proud to have witnessed the Shenfield line open and the electric locomotives he planned come in to service and move Britain's railways into the future.

Aware that many of Gresley's ideas faced much criticism within the railway industry, particularly his use of three-cylinders and streamlining, Spencer provided his own riposte:

They did their jobs very well and proved economical and effective in practice. Three cylinders had many advantages over two (greater hauling power and an increase in mean tractive effort) and these outweighed the complication introduced … Streamlining was seen by many as a meaningless fashion and condemned it for that reason. Yet it was a science still in its infancy, with future applications then barely glimpsed. Gresley saw its potential, as he did many things, and began the process of experimentation with the A4s proving its worth.

To the end, he continued to be Gresley's willing disciple, but he also remained his own man undaunted by seniority or status, ever prepared to question established views or prevailing opinions with great diplomacy. And, as the world moved on, he would continue to test theories and where necessary seek better solutions in circumstances that would test his stamina and skills to the limit.

For a reason which is not recorded, Spencer chose to place these two pictures side by side in an album which ends in April 1941, shortly after Gresley's death. It may simply have been a comparison between the P2s as built (No. 2001 on the left) and in streamlined form (No. 2003) in an easily recognisable and impressive location. Or was it a case of a memorial to Gresley's work? We shall never know so conjecture will have to suffice. (BS)

Chapter 6

Aftermath

In the weeks following Gresley's death, Spencer must have wondered what the future held. After sixteen years working at King's Cross for such a dynamic man and reaching a position of absolute trust and authority along the way, he might have been forgiven for experiencing pangs of concern over the future, exacerbated by the way the war was going. All he held dear was under attack or simply disappearing, and the future held few certainties and the past only fading glories. At only 43, the best life could offer appeared to be in the past, a feeling not helped by the announcement that Thompson would succeed Gresley and be based, for most of the time, at Doncaster. Later accounts suggest that some viewed this promotion with concern, but this would be unfair to Thompson, whose reputation as a good manager, with well-honed skills, was widely recognised. True, he probably did not have Gresley's design skills or ease of working with people from all backgrounds but he was a very experienced and successful production engineer and workshop manager and in wartime there was a huge demand for these talents when speed and quality of output trumped most other considerations. He was also an ex-Army officer who had seen extensive service in the Great War on the Western Front in a senior rank. As a result, he understood the military mind and how best to meet operational needs as a difficult and bloody war of attrition unfolded.

Spencer appears to have appreciated this:

Gresley and Thompson were both very talented men but in different ways. Gresley was essentially a scientist who was engaged by the process of discovery and found the day to day administration of a big organisation frustrating and, it has to be said, an aggravation at times. So he relied heavily on those who had production skills, such as Thom, Stamer,

Britain, and the LNER, at war captured in this photo taken during the conflict for public consumption. V2 No. 4826 was built at Darlington and entered service five months before Britain declared war on Germany in 1939. She began life as a King's Cross engine and moved to New England shed in July 1940, remaining there until 1953. (BS)

Thompson and Peppercorn, to make the workshops operate effectively. He gave them their head in all matters except design which he guarded jealously, rarely trusting anyone except his small team at King's Cross or the Chief Locomotive Draughtsman to assist him or even take the lead. Thompson, in particular, found this limitation quite irksome and sought closer involvement in design tasks. But here he and Gresley had one profound difference. The deputy did not have the same belief in three-cylinders as the Chief, and saw the benefit of adopting other solutions. It was a point of difference that they could not resolve except in Gresley's favour. In May 1941 it remained to be seen how Thompson would take forward his ideas and deal with Gresley's legacy.

Once appointed, Thompson wasted little time in reorganising his department and preparing it for what lay ahead. In truth he had already done much at Doncaster to put it on a war footing and now spread his ideas wider as the true extent of the challenge they all faced became clear. Within a few weeks of his succession to the CME post, the German Army were marching on the Soviet Union and the risk of invasion diminished considerably. Relieved of this stifling pressure, planning for the future could begin in earnest, as could the build-up of Britain's military strength, initially to fight the U boat menace in the Atlantic, then initiate a serious bombing campaign against Germany and, finally, begin pushing Hitler's forces back on land. Achieving this meant placing a heavy reliance on Britain's railway industry – their staff, workshops, locomotives and rolling stock. Thompson had taken on a daunting task and needed good men and women around him if he were to succeed.

Appointments came thick and fast, as Thompson marshalled his resources, his decisions backed by Chairman and General Manager. In due course, and to announce the changes being made, the new CME issued a statement in which he set out his intentions, but, at the same time, paid due respect to his predecessor and all he had achieved:

It will be appreciated that something like a revolution has been made in the methods of conducting work of the department, but there is every reason to think that the departures from the old-established practice will put fresh vigour into the establishment which Sir Nigel Gresley has built up since 1923. He left a great example to his successor and the object of all the arrangements described above is to revitalise the mechanical engineering branch of our railway work and keep the LNER in the forefront as an exponent of modern development, calculated to secure economy and efficiency.

At the same time that Thompson was writing this brief introduction, the Chairman issued his own statement in support of the new CME, in which he outlined the extent of his authority:

There is a general feeling of satisfaction that the directors have chosen for this very important post one who has been associated with the activities of the CME's Department since amalgamation, and who is fitted by training and ability to carry out the tradition of progress created by his predecessor, having had, at one time or another, charge of the company's locomotive, carriage and wagon works in England.

His new responsibilities, covering as they do locomotive, carriage and wagon work, road motor engineering and docks machinery, together with the Chief Chemist's Department, come at a time of considerable difficulty, but he is assured of the loyal support and co-operation of the staff under him who wish him good health so that his energies may be unimpaired by the strenuous task he has been called upon to undertake.

The only change not mentioned in this briefing note concerned the future of Henry Richards and his team. Perhaps aware that electrification projects were unlikely to progress very far while the war lasted, and ever mindful of the huge number of important tasks already facing Thompson, the General Manager set them up as a separate entity. To help them evolve their plans for the future, a small team of draughtsmen were assigned to them, with Tom Street in charge. Even allowing for this sideways move, more than enough remained for the CME to oversee. A little later he issued a note describing the structure of his new senior management team:

Above and opposite above: Although the attacks on Britain during 1940 and '41 were deeply worrying, Spencer seems to have shown considerable interest in the aftermath of the many raids. Where the railways were involved, there would have been some professional curiosity – as there was in investigating accidents. But his interest spread much wider than this and encompassed the effects on society of the bombing and the number of photographs and press cuttings contained in his archive bear witness to this. The photos above are a few of these, four have a railway theme, all of them appearing to be LNER based. The montage of St Paul's Cathedral captures the sheer devastation wrought on London during the Blitz. (BS)

In future there will be five Mechanical Engineers. In addition to Mr Peppercorn at Doncaster, who will also supervise the 'outdoor' carriage and wagon work on the Great Northern Section and the Great Central Section between Sheffield and Marylebone, there will be an ME to supervise Gorton locomotive works, who will report directly to the CME. Mr T Heywood will continue to be styled ME (Scotland). Mr F.W. Carr remains in charge at Stratford. Mr R.A. Smeddle becomes ME Darlington (on promotion from Locomotive Works Manager at Darlington), to replace Mr Peppercorn. Mr J.F. Harrison has been appointed to the new post of ME at Gorton.

Mr Harper will remain in charge of the HQ Office with the title of Assistant to the CME (Clerical). Mr Windle will be in charge of both locomotive and carriage/wagon drawing offices. Mr F Day will continue as Head Carriage Draughtsman and Mr D.D. Gray has been appointed Head Locomotive Draughtsman.

In addition to this, Peppercorn was appointed Deputy CME, thus not repeating the mistake made by Gresley when deciding not to select one after Stamer retired in 1933. At the same time, he also decided to set up a small headquarters team to support him at Doncaster; a move

The partnership that succeeded Gresley in 1941 and guided Spencer's career for the next eight years. (Left) Edward Thompson, who some came to see as a poor engineer intent on destroying Gresley's legacy and others as a principled and very effective leader of the CME's Department in war and peace. (Right) Arthur Peppercorn, his deputy, as well as being Mechanical Engineer at Doncaster, was a production engineer of great skill and, like Thompson, a man of principle. Together they made an outstanding partnership, though neither probably had Gresley's design skills, relying on Edward Windle, the Chief Draughtsman to take the lead in this field, and, later on, Bert Spencer. (THG)

(Left) Edward Windle as he appeared in the years following the war. He was the LNER's Chief Draughtsman from 1941 until the formation of British Railways in 1948 when he went on to play a central role in designing BR's standard class engines. His influence on locomotive design within the LNER has always been understated and yet he was a key player in many Gresley engines, including the A4s, P2s and much else beside. He then led in producing the Thompson Pacifics, including the P2 conversion and the rebuilding of Gresley's first A1, plus the CME's many 'standard' designs including the B1s. Finally, he oversaw the design of the Peppercorn Pacifics before moving on to BR. (Right) Cyril Elwell who fulfilled the role of Mechanical Engineer with special responsibility for the supervision of workshop tasks. It was to this group that Spencer was posted in May 1941 by Thompson and this allowed him to develop a productive working relationship with the highly regarded Elwell. (BS)

probably encouraged by a devastating attack made by the Luftwaffe on London during the night of 10/11 May in which very serious damage was done to King's Cross and the CME's offices there. In selecting this team, he decided to keep Douglas Edge as his principal assistant for the time being, though being a carriage and rolling stock expert meant that his contribution to the locomotive side of business would be slight. In addition, James Blair was chosen to replace Norman Newsome who preferred to stay in London. Meanwhile, the draughtsmen at King's Cross were adsorbed by Windle's team. However, one name was missing from Thompson's list – Bert Spencer. In some quarters this omission has been translated as an act of pettiness at best or vindictiveness at worst – Spencer having been 'Gresley's man' and being damned by association, or so the story goes. The truth, as is often the case, lay elsewhere as Spencer himself recorded in a letter written in 1962:

> Just after Sir Nigel died Mr Thompson sought me out and thanked me very courteously for all my hard work. He wanted to discuss my future and told me that he would be based at Doncaster so wouldn't need an assistant in London. He suggested that I could be posted to Stratford as assistant to the Mechanical Engineer instead. Being concerned about my wife's safety [and his mother, who still lived in Doncaster and was becoming increasingly frail] I didn't wish to remain in London and he proposed that I move to Doncaster or Darlington instead.

He went on to explain that he would have less need for personal technical assistants and because of the pressing need for rolling stock and wartime production he preferred men with this background. He added that the Chief General Manager was of the opinion that there would be little scope for new locomotives whilst the war lasted so my current task would lapse for the duration.

After some consideration, having listened courteously to my views, he suggested that I could be employed in another role in his Headquarters assisting the new Mechanical Engineer there. This suited my wife and I, especially as we both came from the North-East of England.

I was initially employed in planning workshop tasks across the LNER with Cyril Elwell ensuring that all ran smoothly. I was also given responsibility for co-ordinating all 'Government Work in support of the war', which was quite a wide brief, but meant producing monthly reports for Ministry of the Transport departments. However, Mr Thompson suggested that I maintain Sir Nigel's papers and continue working on the ideas he had pursued regarding steam locomotives, but with an emphasis on alternative cylinder arrangements. Later on, I was called to the CME's office and it was agreed that I would work full time on standardisation proposals. Over the next four years I did much personal work for the CME and sat near him in his office at Doncaster. However, the link with Elwell's team continued into 1943.

Spencer was a pragmatist at heart who always did the job to which he was assigned effectively and conscientiously. Such a man is worth his weight in gold and Thompson would have been aware of this and his reasons for directing Spencer towards production engineering at this difficult time are logical. In this case, the new post had the added bonus of being in Doncaster and this allowed him to move Elsie away from London, then still under severe attack. This they quickly accomplished and moved into an LNER property in Thorne Road (No. 157) in June, their house in Barnet being rented out to tenants; sales in time of war being near impossible with the future so uncertain.

In recalling these difficult few weeks, when the organisation underwent such profound change, Norman Newsome recorded that:

'Shortly after Sir Nigel's death most of his staff were transferred to Doncaster. After many years in London I was loath to leave, Bert Spencer less so.

To accommodate our family's needs Thompson interviewed us and offered both of us posts at Stratford. After a few days Bert declined the offer and transferred to Doncaster, but I went there (Stratford) as Assistant Works Manager of the Carriage and Wagon Works. I must say that Thompson was quite decent with me, not though with some people – I can't complain at my treatment. Thompson was a very good engineer, but he had a reputation for upsetting a lot of people.

So, for Spencer and Newsome the arrival of the new CME brought unavoidable change, but it seems to have been managed by Thompson with balance and equanimity. In doing so, he took their personal circumstances and professional needs into consideration and did as much as he could for them. This was hardly the response of a petty-minded man intent on eradicating his predecessor's legacy, but the actions of a serious-minded leader determined to make his organisation work in unbearably difficult circumstances. In truth, he was simply balancing the resources available to him so that he could meet many pressing demands. Within the restrictions imposed on him, he was able to take personal wishes and needs into consideration and ensure no one was disadvantaged by the changes forced on him by such challenging circumstances. If he was Gresley's nemesis, as many came to believe, he seems to have demolished his legacy in a very

(Left) The Spencer's new home in Thorne Road, Doncaster from June 1941. By comparison with London, Doncaster was only lightly bombed during the war and became something of a safe haven for Bert and his wife. But no one could rest easy for long. With its substantial railway workshops, the town was an obvious target for the enemy and so there were occasional raids. (Right) One of the worst occurred just before the Spencer's arrived on 9 May 1941 in Balby when sixteen people were killed and another seventy-three injured. (BS)

strange way – by keeping his predecessor's senior team virtually intact. Only time would tell how he would deal with Gresley's engineering inheritance, but with war raging there was little time for him to do more than simply keep locomotives and rolling stock moving.

If Spencer thought by moving to Doncaster he and his wife might escape the worst of the bombing, the Lutwaffe provided a timely reminder that nowhere was really safe. On 9 May, as midnight approached, Doncaster suffered its worst bombing of the war. In the attack that followed, considered light by comparison with raids further south, sixteen people were killed and another seventy-three injured. Amongst the areas of the town worst hit was Balby, where a single

Having been transferred to Doncaster by Thompson to help manage production targets in the workshops, Spencer and his new boss, Cyril Elwell, were faced with many insuperable problems as the war increased demand and staff left to join the forces. One difficulty that proved most difficult to overcome was created by the destruction of the Carriage Works and other shops on 20 December 1940 by fire. Enemy action or arson were suspected, but the most likely cause was human error. Either way, the result was lack of capacity for building and maintaining rolling stock, which Spencer recorded as 'throwing an added burden on Darlington, Stratford and York at a time when they could least afford to take on this extra load'. Spencer who, seems to have been visiting Doncaster when the fire developed, kept these two press photos of the incident. With the pressures of war, a new works would not be completed until 1949. (BS)

land mine destroyed thirteen houses and damaged another four hundred. Luckily the destruction was not more widespread, but the events of the night would have raised concerns that more raids, of ever-increasing intensity, might lie ahead, especially with the railway works providing such a tempting target. Nevertheless, for the Spencers this seems to have been a risk worth taking, with the added benefit that many members of his family were close by.

After so many years cloistered with Gresley at King's Cross, it must have been strange to be out of the limelight at Doncaster. Admittedly, he sat with Elwell and the planning and production team close to the new CME and had daily contact with him, but this could hardly compare to the central design role he had once enjoyed with Gresley. As things turned out, the change gave Spencer the sort of challenge he had not experienced since the early years of his career as a young apprentice and junior draughtsman. It also helped that Elwell was such an effective leader and from him he must have learnt a lot.

Before Thompson's arrival, Elwell had been the Locomotive Running Superintendent (Eastern Section). The two men were old friends as well as colleagues from their days together at Stratford. As a trusted ally, the CME wasted little time in appointing Elwell to the post of Mechanical Engineer (Outdoors) at Doncaster. Here his tasks included heading a new group which was set up to 'deal with the maintenance and repair of engines across the LNER'. To this task many others were soon added, including oversight of carriage and wagon production and progress chasing myriad war related tasks. In 1958, Spencer described the time he spent working for Elwell:

All the LNER's workshops had to work flat out to meet demand, at the same time as absorb and train many new staff as skilled men left to join the forces. Most of the replacements were women, who soon impressed us with their enthusiasm, hard work and desire to learn. But it still took time to train them to anywhere near the standard of those who had departed, many of whom never returned.

The main crisis did not occur until 1942 when lower maintenance standards and heavy workloads had taken their toll on locomotives and rolling stock and their overall condition had slipped badly. Also by this time the workshops had taken on many additional tasks not related to the railways, such as weapon production and repairs to damaged aeroplanes. All these tasks had to be co-ordinated and production rates monitored, with progress chasing a key part of the daily routine. All this had to be recorded and reported to the CME, who regularly faced grilling's by the General Manager and various wartime committees ever eager to increase production rates. Although our workload was extremely heavy and the hours very long we all felt that our contribution was important and greatly valued by Thompson, who often expressed satisfaction with our work.

All this time I kept hold of many of Gresley's papers on locomotive design, as encouraged to do so by Thompson, and during quiet moments would work on them at home. In some cases, this meant preparing files for the archives, but in others I considered such things as the proposed 4-8-2 and 4-8-4 designs and the next stage of the Pacifics and locomotives to aid the war. Every now and then, as time allowed the CME called me into his office and we sat around his neatly organised desk discussing these ideas. With the war still going badly these meetings struck an optimistic note and were clearly valued for that reason.

Other than these few words, Spencer did not describe his time with the production planning team in any greater depth, but one can easily imagine the pressures he and his colleagues faced each day as the war continued to dominate all their actions. For a man with such obvious design credentials, any frustration must have been outweighed by a sense that what they were doing was equally, if not more, important. Sadly, his partnership with Elwell came to an end very suddenly on 7 May 1943 when he died (one source suggests he was involved in an accident at work, another that he had a massive heart attack). Thompson felt so moved by this death that he wrote:

During the conflict the LNER's workshops gave up much of their capacity to armaments work and ended up producing aircraft parts, guns of all sizes and landing craft amongst other things. Much of this was captured by official photographers, as above, but most of these pictures were not released until after the war for security reasons. (BS)

Of practical work he was a master, of the theoretical side he was a Bachelor of Science [University of London 1911] … He came to my Department as Mechanical Engineer when the decision was taken to add the duties in connection with the Mechanical Supervision of the locomotives … He was invaluable.

We shall miss his very real knowledge and experience. We shall miss his charming personality, his gay humour. We have lost a grand colleague and a very dear friend.

To this Spencer simply added:

He became a staunch friend and ally. Nothing was too much bother for him and during my early months, as I learnt all aspects of production planning – both practical and political – he gave me his entire support. He was sorely missed.

His death came at a time when news from the various battlefronts was getting better. The enemy were being driven out of North Africa, more convoys than ever were getting through and the RAF and USAAF were carrying out huge bombing raids on Germany. There was a feeling that the war in Europe might soon be over in our favour and now was the time to begin thinking about the future.

By the time Elwell died the CME had begun to draw me back into the design world. He wanted me to work on several new ideas he had in mind, his standardisation plans, some locomotive testing and, finally, reviewing the performances of the three-cylinder engines with conjugated valve gear. A consensus had formed in the running department and

With fewer men to maintain or even clean locomotives and rolling stock their outward appearance and inner workings soon deteriorated. The once proud A4s looked particularly awful, as this photo of engine No. 4485 *Kestrel* demonstrates. However, as Spencer reported 'the A4's stood up well to the task, far better than any other types'. (BS)

workshops that they were not lasting well and were causing many unnecessary problems. By this stage [in early 1942] the CME had sought Stanier's advice on the issue and had an independent report conducted by Ernest Cox on the subject to consider. His report, which Stanier counter-signed reached some unpleasant conclusions.

These were easily dealt with by Cox himself, who wrote in his report that:

> The '2 to 1' valve gear although theoretically correct is, in practice, incapable of being made into a sound mechanical job, and rapid wear of the pins, and incorrect steam distribution, are the inevitable results of its use. In view of its inherent defects and the discontinuance of its use throughout the world, a good case can be made for not perpetuating it in any future design.
>
> It is certain that with this arrangement of valve gear it will be necessary to give the engines a frequent overhaul in the Shops and even then it is not possible to eliminate the effect of lost motion due to running clearance required in the pin joints and the effect of expansion of the outside valve spindle on the inside valve.
>
> It is a matter of consideration, therefore, as to whether certain of the classes should not be fitted with an independent inside valve gear.
>
> The excessive inside big end trouble experienced is, in my opinion, due mainly to the design of the big end. The alternative designs already developed by the LNER should alone bring about considerable improvements. The use of higher grade white metal and the elimination of the brass strip across the bearing are also, in my view, worthy of consideration in view of extensive experience with three-cylinder engines on the LMS.

And later on he added an even more sombre note which clearly spelt out the severity of the problem:

> It was an unassailable fact that unit play at each of the eight pin joints was multiplied by eleven by the time it reached the middle valve, and in fully rundown condition the lost motion could amount to 3/8th. This resulted in reduced power at low speeds due to insufficient port opening, while at high speeds the combined effect of overtravel of the valve, plus whip in the combining levers, could produce up to 50 per cent more power in the middle cylinder than in either of the outside. There was also a spate of hot inside big-ends, ten times as many in the inside position as at the outside, six times as many as the LM experienced with the inside big-ends on a comparable number of its own three-cylinder

The pressure of war could be lifted slightly by occasional special events. At Doncaster this included a visit by the King and Queen in 1941 just after Spencer had transferred back there from London. On this occasion, the visitors were escorted by Thompson (talking to the Queen), Peppercorn (between the King and Queen) and the company chairman, Sir Ronald Matthews. (BS)

engines. The high speed engines of the 4-6-2 class suffered the highest proportion of failures, the 2-6-2 and 2-8-2 types also being high. A certain lack of stiffness in the marine big-end arrangement also appeared to contribute to this result.

To this Spencer later added, 'these conclusions came as no surprise to our team, where day to day we had been dealing with problems developing with the Pacifics and the P2s in particular. All of this soon began to attract the ire of the Regional Managers to whom these engines were assigned'. So Thompson had to do something quickly about this ever-worsening situation or face severe criticism. In the short term the problem 'was dealt with by carrying more spares sets of valve gear at sheds and training the fitters in each place to undertake the work. If this had not happened each locomotive would have had to be returned to the main workshops for repair after each breakdown and so spend much longer out of service'. However, increased maintenance could only keep the problem in check for a time, at a cost the organisation could ill-afford with so much else to do. Something more was needed.

After much thought Spencer concluded that 'the best long term solution was to rebuild the worst offenders, which would be costly and absorb precious resources, and replace the 2 in 1 gear in the others with a third set of Walschaerts gear. It was an issue I frequently discussed with the CME who seemed to agree with my summary'.

This proved to be a long running debate that placed Thompson in a very difficult position and on which he needed some honest and skilled advice. As a result, it probably came as no surprise when Spencer was directed by the CME to undertake duties not dissimilar to those he had undertaken at King's Cross for Gresley. There were differences, of course, especially with Windle and his draughtsmen close by to provide direct support to the CME. So in his new post, Spencer did not exercise any control over the design process or act as Thompson's go between when ideas were being considered. In essence he became an advisor rather than an assistant, which in the circumstances may have suited him better.

And with that he moved to a desk immediately adjacent to Thompson's office, in mid-1943, to take on these new duties and begin to re-assert the influence that had once been his stock in trade. But it is probably true to say that Spencer never achieved the level of sway he had enjoyed pre-1941, no matter who was in charge. Nevertheless, his rare skills were again being recognised and, as the war allowed, he re-entered the world of locomotive design where his true calling undoubtedly lay. When Peppercorn succeeded Thompson in 1946, the new CME continued with this arrangement.

No engine, no matter how glamorous its pre-war role, came through the war in anything but a jaded condition. For the multi-purpose V2s this is hardly surprising. Here one of the class, No. 4836, appears to be shunting streamlined stock at Copley Hill sheds during the war. (BS)

So, did Thompson's actions have a negative effect on Spencer's career and could it be said, with any honesty, that the CME behaved maliciously towards him out of spite because he had been Gresley's close associate? All the available evidence says not. In fact, one could say that Thompson behaved with good grace towards Spencer from the beginning, treating him with great respect even when under the most tremendous pressure to get more important things done. When the London HQ had to be shut, he interviewed Spencer, explained what was happening, took his personal needs into consideration and reached a solution that best suited the younger man. Then when the opportunity arose, the CME moved him back into a post to act as his personal adviser. These are hardly the acts of a petty-minded man, but those of an effective and compassionate leader.

With a pressing need for extra freight engines the War Office and Ministry of Supply authorised the construction of a number of LMS 8Fs. These were spread around the workshops including Doncaster and Darlington. Tom Coleman, from Derby, oversaw this work and for a short time was seconded to the LNER. He duly collected many photos of this work of which this is one. (TC/ML)

In considering this issue there are two other points that might help cast some light on the subject. Firstly, in all the letters and documents he left, Spencer does not complain about his treatment or criticise Thompson in any way. In fact, be later wrote:

> He always had the good of the department at heart and could be ruthless in the execution of his duties when necessary. But there was another side to him which was considerate and accommodating. He appeared to think deeply about the future and introduced many changes to improve productivity and working conditions. These were aspects to which Sir Nigel and Bulleid gave little attention, preferring questions of locomotive design to the day to day tasks undertaken in the workshops. Thompson was a good forward-thinking manager and a good workshop manager. However, he was also an average, well intentioned engineer who relied upon Windle, in particular, for guidance when it came to locomotive design. The part played by Windle has been underestimated, as was his role in BR's standardisation plans.

Secondly, and this only came to light when IMechE records were consulted, there is evidence to suggest that Thompson actively encouraged Spencer in his professional endeavours. Early in his career, before joining Gresley at King's Cross, Spencer twice sought to become a member of the Institution, but failed to do so on both occasions. He did not apply again until 1944:

> The CME, who was a member, urged me to do so with the words 'with your background and skills it would be a waste not to, and membership will undoubtedly help you in your career'. He then became my proposer, [seconded by Peppercorn, with Bulleid and T Henry Turner as additional referees] provided a strong reference and urged the Institution to accept me, which they did making me an Associate Member in July.

Spencer then added a short but interesting note. 'Whilst with Gresley I did occasionally consider re-applying for membership, but he thought I would be better off with the Institution of Locomotive Engineers and so until Thompson encouraged me I followed Gresley's advice. Rightly or wrongly.'

We shall never know why Gresley advised Spencer in this way and speculation will take us in many directions not all of them helpful. Was it simply good advice to help avoid disappointment

Spencer took or kept many photos of locos during the war, presumably to record the great effort being made by the company and its staff. Most of these, including this picture of ex-Great Eastern, Holden designed, Gresley rebuilt Class B12 4-6-0 No. 7476, have survived without any details to show time or place. In this case the photo appears to have been taken in the latter part of the war by which time the LNER markings on the tender had been reduced to NE. (BS)

or was it some deeply held belief that Spencer was not quite good enough for the IMechE? And here there is one other issue to consider which might throw some light on the matter. Before joining the CME in London, Spencer, encouraged by William Elwess, submitted papers to the ILocoE and personally presented three of them to members. During his time as Gresley's assistant, no others appeared and one wonders why. Was it a case of insufficient time and more important duties taking up his time? Perhaps the truth is as Spencer suggests when he later wrote:

> The CME thought it important that he present papers to learned bodies to underpin the work he was doing and the advances being made. He was a theoretical man and inventor at heart and placed great store in such things, but being such a busy man he did not have the time to set his thoughts down on paper and required assistance in doing so. I found supporting him in these extra-curricular tasks fascinating and absorbing.

When reading these words, I was struck by the thought that Spencer was essentially a team player and had no ego to be flattered or assuaged. Doing a job well and advancing in carefully considered and practical steps was all that appeared to matter to him. By comparison, Gresley seems to have seen himself performing on a far bigger stage. Here, through persuasion and debate, he could advance ideas that he thought important, but would also enhance his reputation – both personal and professional. If so, it is hardly surprising that this partnership worked so well, but it only did so because Spencer was prepared to comply, play second fiddle and not seek the recognition he so richly deserved. Thompson, it seems, took a more balanced, less self-serving view and helped promote the career of his assistant. This is borne out by a letter he wrote to Spencer following his presentation in 1947 to the ILocoE, which Thompson appears to have attended as a guest:

> Well done on your masterly performance. Your thoughts and words did Gresley great credit. You must submit your paper to the Mechanics where it will reach a far bigger audience. Before I retired we spoke at length about our many years together, the ups and downs, the politics and the challenges. However, I did not thank you fully for all you did for me at Doncaster in such difficult circumstances and how valuable your advice on locomotive matters proved to be. I hope you go on to greater success, even though Nationalisation may significantly change how the industry operates. I hope we can continue to meet in London at Birdcage Walk to discuss old times.

Trying to untangle the nature of relationships so long after the event will always be difficult. There is a constant danger that too much or too little emphasis will be placed on certain issues, with the result that any conclusions reached might appear prejudiced. It is also a debate coloured by the fact that both Gresley and Thompson were strong, powerful and ambitious men who expected unquestioning obedience from their subordinates. They were products of the Victorian world where deference and compliance were expected and, although times were changing in the post-Great War world, throwing off the shackles of this conformity was proving difficult. So for Spencer, acceptance of his position in society was quite natural with any ambitions he might have had being subordinated to the will of an employer and the concept of service.

Did he wish for more? We shall never know but having been imbued with a strong work ethic and an obligation to serve, no matter what the consequences, meant that he laboured at Gresley and Thompson's pleasure. And so he left it to them to decide how he might contribute and hope for the best when plaudits were handed out. Gresley seems to have fulfilled this role with some circumspection. He certainly allowed Spencer leeway as an advisor, but then benefitted greatly from his outstanding and largely uncredited contribution. In so doing, he advanced his own cause without allowing his talented junior to do the same. Thompson also profited from Spencer's efforts but was more generous in boosting his assistant's professional standing and career when the opportunity arose. He seems to have done this without thought of the benefits that accrue for himself, happy that due credit would

For some reason, wartime dirt and grime looked slightly better on non-streamlined Pacifics than the A4s, though neither types could be said to be looking their best. Here A3 No. 2580 *Shotover*, now with its ACFI removed, is captured working hard late during the war. According to her maintenance records she seems to have spent less than 150 days undergoing general or light repairs during the conflict. This 1924 built, 1927 converted engine remained in service until 1962 and was cut up at Doncaster the following year. (BS)

go those who earnt it. For a man who gained an unenviable reputation as something of a martinet, in the years following his death, such understanding and generosity of spirit is quite surprising.

In many ways, Spencer's transfer from the production side of business to design was a godsend for Thompson, who was struggling to keep the locomotive fleet running and plan for a future beyond the war. By the time Spencer was in this new post, the CME had made some headway but sparked a controversy that still echoes today in the process. Under pressure to improve their performance, he ordered the P2s rebuilt as Pacifics. In an interview years later, Thompson explained his reasons for doing so:

> This conversion was instigated chiefly by troubles with the conjugated gear, although tyre wear and performance were also contributory factors. The availability of the engines for the 12 months prior to rebuilding had been more than 47 per cent and on one occasion, three of the six were under repair at Doncaster [engine Numbers 2003, 2005 and 2006 all between September and October 1941].

With problems appearing to increase, the CME recorded that he contemplated rebuilding one of them to Pacific configuration as a means of eradicating the problems, rather than tweak the existing design. But he also believed that this would 'extend their range of operations in Scotland by making the engines less wasteful of coal'. To test this theory, he submitted a scheme to the company's Locomotive Committee in late 1942, seeking permission to modify the engines. He later reported that his 'original proposal was at first opposed by Andrew McCosh, the Chairman, who eventually said "Well, rebuild one". A few months later, having received favourable reports from every driver he had spoken to, insisted on all six examples being rebuilt.'

Although not directly involved in this decision or the rebuilding work, Spencer believed the course of action taken was the correct one:

> Exacerbated by the war the P2s had simply become too much of a liability – costly to run and requiring too much workshop time. There was also increasing concerns over their safety with an ever growing number of crank axles fracturing in service; a problem Bulleid's

Pacifics also suffered from and which led to their rebuilding in the 1950s. Thompson had to take action and converting the 2-8-2s to Pacifics was a logical and timely step. It also allowed him, through Windle, to develop one part of the standardisation plan – a new three-cylinder Pacific with three independent sets of valve gear. Few at the time objected to this particularly at the sheds where men had to work and maintain them. By the time I became Thompson's assistant this project was well underway and was quickly followed by proposals for a number of other standard classes.

By 1942, standardisation had become a hot topic. This is a view highlighted by Charles Newton, who replaced Ralph Wedgwood as General Manager in 1939. On the cover of a post-war planning strategy paper on the subject he has written, 'Standardisation of locomotives and rolling stock is essential if we are to make this work …' He then sent a memo to Thompson urging him to 'press ahead with this work in all haste, but with due regard given to other priorities'. In the circumstances, it is not surprising that he turned to Spencer for help and with his arrival the level

(Above) 2001 *Cock of the North* before and after rebuilding. To some, the conversion of the P2s into Pacifics, led by the Regional Manager responsible for them and accomplished by Thompson and Windle, seemed a travesty. To others it resolved a long running problem in a practical way. Their new looks also caused controversy, but bearing mind that beauty is in the eye of the beholder this is an issue unlikely to be resolved. On the issue of rebuilding, Spencer believed the correct action had been taken; on the question of looks he remained silent. Either way, the rebuilt 2001 *Cock of the North* looked impressive in wartime black. (BS)

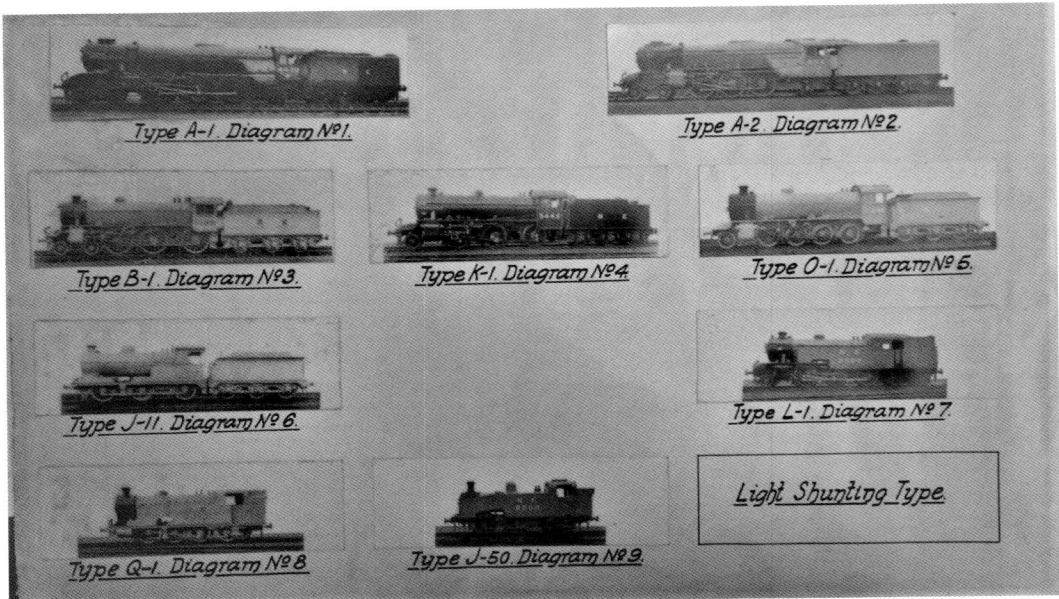

A photographic summary of some his ideas for standardisation as presented by Thompson in 1946 but prepared by Spencer who spent two years working on this project as the war came to an end. Although not included in this group, the CME made mention of the continuing need for Gresley's Pacifics, but did not rule out the possibility of modifications to their valve gear. (ET/DN)

of experimentation increased as options were explored and the number and types of engines to be included in this plan were narrowed down. In tackling this project, Thompson set out a number of guidelines in a draft paper for Newton; it was a document that Bert Spencer kept, suggesting he was involved in the drafting process:

> Standardisation is not intended to lay down hard and fast rules from which there can be no departure. It is only necessary to see where the bulk of the traffic can be dealt with by a limited number of locomotive classes, keeping in mind the necessity for continuous study and testing to judge whether improvements or modifications are required from time to time.
>
> By this means the advantages of standardisation can be secured without involving the stagnation so far as research and development are concerned. If improvements were considered desirable in one of the standard types, one or two locomotives would be selected for experimental purposes. These, after modification to incorporate the new devices and new ideas, would be tested against unaltered engines, and if they proved satisfactory would form the basis for a change in the standard.
>
> From this point we need to consider a more comprehensive policy, the first step being to divide locomotive types, totalling 166, into three Groups:
>
> The new standard types which will be constructed when it has been established that a demand cannot be met by one of the existing types.
>
> The second group includes existing locomotive types which are considered worth maintaining until the end of their useful lives – new boilers will be built for them as required and they will not be broken up until they become obsolete (there are eleven types in this group - the A1 (later called A10s), A3, A4, B17, D49, B16, K3, V2, O4, V1 and V3).

The third group includes all the remaining locomotive types, all considerably older types which are no longer satisfactory or whose work could, with advantage, be transferred to one of the new types in group one. Nevertheless, this is only a general policy, and not an invariable rule.

Having been presented with his terms of reference, Spencer set to work, conscious of the possibility that all might quickly fall apart if the war, which was still on a knife edge, went badly. He later wrote:

I was intrigued by my new job, but felt as though I was on the side lines of the war, contributing little to its success by what I was doing. However, Thompson did occasionally seek my opinion on production matters and I would act as his sounding board when he was considering papers presented to him by Windle. These included the P2 rebuilding programme, a new Pacific, plus other classes of locomotive then being planned. I was greatly relieved when the ideas I was working on became a physical reality.

It is difficult to say how closely Spencer was involved in day to day design matters in his new post, or, more importantly, how far Windle, who seems to have been a strong presence, would have allowed him to become so. All parties concerned remained mute on this point, for the most part. But it is quite conceivable that Spencer's contribution was limited to establishing the broad principles of standardisation with Thompson, consider the requirements, agree the types needed and then formulate a strategy. A time consuming and complex planning task, but one that Windle and his team would develop when the time came. And this proved to be the case, even when Thompson retired in June 1946 and Peppercorn took his place. So Spencer occupied a position of some importance, but essentially one where his design skills were, with one exception, not tested to any great extent. If Thompson had chosen to remain in London with a small team around him, as Gresley did, things might have been very different.

Spencer did not bemoan the lack of opportunity to design new engines, but he probably looked on with some frustration as others did. A letter he wrote in 1959 offers us a brief glimpse into his world during the last few years of the LNER's existence:

The main effort in developing the locomotive fleet was applied by Windle. Thompson certainly set him some broad guidelines but then allowed the Chief Draughtsmen to interpret them as he saw fit. Peppercorn did likewise and both men seemed pleased with the outcome. All six P2s became Pacific class A2/2s during 1943/44, then the last four V2s appeared as 4-6-2s [designated A2/1s] in '44 and a Gresley A1, 4470 *Great Northern*, was rebuilt in 1945 to test the efficacy of some elements of the standardisation programme. This conversion was deemed a success and work soon began on what Thompson and Windle hoped would be the standard Pacific and in 1946 the first of the A2/3s, as they were called, appeared.

There were long discussions about converting all the remaining A1s to A2/3s or simply completing their modification to A3 standard, as had long been planned. For reasons of cost Thompson chose the latter course and this programme was given much added weight. The future of the A4s also came up and Windle was keen to de-streamline them when removing Gresley's conjugated valve gear. Thompson was not prepared to sanction these changes and preferred to keep them as they were. Statistically they had performed well during the war, this, despite the very difficult working conditions. In fact, the valve gear had held up well, far better than on other engines. This convinced the CME that all they needed was remedial work to help overcome the detrimental effects of poor maintenance in the war and nothing else. This may simply have been a business decision, but I was left with the impression that

(Top) Thompson's first stab at producing a new standard class Pacific. In 1943/44 he was given permission to build the last four V2s as 4-6-2s. Here the first of these engines, No. 3696 *Highland Chieftain*, enters service in wartime livery. (Second from top). Sad for some but an acceptable conversion to others. Thompson wished to see how his and Windle's developing ideas would work on the A1s, many of which still had to be upgraded to A3 standard. 4470, Gresley's first Pacific was unfortunately chosen for this work in 1945. Was it an act of vandalism or just simply the Works taking the next old and tired A1 in line for rebuilding? Spencer remained mute on this point. When completed the 'new' Great Northern certainly looked impressive. (Bottom) Engine No. 500, the first of the A2/3s and soon to be named *Edward Thompson*, photographed in 1946 at Doncaster. Another fourteen would follow before the design underwent further modifications under Peppercorn and Windle. (BS)

he regarded the A4s as being too good to touch. He even made reference to them in the standardisation plan as worthy members of the new fleet.

Perhaps the biggest design achievement of Thompson's time as CME was the construction of the B1 4-6-0s; a powerful two-cylinder mixed traffic engine with wide route availability that was long needed by the LNER. Here he was influenced by Stanier's Black Fives and the work of Tom Coleman, who had come to Doncaster for a while during the war when his 8Fs were being built in our workshops. Thompson was eager to follow the LMS's example and drew heavily on Coleman's expertise. In this case the CME involved me quite closely in the work and it was one occasion when I used my draughtsman skills, albeit at home in my office there, to prepare outline schemes. Windle, who was by then overloaded with other pressing tasks was happy for me to do this. It was the only occasion that this happened. Four hundred and ten of these successful engines were built between 1942 and 1952. Some criticised the quality of their ride, but I never found this so on the many occasions I rode on the footplate.

You asked about streamlining and wondered if the war put paid to this work? In part yes it did, however, it remained a constant theme occasionally explored by both Thompson and Peppercorn, though the latter with perhaps less enthusiasm. The former was convinced of its merits when applied to high speed services and allowed me to keep developing these theories with the new Pacifics. Peppercorn was more heavily influenced by Windle who was more conventional and practical in his thinking and preferred a more traditional form in his designs. He saw it, primarily, as a means of smoke lifting and applied solutions that reflected this – so smoke deflectors of one sort or another, not streamlined casings were the order of the day when he was involved.

In a letter written in 1961, Spencer, added a little more detail to this summary:

Streamlining was not forgotten in plans for the new Pacifics – the A1/1, A2/1s, A2/2s and A2/3s – and led to some modelling and wind tunnel testing to see if it could be included in the designs. Thompson was very keen on this, Peppercorn and Windle much less so,

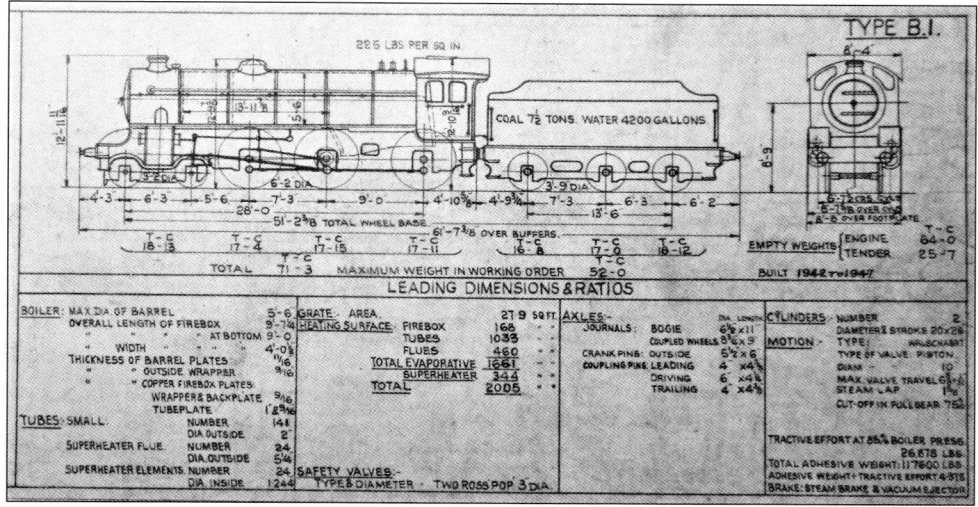

Thompson and Windle's B1 was described by Spencer as being 'the biggest achievement of Thompson's time' and by Robert Riddles (BR's first CME) as being 'probably the most useful engine ever built on that line (the LNER)'. Such was its success that 410 would be built between 1942 and 1952. It seems that this was a project in which Thompson sought Spencer's help during the design stage. If so, this might account for the project's success and the engine's wide acceptance by BR and its continued construction when many other inherited designs were discarded (BS)

seeing it as an 'unnecessary extravagance', as the Chief Draughtsman put it. However, when considering a bigger A4 I did discard the three cylinder/conjugated valve arrangement and prepared sketches showing three independent sets of Walschaerts valve gear instead and other changes. I showed these to the CME, shortly after becoming his assistant, when he was considering his new Pacifics and these then went to Windle, who, at the time, was not wholly convinced that the Gresley solution should be dropped.

At this point the CME, armed with Stanier and Cox's report, and a substantial bank of evidence Elwell and I had been collecting, and under pressure from Newton, took the decision to discard the 2 to 1 gear and go for the three independent sets of valve gear instead in the rebuild of the P2s and the new Pacifics. But at the same time he still wished to continue exploring any benefits that might accrue from streamlining, despite Windle's reservations. This led to some modelling and wind tunnel testing to see if it could be included in the new designs. But all this was quietly dropped when Peppercorn became CME.

So the A4s were safe while Thompson remained CME and streamlining, whether to further scientific research or simply as a PR exercise, was given a brief afterlife. However, the more important question of removing Gresley's conjugated valve gear and fitting a third set of Walscherts was carefully sidestepped. Bearing in mind the reported deterioration of the locomotives with three-cylinders and the 2 to 1 gear, and the problem of maintaining them in good condition, this is interesting. Perhaps it was, as Spencer later recorded:

> ... a matter of cost, it being much more expensive to rebuild the engines than meet the expense of the increased servicing involved. In any case, after the war when proper maintenance routines were restored and many trained men returned to do the work, the engines were kept in much better shape and the problems decreased slightly. In this position the Chairman felt that the cost of rebuilding so many engines could not be justified. It was a view that was restated when Peppercorn took over and sought to take action.

When Peppercorn took over in 1946 little changed and the 18 months to Nationalisation saw him continuing to develop Thompson's ideas. Key to this programme was the refinement

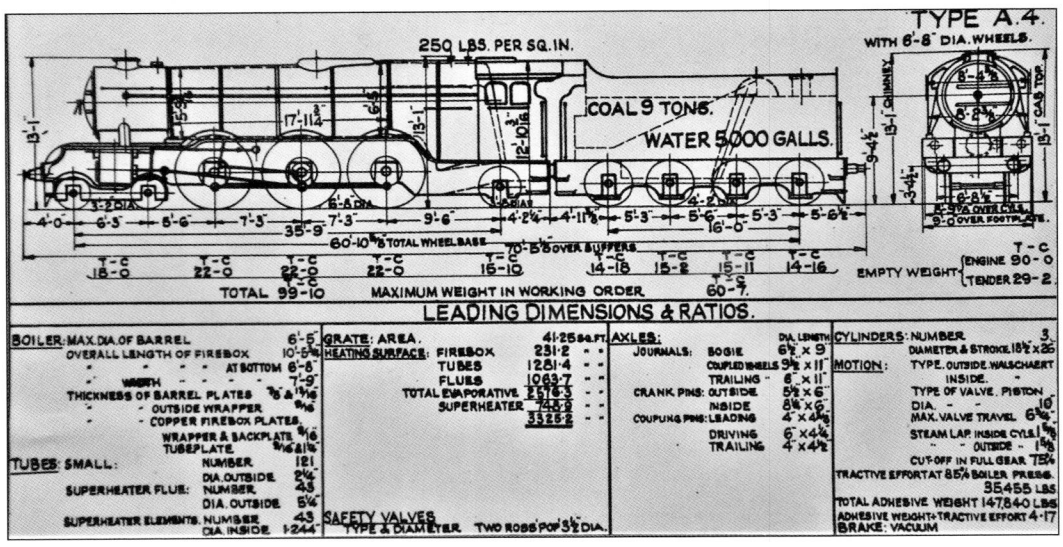

Windle's view of the future for the A4s – de-streamlined and built to a more traditional design. It was a move Thompson felt unnecessary, could not support and it was quickly dropped. (PA)

of the design of the new Pacifics, which continued to appear until 1949 adding substantially to an already oversized fleet of 4-6-2s.

The Standardisation Plan which I continued researching and then writing throughout 1944/45 found wide acceptance and quickly became company policy, with annual updates issued until 1947. However, little could be done to implement its recommendations before BR came into existence; such plans being put on hold while future policy was being decided. Post-1948 work on a new BR wide standardisation plan began and until the end of my career became a central part of my day to day routine.

Although Spencer did not retire until 1958 he left fewer words, in letters or personal papers, describing his life during the last years of his career other than those quoted above. One can only guess why. It was not as if he had moved away from an area of work that suited him best – designing and testing locomotives – quite the opposite, in fact. So perhaps it was a reaction to being absorbed by a new, giant organisation where few decisions were delegated from the centre. Instead of being masters of their own destiny, the 'Big Four' had been taken over by a large unified

Peppercorn's commendable contribution to the Pacific story and the types final evolution as far as the LNER was concerned after more than twenty-seven years of development. (Top) A1 No. 60130 *Kestrel*, one of forty-nine built between 1948 and '49, is posed with some of the men who built her at Darlington in 1948. (Below) A2 No. 525, soon to be named *A.H. Peppercorn*, one of fifteen built during 1947 and '48. (BS)

Peppercorn and some members of his senior team pose for a group of photos taken on a cold, snow dusted 31 December 1947, the last day of the LNER's life, in front of engine No. 525, the first of the CME's new A2s. (Top) In the front row sits Edward Windle (front row sixth from the left), then John Harrison and Peppercorn. Spencer is second from the right front row. (Below) A much larger group with Peppercorn remaining in the centre of the front row, with Spencer having moved to the periphery of the group (seventh from the right front row). Spencer recorded that 'Thompson was an honoured guest and had to be persuaded by Peppercorn to join the group for one photograph' (front row, twelfth from the left). (BS)

bureaucracy, which issued commands and instructions that were prescriptive and authoritarian in nature. This had the effect of stifling initiative and individual ambition in offices grown used to a high degree of freedom. In this situation, a man such as Spencer would have found his creative edge blunted and feel less engaged. So, while continuing to work hard, he may have found the new world far less inclusive and challenging than the old.

However, during this period he did record more of his thoughts in official documents, but for reasons of discretion these are carefully considered, avoiding anything that might be deemed contentious. Despite this, they still contain much of value in helping us understand some of his underlying views and feelings in the last years of his career.

During 1947, and in recognition of his work over the years, Spencer was promoted by Peppercorn to be Mechanical Engineer (Outdoors) at Doncaster. Here he was made responsible for all 'Mechanical Work with the Running Superintendents'. This was an interesting appointment, most importantly because its primary focus was to provide Peppercorn with an effective link with a group of men who exerted considerable influence over what the CME did. During Thompson's time this had proved to be a matter of some concern, so it would seem that Peppercorn considered the astute, widely respected, diplomatic and talented Spencer ideal for such a difficult role. Within months, Peppercorn would re-label this post Technical Assistant to the CME and in November that year, on the eve of nationalisation, he further rewarded all Spencer's hard work by making him Assistant to the CME (Locomotive and General). And so, as they entered the new government

For most of his career, Spencer managed to stay in the background and avoid the camera's closest gaze. He was not a self publicist and so it is even more interesting when this retiring man shows up, even as here on 31 December 1947 in a group shot. Although smiling, his expression gives little away. (BS)

controlled world he filled a role akin to that of Bulleid when Gresley was CME.

With BR's birth, any plans the LNER had to build any other locomotives were put on hold by BR, conscious of the array of building projects they had inherited and the sheer volume of locomotives on their books. In an article dated May 1948, the editor of the *Locomotive Magazine* gave the total numbers as 12,490 tender engines of various types and 7,536 tanks of 34 different wheel configurations. Of these, some 6,500 were LNER engines. There was clearly a need for some rationalisation and a master plan that drew the old companies together in a practical and rational way. The task was a daunting one that would not be resolved quickly or cheaply, let alone the longer term need to introduce other forms of locomotion. And in the background lay the pressing issue of wear and tear inflicted by the war and how it might be corrected.

The first sign of how this might be managed came when a set of locomotive comparability trials was commissioned by BR in 1948; later known as the 'Interchange Trials'. The concept was a simple one. Take the best of the types then in service and match them, by group, in a series of tests over each region's main routes. Armed with this information it was hoped that the most effective elements of each design would be established, and these be fed into plans for a new group of standard class locomotives. Rather strangely, this all-encompassing ambition did not seek to assess new technologies, choosing instead to focus solely on steam. On reflection, this seems a rather short-sighted, though understandable, approach considering the country's dire financial position and the importance of its coal industry.

During the trials, each of the old companies was represented by a man from each new region, supported by a small team. Peppercorn chose Spencer for this co-ordinating role, and very soon he was selected by BR to be chairman of the Locomotive Testing Committee which oversaw and controlled the whole programme. It proved to be a wise choice. It also reflected the esteem with which he was held by many in the industry, perhaps greatly enhanced by his 'masterly' presentation to the ILocoE the year before.

Whilst this was happening, BR selected the locomotives to be tested, taking into account the views of each regional chief. As a result, three LNER classes were chosen – the A4, in the express passenger category and Thompson's B1 and 2-8-0 Class

Thompson A2/3 No. 516 (later 60516) *Hycilla* soon to be a BR engine with new logos and number. (BS)

O1 in the mixed traffic and freight groups respectively. The choice of individual engines for this task was left to the CMEs and their staff to decide, but conditions were applied to this process by Ernest Cox, who had recently been appointed to a senior position in BR. He issued instructions that engines selected should not undergo any 'special preparation' and be 'taken direct from traffic having run between 15,000 and 20,000 miles since their last general repair'.

On selecting A4s for the task, Spencer recorded:

> The powers that be just wished to take any A4s available. I then pointed out that the trials were primarily to establish which parts of which locomotives were good enough to feature in future standard BR designs. In this case the A4s chosen should be those fitted with the double chimney arrangement. Agreement was reached and so 60022 *Mallard*, 60034 *Lord Faringdon* and 60033 *Seagull* were chosen to represent the LNER in the express passenger group. Although we were now BR, old rivalries were hard to give up and we at Doncaster wanted our engines to be best!

During the Interchange Trials in 1948, Spencer was a constant presence on the different engines that were tested. His archive contains masses of information and photographs covering these events, not surprising when considering his role as Chairman of the organising committee. The pictures above capture some of the classes that 'competed' in the express passenger group, all of which Spencer rode behind, some on more than one occasion. Top left – 46162 *Queen's Westminster Rifleman* about to depart from King's Cross. Her sister, engine No. 46154 *Hussar*, would be involved in some of the later trials. Top right – 60033 *Seagull* awaits departure at Waterloo on a preliminary run. According to the notes with this picture, Spencer is in the group of men on the right. Bottom left – the sole GWR King Class engine included in this group – 6018 *King Henry VI* pulls away from King's Cross. Bottom right – 46236 *City of Bradford*, the sole Coronation Pacific involved in the trials, storms away from Waterloo with dynamometer car attached. (BS)

By March, the programme had been agreed. However, it seems that some doubts were then expressed over the benefits of whole exercise. The official report touched on this issue:

> From the outset it was realised that these indications [of the most desirable features of each locomotive] would be of a very broad nature ... It was also realised that inequalities which are liable to be experienced in any variable speed testing on the track would be present and affect some locomotives more than others.

Nevertheless, the trials went ahead and ran from April to September, with some tests over Western Region metals being repeated in November and December. It was even suggested at one stage by the committee that it might be beneficial to undertake 'further testing on the Rugby and Swindon Testing Plants and with Mobile Testing Plant', which opened that year, to supplement or confirm the earlier results.

In early 1949, the final report was being considered by all those involved, with Spencer still fulfilling his co-ordinating role and trying to reach some sort of consensus and agreement on future policy. For those who doubted the validity of the exercise, and there appear to have been many, they would have found ample ammunition to support this view. When finally issued, the tone of the report was probably summed up in the opening pages, which recorded that the trials 'provided valuable and interesting information'. Yet the nine conclusions reached were, with few exceptions, nebulous to say the least.

Spencer probably caught the general feeling of the time when he wrote:

> The trials were useful up to a point, but did not really tell us anything we did not know already. Each class had its own strengths, but the variables involved in such trials made such a broad comparison most difficult and speculative in nature. By this stage the new Test Centre at Rugby was finally opening and it was hoped that this facility would soon provide more information. But it was not until January 1950 that serious testing of any of the Interchange engines took place, by which time standardisation plans had been formulated by Cox and his design team, which included Windle.

One immediate outcome of the trials was a slight relaxing of the restriction on building new locomotives, as BR considered its standardisation plan in greater depth and argued a case for its acceptance. At Doncaster, this allowed Peppercorn to complete his Pacific programme, though the

Spencer was keen to recognise the contribution made to the Interchange Trials by the footplate crew and arranged a series of special 'luncheons' to thank them for all their efforts. Photographs of some of these events and a short article soon followed, as witnessed above. (BS)

last twenty A2s were cancelled. So, in the run up to his retirement during March 1949, the last of the new A2s appeared, with the A1 programme completing in December that year also.

As these designs had evolved from the Thompson/Windle Pacifics, there must have been a temptation to draw comparisons. For some reason which is not clear, Spencer only chose to comment on the A2/3 to A2 programme The most obvious difference between the two lay in the position of the cylinders. The A2/3 like the A2/1s and A2/2s, had these set back behind the front bogie, giving the engines an unusual, stretched look. For the A2s, and later the new A1s, this was changed by, as Spencer recorded:

> The simple expedient of moving the outside cylinders forward over the leading truck and by amending the steam ducts. In doing this the wheelbase was shortened and the smokebox reduced in length. However, it retained the cylinder and valve gear arrangement introduced when Thompson was CME; divided drive with the middle cylinder acting on the leading coupled axle and outside cylinders the middle axle. This could only be achieved in the space available on the A2s by discarding the Kylchap exhaust or the self-cleaning device in the smokebox.

Windle decided that the former could go, and this, apparently, had the added benefit of improving the passage of smoke over the cab so enhancing the footplate crews forward visibility.

However, Spencer felt this was wrong and later wrote that:

> This was a false economy. The Klychap double blastpipe and chimney, which Gresley strongly advocated, had proved its value when fitted to some of the A4s in the 1930s and some of the A3s. Thompson had seen the wisdom of this and his Pacifics were so fitted also. However, Windle was not a strong supporter of this design and his view prevailed when the A2s were being designed, although five were equipped with a double chimney. Consequently, they tended to steam poorly and only at the end did my advice prevail and the last A2 [No. 60539 *Bronzino*] was fitted with a Kylchap.

For a mild-mannered man these represented strong words, suggesting a degree of frustration with Windle's methods. In many ways, the debate was a repeat of the long running saga over Gresley's conjugated valve gear and the lap long issue that played out in the 1920s. This was resolved by trial and error and by the CME eventually adopting Spencer's long-argued solution. In this more recent

At Spencer's insistence, it was eventually agreed that one of Peppercorn's new A2s should be fitted with a Kylchap double blastpipe and chimney to help enhance its performance. The last of the class, 60539 *Bronzino*, was chosen and rolled from the workshops at Doncaster in the summer of 1948. The engine is captured here in the early years of the 1950s before the final form of BR logo was applied. (BS)

case, Windle seems to have been equally unconvinced by Spencer's arguments and was unprepared to give way until the evidence began to mount in his favour. It is a small point, but one wonders whether this difference of opinion pointed towards a deeper malaise between the two men. If this was the case when their paths crossed over the next few years, which they are bound to have done, might other differences have arisen? Possibly not, because from 1949 onwards, although remaining at Doncaster and leading the design team there, Windle's primary task would have been to focus on the nationally managed standardisation programme. This remained the case until he retired.

Meanwhile, Spencer, though participating in the construction of BR's new standard class engines, played little or no part in the design process. Instead, he focussed on production and testing of these locomotives, plus the development of new electric and diesel motive power. This is not to say that he did not have thoughts and views on the way steam design was going and might have aired any concerns he may have had, but with so much else to do, this was no longer his main concern.

And so, Peppercorn departed the scene for a well-earned rest. Sadly, it was not destined to last long. On 3 March 1951, he suffered a coronary and died a little later that day. Spencer was amongst many old friends and colleagues who attended his funeral in Doncaster and in the weeks that followed wrote a short, informal obituary for his much admired leader and friend:

> Peppercorn seemed relieved to be retiring and had not been well for some time. However, this didn't stop him enjoying his food, a cigar and his last few months at work. He would often reminisce about our time together with Gresley and Thompson, the latter being an occasional and welcomed visitor to Doncaster especially when Pep retired.
>
> In 1946 and '47 Pep encouraged me to prepare a paper for the Institution of Locomotive Engineers describing all the engine development programmes undertaken by Gresley. This I did and towards the end of his time I suggested that I continue this exercise to include the years 1941 to '49. He laughed and said 'No one will be interested. The war then nationalisation put paid to all our plans. It will all be diesels and electric trains from now on.'
>
> When he went we wished him a long and happy retirement. Sadly, it wasn't to be.

In terms of succession, it is interesting that during Peppercorn's last six months of service there was probably an easing of pressure, with BR now well into its stride and orchestrating all that

Peppercorn's retirement in 1949 was accompanied by much celebration but tinged with sadness that such a good man was leaving the service. Many old friends, including Edward Thompson and Spencer, gathered at Doncaster to wish him a long and happy retirement. Sadly, it was not to be and he died in 1951. Here John Harrison presents a clock and radiogram to Peppercorn with Luther Reeves, T. Henry Turner and Spencer in attendance. (BS)

happened. He also had the young and vigorous John Harrison sitting at his elbow gradually taking on more responsibility; having been appointed Assistant CME in 1947, on promotion from Mechanical Engineer at Cowlairs – a post he had held for only two years. So, although Peppercorn was nominally in charge as CME (now known as Mechanical and Electrical Engineer, N&NER) until 31 December 1949, the transfer of power to Harrison would have been well under way by then. However, as things turned out Harrison only remained at Doncaster for a comparatively short period, leaving to take up a similar position at Derby in 1951, being replaced by Kenneth Cook from Swindon – a GWR man of long standing.

Throughout this period, up to his retirement in 1958, Spencer carried on with the work begun by Thompson, continued by Peppercorn and inherited by BR. His new masters soon began implementing their standardisation plans for steam locomotives, in the process choosing to spread the design task evenly around the regional centres at Doncaster, Derby, Swindon and Brighton. Ernest Cox, who was one of the leaders in pursuing these ideas, described the rationale behind this strategy and the outcome when he wrote:

> Each design office was made a parent for a particular locomotive type or types [of which there would eventually be twelve] for which it had to undertake the complete production drawings. Superimposed upon this, each office was made responsible for a range of components applicable to all types ... Although this sounded complicated it worked like a charm.'

In practice, this meant that staff at Doncaster were made responsible for the overall design of a Class 5 4-6-0 initially, with the Class 4 2-6-0 added later. In addition, Windle and his team would bear responsibility for the scheming of a number of standard components, including cylinders, coupling rods, valve gear, slidebars and crossheads. Of the other drawing offices, Derby acquired the lion's share of the work, with five classes of engines, including three types of Pacific, and a range of components, including tenders, wheels and bogies. To Spencer this was not unpredicted as he related later:

> With BR's senior design team dominated by men from the LMS [Robert Riddles as CME and Railway Executive Board member, Roland Bond as Chief Officer for Locomotive Construction and Ernest Pugson as Chief Officer for Carriages and Wagons] it didn't surprise me that so much design work and new construction went there. If my old friend, Tom Coleman, who was the best designer and Chief Draughtsman BR had by a long way, was still running the show this would have been understandable. But he had retired suddenly in 1949 following the death of his son. His great skills and influence were sorely missed as the design programme slowly gathered pace.

With these extensive plans in place, there would have been an expectation that a fair balance of construction work would then fall to each centre. With worry over cutbacks unavoidable, in the wake of nationalisation, there would have been some gnawing concerns that each share would be insufficient, leading to closures and redundancies. As things turned out, the programme did not get underway until 1951, with 89 engines built that year, and then run on until 1960, when the last of the 999 standards engines finally appeared. With so many large workshops available to undertake the task, there was barely enough in this programme to keep them all going, but was a useful fill-in while it lasted.

For the shops at Doncaster, the demand proved to be lighter than expected, even more so at Darlington. The former built a total of 137 new standard engines between 1952 and 1957. There were three types involved – the Class 5 4-6-0s, Class 4 2-6-0s and Class 4 2-6-4Ts. Meanwhile Darlington managed just seventy-five over the same period – Class 2 2-6-0s and Class 2 2-6-2Ts. However, there were still some inherited programmes still running which gave the ex-LNER shops

When the first of the new standard Class 7P 4-6-2s (No. 70000 *Britannia*) appeared in 1951 Spencer, as Chairman of the Locomotive Testing Committee, was invited to participate in test runs between Crewe and Carlisle. He kept a number of photos of these events including these two. (Left) The engine after pulling the 8.20 am from Carlisle to Crewe North Junction on 11 May. (Right) The next day 70000 is captured being prepared at Crewe before another run to Carlisle pulling 442 tons, including a dynamometer car. Spencer was on board on both occasions. (BS)

some much needed work. Although the Thompson B1 4-6-0s were mostly built by North British under contract until 1952, ten were produced by staff at Darlington in 1950. In 1951/52 the same workshops also built thirty-six LMS designed Class 2F 2-6-0s and thirty-six Class 4F 2-6-0s. Over the same period, Doncaster picked up some of this work and built fifty of the 4Fs of the 162 constructed. In addition to this, there was still a substantial locomotive maintenance task which helped tide them over this difficult period of re-organisation and rationalisation. However, the writing was probably on the wall by then and as the years slipped by a gloomy view of the future would have formed across the workshops. It was a feeling magnified by the inexorable march of the road industry and its increasing ascendancy over rail transport.

The production of even more steam locomotives at this time seems to reflect a business that was out of tune with a rapidly changing world. It was, as Spencer related, 'a waste of time, money and effort when a more rapid advance on electrification and dieselisation could have been made and taken the railways forward. It was a huge mistake, even though many of the new standard engines, especially the 9Fs, were quite outstanding'.

But the die had been cast and BR remained committed to a programme in which the doubting Spencer would pay a full part. As Harrison, then Cook's Chief Technical Assistant for all Mechanical and Electrical matters in the Region, with a staff of forty-two, he would oversee all new production at Doncaster and Darlington of steam, as well as diesel and electric motive power. It was a task that involved working and corresponding with such companies as English Electric, Napier, Sulzer and Brush as his papers reveal. In some cases, it was simply to acquire their latest brochures and detailed descriptions of their developing products, in others, he seems to have become involved in the design and production of new engines. This was particularly so with English Electric and their Diesel Prototype No. 1 which evolved into the main line Deltic class.

By 1951, the company had many years of experience building and selling diesel and electric engines and the DP1 can be seen as a speculative venture in producing a large locomotive that might be sold to markets around the world and so expand their business. The design concept for this prototype was first explored by the company in 1950/51. Such was their confidence in the proposed design that an order for four engines to power them was raised with Napier's, a subsidiary of EE. In November, this led to an internal contract being issued by the company's Tractive Division at Bradford for a single prototype to be built at EE's Preston Works.

While the development of steam engines continued to dominate BR's thinking the results of Gresley and the LNER's electrification plans finally reached fruition. In 1949 the Liverpool Street to Shenfield commuter line opened with ninety-two three car sets (above left). This was followed by the Woodford electrified line which opened fully in 1955 with fifty-seven EM1s (above right) for freight work and seven EM2s to work the Sheffield Victoria to Manchester express services. All these were assembled at the ex-LNER Gorton Works. Spencer recalled that 'my involvement with this work was mainly in supporting the design and then production of the EMUs and locomotives, making sure, amongst other things, that all were produced on time. This included overseeing the test and modification programme that followed, particularly on improving the ride quality of the EM1s'. (BS)

Production of this engine proved to be a long drawn out affair, not unusual when a new design is being developed. In this case, the project was accompanied by as many revisions as new avenues explored. Couple to this, a lack of any potential customers for the locomotive would have encouraged a certain amount of drift in the programme, which a commercial imperative might have helped assuage. So the project struggled on, with the prototype finally being ready for trials in November 1955.

It was sometime in 1953 that Spencer first enquired about this engine and received a substantial pack of material relating to its development from EE. Why he began gathering this information is unclear. It may simply have been personal interest that encouraged his actions or, more likely, he was carrying out a task delegated to him by one of several BR committees on which he sat. Either way, he seems to have become something of a focal point within BR for this project, and his papers record regular visits to Preston as DP1 slowly emerged, followed by participation in the engine's trials. In the same way he also became involved in the projects that resulted in the Brush Type 2 (BR Class 31) and the EE Type 2 (BR Class 20), which both began entering service in 1957.

As his career moved towards a close, these diesel projects remained for him an interesting sideshow, with his work producing or maintaining a substantial fleet of steam engines still dominating his days. And his extensive knowledge of testing drew him into a constantly expanding trials programme, now including the recently opened Test Centre at Rugby. Spencer's close involvement with this work was reflected in his membership of the Locomotive Testing Committee, a proactive group which he chaired for nearly three years before handing over to Ernest Cox in 1951. During this time, many talented BR railway engineers from across the regions contributed to its work. These included Sam Ells from Swindon, Ron Jarvis from Derby then Brighton, Dennis Carling, Superintending Engineer of the Rugby Test Centre, Frederick Abraham, the LMR's Motive Power Superintendent, Tom Herbert Head of Research at Derby and Clifford Cocks of Brighton and then Derby as Chief Draughtsman, replacing Tom Coleman.

Spencer's position at the head of this prestigious group, as it set out the testing policy for BR and then implemented it, confirms the high regard in which he was still held by his contemporaries. When he did relinquish the post, he made it clear in a letter to Robert Riddles that he did so because:

Aftermath 229

The production of DP1 by English Electric was accompanied by a great deal of publicity material in the hope of encouraging interest at home and abroad that might lead to sales. Spencer collected many of these brochures and technical assessments including various versions of this cutaway illustration. (BS)

> Of pressure of work at Doncaster and a wish to see that the Testing Committee continues to undertake this most important of tasks. In my place it will be led by someone with the time and seniority to focus more fully on this trials work for both steam and diesel locomotives. In so doing, he can seek to increase the combined knowledge of design and establish how existing types might be improved and future locomotives made better. However, I will still be an active member and continue to make my own modest contribution to the work of the committee.

In reality, the creation of this all-encompassing test regime probably came too late to be of much use for steam engines. With the publication of a series of Modernisation Plans during the 1950s, BR and the Transport Ministry made it clear that steam's days were numbered. Even as early as 1955 it was projected that 2,500 diesels would be built over ten years and electrification was again on the agenda. Steam still had a part to play but it was a diminishing role. In the meantime, Spencer took on the tasks assigned to him, always giving his best and taking a great interest in all that was going on around him, which meant getting involved in trial runs of new steam and diesel locomotives.

According to his records, he accompanied engine No. 70000, *Britannia*, the first of the new Class 7P 4-6-2, in January 1951 on a return trip between Crewe and Carlisle, pulling slightly in excess of 440 tons, including a dynamometer car. Of this experience he later wrote 'it was a good engine even when still running in, but would struggle to compete with an A4 even one that was badly worn'. From here, he went on to observe various other engines under test at Rugby, Swindon or on the road. Most notably these included another Class 7P, No. 70005 *John Milton*, in 1951, a Bulleid Merchant Navy Pacific, No. 35022 *Holland America Line* in 1952/53 and a Stanier Duchess, No. 46225, during 1956.

Bearing in mind his work with LNER Pacifics over nearly twenty-five years, this interest is, perhaps, unsurprising. But he did not limit himself to these classes of engine and by the time he retired he had seen first-hand most of the standard designs being tested, as well as a B1 and V2 (at Swindon). He also had the opportunity to observe Bulleid's experimental Leader Class running, follow the progress being made by English Electric with their GT3 gas turbine engine and assess

For the last decade of his career, Spencer was closely involved in locomotive testing and the work of the centre at Rugby. Here he witnessed many engines being evaluated and retained copies of all reports, plus many photographs of which these are three. (Top) The sixth member of the new class of 7P 4-6-2s – 70005 *John Milton* – photographed in 1951 when undergoing tests with live steam injectors. (Middle) One of Bulleid's Merchant Navy's, 35022 *Holland America Line*, followed in 1952/53. (Bottom) A Coronation Pacific being prepared for testing at Rugby. 46255 *Duchess of Gloucester* spent 4½ months at the centre and was run for 7,205 miles. For reasons that are not entirely clear, no formal bulletin was compiled, as happened with other engines. Spencer retained many papers, however, and personally took part in many tests at Rugby and on the mainline. (BS)

One of many of Spencer's undated photographs, thought to have been taken at Waverley Station during a holiday to Scotland in the mid-1950s. It is a typical, but atmospheric view of life on a main line station in the age of steam, here with the added benefit of displaying many locomotives on which he had worked during a long career. (BS)

the performance of the Southern Co Co mainline diesel electric No. 10202 when running between Waterloo and Exeter in 1952

Unfortunately, any notes that Spencer kept recording his thoughts or impressions of these events have not survived or have not yet to come to light. As a seasoned campaigner, they would make interesting reading, especially where Bulleid's locomotives were concerned. But perhaps, on this occasion, discretion was the better part of valour, there being plenty of others in BR who were less than enamoured with Bulleid's work and publicly expressed their critical thoughts.

From a personal point of view, it was probably too late in his career to make much use of the information he had carefully collected over so many years, as far as new designs were concerned. In the circumstances, Spencer would probably have submitted any observations he made to the Superintendent of the Test Centre or Cox, who would have included them in any report that was compiled. As with Gresley, Thompson and Peppercorn, Spencer seemed happiest when working quietly behind the scenes and avoiding the limelight. There is one exception to this though, and this concerned DP1 which, after a long running development programme, was finally ready for trials with the London Midland Region during 1955, having been re-painted powder blue, after EE had initially applied a green and cream livery.

Spencer had an eye for diesel developments in the post-war years and took whatever opportunities that arose to see them in action. This included locomotives developed by the Southern Region by Bulleid and team. In 1950/51 two Co Co engines appeared numbered 10201 and 10202 and went into service. A third was added in 1954. All three had English Electric engines and transmissions but were in every other respect Bulleid designs. Spencer rode on them a number of times including (right) engine No. 10202 when assigned to the Golden Arrow for a short period. (BS)

Having followed its development with interest for several years, Spencer obtained permission to travel on this engine in March 1956 and several more times in 1957. Finally, in the few weeks before his retirement, he was invited to join the engine one last time on a run from Liverpool Lime Street to London. By this stage, a discussion between EE and BR regarding the construction of more of the type was well underway, for use on the East Coast Mainline. This resulted in a final order for twenty-two locomotives being agreed, with contracts exchanged in May 1958, delivery to begin in March 1960. While this was happening, the prototype remained with the LMR, but all this changed in January 1959. After a major overhaul, the Deltic was delivered to Hornsey depot for testing by staff on the Eastern Region in anticipation of the first of the new engines being delivered. Although by now departed, one wonders whether Spencer's expert assessments of the Deltic played any part in the development programme and their use along the East Coast, where they would soon begin to displace the A4s. Of this he wrote:

> Although it would have been easy to cling to the past and see steam locomotives in service for many more years, by 1958, when I retired, the lack of real progress towards diesel or electric replacements was something I regretted. The technology was sufficiently advanced to have achieved much more and the money spent on all those new standard engines could have been better invested on diesels. I was impressed by Ivatt's two Co Co engines, Nos. 10000 and 01, that appeared in 1947/48, though rough around the edges they should have been refined and built in greater numbers. Likewise, the Deltics could have entered service much earlier than they did. Luckily there were companies prepared to invest and experiment in new technologies which meant that when BR finally bit the bullet they could tap into their work. I did find the Deltics interesting and enjoyable and rode in the cab of the prototype on a number of occasions, most notably on 26th March 1958 when running from Liverpool to London. A detailed report of which I submitted to John Harrison at Derby, soon to be BR's CME.
>
> As a rule, I was never too fond of the dirt and grime of a steam engines footplate and did not envy the lives of drivers or firemen which were hard to say the least. Being able to ride on a diesel with their pristine cabs, instantly starting and then harnessed to all that power was much more to my liking and theirs, if the many accounts I read are to be believed. Nevertheless, I was sad to see the Pacific's go having been central to my life for so long and wished that Doncaster had been chosen to design and build the standard Class 6, 7 and 8P 4-6-2s. With all our experience of the type the task would have sat well there.
>
> Just before I retired I travelled one last time on the footplate of an A4, rather appropriately No. 60014 *Silver Link*, from King's Cross to Waverley. She ran well and had many years of active left to her, but would be withdrawn and scrapped only four years later having been replaced by the fleet of Deltics. These were sad days, but change is inevitable and must be embraced.

On 26 March 1958, shortly before he retired, Spencer was invited to join the prototype Deltic on a special run from Liverpool to London. He remained in the cab for the entire journey, later commenting that it was 'interesting and enjoyable'. This photo captures the train awaiting departure on that day. (*BS*)

Another view of DP1 that Spencer kept in his archive. On the back he has simply written '1959- running on LNER metals'. The engine was transferred for use on the East Coast Mainline following overhaul for evaluation. This led to an order for twenty-two being signed; the first arriving a year late in 1961 to begin replacing the Pacifics. (BS)

After forty-five years of important and successful service, some public fanfare might have been expected when he walked through the gates of Doncaster for the last time. But this was not Spencer's way. He preferred to slip quietly from the scene to begin a new life, allowing any credit he had earnt to rest on the shoulders of the men he'd served so well. And here he always remembered Gresley and trumpeted his achievements for the rest of his life. Nevertheless, and despite his natural modesty, he might have been pleased to read Ernest Cox's description of his contribution to railway history in *Locomotive Panorama*, which appeared in 1966:

> To such men as Gresley, Maunsell, Stanier, George Ivatt and Riddles, the historian must rightly accord the direction and authority which made this work possible. To the lesser known names of Tom Coleman, Bert Spencer, James Clayton and Sam Ell, among other unsung heroes, goes the credit for the original thought and application which assured its success.

High praise indeed for Gresley's master engineer.

Spencer has written on the back of this print 'celebrating the last steam locomotive built at Doncaster'. In this case it is standard class 4 2-6-0 No. 76114, one of seventy built at Doncaster between 1952 and 1957. To mark the occasion, a number of photographs were taken and published. This one shows senior members of the Management team and supervisors, including Spencer who sits in the front row, near the centre fourteenth from the left. This historic day was perhaps the appropriate moment for him to bow out. (BS)

Epilogue

Retirement for Bert and his wife meant a change of location. After so long in the North-east they might have been expected to stay in an area they knew so well. But it seems they had a long-held dream to move to the West Country and this is what they did. A loosening of ties with Doncaster may also have been encouraged by the death of his mother at the age of 86 and his brother Harry's move to Shaldon in Devon. Added to this, his sister Edith and brother Fred had died in 1943 and 1956 respectively. And so, an important link came to an end and after a brief search they sold their house in Yorkshire and found a newly built bungalow called Claverdon on Higher Ringmore Road, which had a wonderful view over the River Teign, to the main line from Exeter to Plymouth. Whether this was a deliberate move or a happy chance is not known, but it must have been pleasant to have this permanent reminder of a long and rewarding career so close by.

Harry, who had been a near neighbour of Edward Windle in Doncaster for many years, now lived within three hundred yards of Bert. They, according to Elsie, had always been very close and now occasionally joined each other on 'expeditions by car and train to various parts of the country with Bert continuing to take photos of steam engines of all sorts and now diesels of which he became quite fond'. By chance, he now found himself living within a few miles of Oliver Bulleid, across the Exe estuary in Exmouth. Whether he knew this is unclear, but they do not appear to have met or re-established a relationship forged at King's Cross over so many years. Perhaps it was a case of ships that pass in the night; they had much in common, and fought for a common cause, but they were very different characters.

Spencer remained a member of the IMechE and ILocoE to the end of his life but appears not to have attended meetings or felt the need to present any new papers to either body. The one exception was the 50th Anniversary celebrations for the ILocoE held at Marylebone in May 1961. He later recalled:

> I was persuaded to go against my better judgement, because I felt it would be living in the past, but it turned out to be a highly enjoyable three days. Many of my old friends were there and I was able to catch up with William Stanier, Ernest Cox and many others and

The Spencers' retirement home in Shaldon, Devon, with views over the River Teign towards the old GWR mainline, then dominated by the Western Region's Class 42 and 52 diesel hydraulics. Judging by his photographic collection, these interested Spencer greatly and he travelled behind them on a number of occasions. (THG)

The 50th Anniversary of the ILocoE's life was a major event attended by many VIPs and members, including Spencer. He seems to have found it interesting and particularly enjoyed seeing 60022 on display especially with Tommy Bray in attendance (top left). The general scene as captured on 12 May (top right and lower left) (Lower right). The day before, some members, including Spencer, took a special train to Bath, pulled by the Warship diesel hydraulic *Zebra*. A tour of Longleat was preceded by lunch at the Limpley Stoke Hotel. (BS)

reminisce about Gresley and the great days now gone. Interestingly, amongst all those new and gleaming engines Mallard still stood out and attracted large crowds, including the Duke of Edinburgh, eager to jump on her footplate. I was also pleased to see Tommy Bray, now a driver, and together we remembered the record run of 3rd July 1938. After that it was curious to stand on the Deltic then John Hughes' GT3, This looks a strange beast but seems, from what he told me, to be working well though its future is far from certain. I was also taken with the new 3200 hp AC Electric West Coast Mainline Locomotive, which I assume will soon be replacing Stanier's Pacifics.

After three very busy days I was glad it was all over, but pleased I went.'

Despite the lack of regular contact with the institutions Elsie recalled:

He was very proud to have received an award from the ILocoE in recognition of his 1947 presentation about Gresley, to which he added many additional notes and photographs over the years. When journals arrived he would devour their content as he did scientific books

An undated Spencer photograph this time of engine No. 60112 *St Simon* which first appeared as A1 No. 1481 in September 1923, and was upgraded to A3 standard in 1946. By the time this picture was taken, the engine had been fitted with a double blastpipe and small smoke deflectors. This engine was finally scrapped in February 1965. (BS)

and magazines. He never lost his sense of curiosity or desire to learn and often wished he was young enough to still be working for British Railways.

My late uncle, Ronald, who had corresponded with Spencer for many years, visited him at least twice during his last years when passing by car on holiday, recalled that:

[Spencer was a] kindly, courteous and intelligent man who seemed more interested in you as a person than in recalling his own life. He had no sense of self-importance or vanity and was very easy to talk to about many things. He was also very generous to other people when recalling his working life, claiming no personal credit, even though it was clear that his influence on events had been considerable and crucial to success. When he spoke about past events he always seemed to prefix his words with 'Gresley, Thompson or Peppercorn thought this solution up and did this or that', when it was clear that the credit was rightly his. But he appeared to feel no anger or frustration at this and revered all three men commenting that 'they all managed at very difficult times, Thompson particularly, and always did their best for the LNER and its employees. They did fall short at times and Gresley, in particular, may have stuck too dogmatically to an idea when a better solution was available. But they did

Another Spencer photograph taken towards the end of steam on the East Coast Mainline. On this occasion, a rather grimy A4, No. 60012 *Commonwealth of Australia*, comes to a halt at some unrecorded destination sometime towards the end of its service in August 1964 when based in Aberdeen. (BS)

so for the right reasons and would, if a case was carefully and diplomatically made, change their minds'. Such is always the way of generous, self-effacing, clever men and women.'

Spencer enjoyed ten years of comparatively healthy retirement, but as the decade drew to a close he developed a slight heart problem that restricted him a little bit. Nevertheless, as Elsie recalled, 'Bert still liked to go out and stand on the seawall between Dawlish and Teignmouth watching and photographing the trains that passed by. He never lost his fascination with locomotives and still worked on plans for new types right up to the end.' This came on 20 July 1968 when he suffered a 'myocardial infarction followed by cardiac arrest' and died at home with Dr Firth in attendance. A day later his niece, who was living with Harry Spencer nearby at the time, registered his death on behalf of her aunt, so drawing Bert's story to a close.

In the weeks that followed there were no obituaries or memorial services, only a very quiet and modest funeral to mark the going of this exemplary man and talented engineer. But there was a memorial of sorts to mark his life and work in the locomotives he helped design and build. Luckily some of them survived BR's cull during the 1960s to find their way to museums or into the preservation movement. Through them we are left with a lasting reminder of the many engineers who, like Spencer, struggled for success often in the most difficult circumstances, achieving much in the process.

Sadly, the Spencer family soon had to face another loss when Harry died in 1969. But Elsie lived on in her house in Shaldon for another eighteen years, reaching the end of her life on 2 September 1986. To the end she was happy to talk about her husband's many achievements. She also made sure that his papers and other items relating to his work were conserved and then passed to others for assessment and preservation.

It is in the nature of things that history tends to record the deeds of great men and women in the world of science as though they lived and worked in splendid isolation without the support of others while awaiting that eureka moment. It is a romantic image, but one rarely with foundation. More often than not, these moments came after years of hard work by a well led, very capable team slowly developing ideas and solutions by trial and error. This was none more so than in the GNR and LNER design offices over which the multi-talented Gresley benevolently ruled for so long. To him fell the task of managing a team in such a way as to meet the many challenges set him by a Chairman and board eager for commercial success. This meant innovation, modernisation and a hard sell, all within the boundaries of a limited budget and in a world still struggling to overcome the wounds of the Great War. Here expectations had been heightened by the sacrifices made during the conflict, with greater rights and consumerism becoming ever more important to the masses. An old order was being swept away and new demands had to be assuaged. The railways, as they had been since their 'Great Boom' of the nineteenth century, were at the centre of these social and economic changes. Gresley rode this wave with great skill and dexterity, but he did not do it alone and needed excellent deputies and assistants, from many specialisations, to achieve as much as he did.

At the centre of all this activity lay Gresley's team at King's Cross. It was they who had to translate orders and ideas so that workshops could produce locomotives and rolling stock that met current and future needs. To do this, they had to manage all elements of design, construction, testing and maintenance of a large and varied fleet. But to do this they also had to manage the dominating figure of Gresley, with all his dynamism, brilliance and obstinacy thrown in. To do this he needed men of equal or higher intelligence, plus scientific skills on a par with his own. Spencer proved to be just such a man and his selection as the CME's assistant proved to be an inspired choice.

John Bazin and William Elwess saw all that the young man had to offer, trained and counselled him as he grew to maturity and recommended him for high rank. But Spencer was not a personally ambitious man, possessed of no overpowering ego, unlike many around him, so fame and very

Spencer remained interested in all aspects of life on the railways in retirement and, according to his wife, 'sought out locomotives whenever he could until very near to the end of his life'. These two pictures probably capture two of the best of the Big Four and BR's express passenger locomotives. Left Coronation Pacific No. 46225 *Duchess of Gloucester* and Class 7P No.70052 *Firth of Tay*. Dates and places are not given. (BS)

senior rank, such as CME, were unlikely to appeal to him. He was in the truest sense a backroom man, who simply wanted to design locomotives and serve those who led faithfully, honestly and to the best of his ability. Such a person, especially one so talented, will always be highly valued because such a mixture of skills, abilities and personality are most unusual. But Spencer was much more than this as his years with Gresley soon revealed. And his contribution did not end with the CME's death, though its nature changed to reflect the character of the leaders who followed and the times through which they lived and worked.

When describing Gresley's life and work in an earlier book I suggested that 'Spencer without Gresley was unthinkable, but so, I believe, is Gresley without Spencer' when it came to locomotive design. Since then I have thought more deeply about their partnership, for that is what it was, and believe this statement to be more apposite than I first thought. In researching *Gresley's Master Engineer* I was able to look more closely at their complex but meaningful association and consider what made it work. As a result, I came to see it as a relationship between two sides of the same coin – each with great strengths that seemed to complement each other. Essentially, they were both good scientists with very keen analytical skills, which were informed by a constant study of engineering practices and new developments around the world.

However, where Gresley had ambition, dynamism, great energy, political acumen and strong leadership skills, Spencer had the ability to apply a careful hand to the process and allow ideas to form possibly in a more cogent way. In doing so, he often translated and deciphered concepts Gresley outlined in the roughest way, often when scribbled down on any old piece of paper that came to hand as he rushed around keeping his vast organisation going. These Spencer then passed to the Chief Draughtsman, adding his own thoughts and ideas in the process.

It was not a partnership of equals of course – the gap in rank was too big and the scope for influencing events too wide for that – but Spencer provided an essential filter that worked in a number of ways. It gave the CME protection from the minutiae of daily life, allowing him to think and develop new ideas without disturbance. He knew, as a talented engineer and a very

During his travels after retirement Spencer occasionally visited old haunts, with King's Cross being a particular draw, though now in the process of massive change as steam gave way to diesel. What did he think as he stood on those old familiar platforms – the scene of so many memorable triumphs? One can only imagine what these may have been but it must have been deeply thought provoking whatever scenes flashed through his mind. On this occasion ex-A1 No. 2562 now 60063 Isinglass rebuilt as an A3 in 1946 appears to be backing down from the platform to be turned ready for her next duty. She will be condemned and cut up during 1964. (BS)

clever man, how to get Gresley's full attention and by slow degrees direct his thought processes, perhaps more effectively than any other subordinate. The length of lap gear debate, shortly after the A1s were introduced, was just such an occasion and Spencer's suggestion, which Gresley eventually accepted, made a good locomotive even better. And much more followed in the same vein as the partnership grew and the CME learnt the extent to which his young assistant could help and support him.

As time passed, it seems that the importance of Bulleid's role in the day to day business at King's Cross began to fade. Though his relationship with Gresley remained affable, it seems that from the late 1920s onwards the two men began to move in different directions. Perhaps the one issue that demonstrates this best was streamlining, which Bulleid thought to be a fad and Gresley a serious concept worth evaluating in some detail and applying wherever he could to steam locomotives. Spencer caught a flavour of Gresley's thoughts when he wrote:

> Streamlining was seen by many as a meaningless fashion and condemned it for that reason. Yet it was a science still in its infancy, with future applications then barely glimpsed. Gresley saw its potential, as he did many things, and began the process of experimentation with the A4s proving its worth.

When Bulleid criticised the streamlining concept, at a well-attended gathering of the IMechE in London, arranged by Gresley as the A4s were being built, the gulf between the two became only too apparent. Nothing was guaranteed to upset the CME, who valued loyalty very highly, more than the criticism by a subordinate in such a public place. And Bulleid seemed unable to rein in his criticism as the months passed, so perhaps distancing himself from Gresley even more. But

A reminder of great days to provide warm memories of a past life during retirement. Spencer had this picture, taken in the mid-1930s, framed and displayed in his 'office' at home. Its value rests in the fact that it captures four of the key players in the LNER's history together – William Whitelaw, the Chairman, Gresley, Robert Thom and Spencer – which is something of a rarity. Gresley stands in the background in the middle of this group with Whitelaw to his right and William Stanier four down on his left. Spencer sits at the table in the foreground (right side second from the left), with Thom on the next table turning in his chair towards the camera and immediately behind Spencer. (BS)

Bulleid was undoubtedly an ambitious man who wanted to be a CME. As a perpetual assistant, he was probably perturbed by the limitations this placed on his creativity and was frustrated by the lack of opportunities for promotion he faced in an industry with so few senior posts for which he was suited. But as his role diminished, so Spencer's star rose even higher at King's Cross and the course set fair for him and Gresley to accomplish great things together.

Sadly, this was not to last and as Gresley's health declined, Spencer's role subtly changed. There were still ideas to be pursued and concepts explored, but the zest for these things diminished with each passing year. As this happened, Spencer became more an aid than an assistant and later wrote:

> By 1936/37 there was a noticeable slackening in the CME's workload. He was, of course, getting older and even the busiest person will have slowed down by then. But his health was in sharp decline and this made it increasingly difficult to complete tasks he once managed so easily. This was distressing to witness and made Harold Harper and I more determined to support him as long as he wished to continue working. As a result of all this, Gresley worked from home more and more and we travelled there, often daily, to do his bidding.

Some would have taken an easier route, but this was not Spencer's way. He was committed to his leader and would remain so until the end, no matter how inconvenient or tiring this proved to be. As Elsie Spencer wrote, 'for Bert nothing was too much bother when it came to Sir Nigel, who he would have followed him anywhere no matter what the cost. He was very deeply saddened when the "Chief" passed away and missed him until the day he died.'

Such was his nature in good times and bad – perceptive, generous, honourable, professional, unassuming, dedicated, intelligent and wise. So it is little wonder that Gresley valued him so

According to Elsie Spencer, this press photograph, which is thought to have been taken at New Barnet in 1937, was one of her husband's favourites. Although sentimental in nature, it captures the fascination with locomotives that must have gripped Spencer as a child in Doncaster at the turn of the century. Perhaps this is why it appealed to him. (BS)

highly and kept him close by for so many years, even in his declining years. In so doing he entrusted his assistant with much more than locomotive design issues. He trusted him to be his go between and his mouthpiece as his powers faded. Here and in all his other duties Spencer never let Gresley down. He supported the CME no matter how difficult this became and always gave him practical, down to earth advice on many engineering issues, patiently and with good grace. But, most importantly, he never backed down when he knew he was right and used his considerable skills to change Gresley's mind when he thought this necessary. He was, perhaps, the only person in the CME's entourage who could do this and so his influence on the course of events was considerable. So, bearing all this in mind, I believe Gresley without Spencer, as an axiom, is true and railway history gained much as a result.

For the young boy growing up in the hard-pressed backstreets of Doncaster, without the benefit of wealth or position, who rose to become a man of great substance and reputation in his chosen field, this is quite remarkable. So to Gresley go the plaudits and statues, but to men such as Spencer must go many accolades too.

Reference Sources

The National Railway Museum (Search Engine)

Records Consulted
Corr/LNER/1 to 6.
Calc/LNER/1
Loco/LNER/1 to 9.
Spec/Don/7.
Spec/LNER/1 to 7.
Test/LNER/1 to 10.
The R Bond Collection.
The E.S. Cox Collection.
The R. Riddles Collection (donated by author).
The Immingham Collection (donated by author).
The E. Thompson Collection.

Other Collections
National Archives
Museum of Science and Industry, Manchester.
Science Museum, London.
Institution of Mechanical Engineers, London.
R.A. Hillier.
D. Neal.
T.F. Coleman/M. Lemon.
B. Spencer.
Dr F. Johansen
R.A. Thom.
N. Newsome.
R.H.N. Hardy.
A. Ewer.
Paget Archive.

Books and Other Publications
IMechE/ILocoE Journals
The Engineer
The Gazette various dates.
The Meccano Magazine
Steam World
The Stephenson Society Journal
Allen, J.R. and Bursley, J.A., *Heat Engines; Steam, Gas, Steam Turbines and Their Auxiliaries* (1941).
Bannister, Eric, *Trained By Sir Nigel Gresley*, Dalesman (1984).

Reference Sources

Bond, R., *A Lifetime With Locomotives* (1975).
Brown, E.A.S., *Nigel Gresley. Locomotive Engineer"* Littlehampton Book Services (1961)
Bulleid, H.A.V., *Master Builders of Steam*, Ian Allan, (1963).
Bulleid, H.A.V., *Bulleid of the Southern"* Littlehampton Book Services (1977).
Bush, D.J., *The Streamlined Decade*, George Braziller (1975).
Chapelon, A., *La Locomotive a Vapeur* (1952).
Coster, P., *Book of the A3 Pacifics*, Irwell Press (2003).
Coster, P., *Book of the A4 Pacifics*, Irwell Press (2005).
Coster, P., *Book of the V2 2-6-2s*, Irwell Press (2008).
Cox, E.S., *Locomotive Panorama Vols 1 and 2*, Ian Allan (1965/66).
Cox, E.S., *Chronicles of Locomotives*, Ian Allan (1967).
Cox, E.S., *Speaking of Steam*, Ian Allan (1971).
Dalby, W.E., *The Balancing of Engines* (1920).
Dalby, W.E., *British Railways: Some Facts and A Few Problems* (1910).
Grafton, P., *Edward Thompson of the LNER*, Oakwood Press (1971 & 2007).
Hillier-Graves, T., *Gresley and His Locomotives*, Pen and Sword Transport (2019).
Hillier-Graves, T., *The A4 Pacifics After Gresley* Pen and Sword Transport (2023).
Hillier-Graves, T., *Gresley's Silver Link*, Pen and Sword Transport (2022).
Hillier-Graves, T., *Peppercorn. His Life and Locomotives*, Pen and Sword Transport (2021).
Hillier-Graves, T., *Thompson. His Life and Locomotives*, Pen and Sword Transport (2021).
Hillier-Graves, T., *Tom Coleman. His Life and Work*, Pen and Sword Transport (2019).
Hardy, R.H.N., *Steam in the Blood*, Littlehampton Book Services (1971).
Haresnape, B., *Gresley's Locomotives*, Ian Allan (1981).
Holcroft, H., *Locomotive Adventure Vols 1 and 2*, Ian Allan (1962).
Hughes, Geoffrey, *Sir Nigel Gresley*, Oakwood Publishing (2001).
Martin, S.A.C., *Edward Thompson. Wartime CME*, Strathwood, Ltd (2022).
McKillop, Norman, *Top Link Locomotives*, Thomas Nelson and Sons (1957).
Nock, O.S., *The Gresley Pacifics*, David and Charles (1973).
Nock, O.S., *Locomotives of Sir Nigel Gresley*, (1945).
Pope, A., *Wind Tunnel Testing* (1947).
RCTS, *Locomotives of the LNER – Vols 2A, 2B & 6B* (1973 & 1983).
Rogers, H.C.B., *The Last Steam Locomotive Engineer*, Allen and Unwin (1970).
Rogers, H.C.B., *Thompson & Peppercorn. Locomotive Engineers*, Allen and Unwin (1979).
Rogers, H.C.B., *Transition from Steam*, Allen and Unwin (1980).
Townend, P.N., *East Coast Pacifics at Work*, Littlehampton Book Services (1982).
Townend, P.N., *Top Shed*, Ian Allan (1975).
Yeadon, W.B., *Yeadon's Registers* – Nos 1,2,3,4,5,8,9,10 and 25 (various dates).

Photographic Sources/Credits

B. Spencer (BS), R. Hillier (RH), T. Coleman (TC/ML), Author (THG), H.A.V. Bulleid (HB) and D. Neal (DN).

Copyright is a complex issue and often difficult to establish, especially when a photograph or document exists in a number of public and private collections. Strenuous efforts have been made ensure each item is correctly attributed, but no process is flawless, especially when many of these items are more than seventy years old with photographers or authors long gone. If an error has been made, it was unintentional. If any reader wishes to affirm copyright, please contact the publishers and an acknowledgement will be included in any future edition of this book, should a claim be proven. We apologise in advance for any mistakes. A number of documents held by the NRM have been quoted in this book. My thanks to the museum for permission to do this.

Index

Abraham, Frederick – 228.
ACFI Feedwater System – 7, 131, 138, 212.
Adams, Frederick – 113.
Adkinson, Bernard – 188, 189.
American Locomotive Association (ALC0) – 86.
Allen, Cecil – 28.
Altoona Test Centre – 134.
Amalgamation of Railway Companies (1923) – 32.
Association of Railway Engineers (ARLE) – 58, 69.
Aspinall, John – 20, 113, 114.

Baltimore and Ohio Railroad – 87.
Bannister, Eric – 18, 40, 46, 107, 108, 156, 157, 185, 188, 189.
Barnes, C (Driver) – 159.
Barrington-Ward, Victor (Sir) – 130, 158.
Bazin, John – 9, 17-21, 23, 24, 237.
Beames, Hewitt – 69.
Belpaire – 37.
Bernoullie, Daniel – 113.
Billington, J – 21, 22, 88.
Blair, James – 202.
Boiler Trial 1928 (A1) – 67-69.
Bond, Roland – 184, 226.
Brackenbury, A – 162, 163.
Bray, Tommy (Driver/Fireman) – 188, 235.
Broughton, Harry – 24, 34, 44, 108, 127.
Budd Company - Zephyr development – 123.
Bugatti, Etorre – 57.
Bulleid, O V S – 7, 33, 34, 37, 38, 40-42, 51, 56, 58-60, 64, 69, 77, 107-110, 114-118, 121, 127, 135-140, 142, 143, 161, 162, 169, 170, 175.
Burlington and Quincy Railroad – 123.

Calder, James – 125.
Calthrop, Samuel – 113.
Campbell, Malcolm (Sir) – 105.
Cantile, K Lt Col – 69.

Carling, Dennis – 228.
Carr, F W – 201.
Cartazzi Slides – 154, 185.
Cassidy, Maurice (Sir) – 156.
Cayley, George – 113.
Chapelon, Andre – 56, 57, 127, 134, 135, 183.
Churchward, George – 24-26, 62, 66, 77, 149, 196.
City and Guilds Engineering College, London – 120, 139, 135.
Clayton, James – 233.
Cocks, Clifford – 175, 228.
Coleman, Tom Francis – 9, 122-124, 175, 209, 216, 226, 233.
Conjugated Valve Gear – 26, 27, 45, 46, 156, 166, 176, 177, 207, 208, 218, 224.
Cook, Kenneth – 226, 227.
Corridor Tenders – 72-75.
Cox, E S – 21, 27, 218, 222, 223, 228, 231, 233, 234.
Cramlington Rail Crash (1926) – 53, 54.

Dalby, W E (Prof) – 56, 57, 121, 122, 156.
Day, Frank – 38, 201.
De Havilland, G – 105.
Delaware & Hudson Railway – 86.
Doncaster Aviation Pageant -13.
Dorpmuller, Julius (Dr) – 171, 187.
Duddington, Joseph (Driver) – 187.
Duke of York (later King George VI) – 117.
Duncan, William – 112.

Edge, Douglas R – 142, 168, 169.
Electrification (GNR & LNER) – 61, 171-173.
Electricity Supply Act (1926) – 61.
Ell, Sam – 228, 233.
Elwell, Cyril – 202-206.
Elwess, William – 9, 18-20, 23, 24, 28, 35-37, 44, 108, 122, 211, 218, 237.
Emerson, Alexander – 61.

Fowler, Henry – 69, 88.

Gass, Edward – 21, 22.
General Strike (1926) – 50-55.
Germany (and Nazism) – 141, 170, 191.
Glenn, G (Fireman) – 159.
Golightly, W – 54.
Gray, D D – 201.
Great Southern and Western Railway (GSWR) – 21.
Great War – 17-19, 51. 111, 113, 198, 211, 237.
Gresley, Herbert Nigel (Sir) – 7, 8, 17, 20-33, 35-45, 47-49, 51, 52, 60, 62, 64, 65, 69-72, 75, 77, 82-84, 88-94, 129-136, 140-150, 153, 157, 158, 163-167, 169-173, 176-190, 193-198, 205, 208, 209, 211, 218, 225, 231, 233, 236, 237-241.

Harold Wood/Brentwood Rail Crash (1941) – 195, 196.
Harper, Harold – 40, 142, 143, 240.
Harrison, J F – 201, 225-227, 232.
Hart-Davies, Rupert – 107.
Hartley, Harold (Sir) – 122.
Hay, Will – 109.
Herbert, Tom – 122, 228.
Heywood, T – 201.
Hitler, Adolph – 141, 170, 171, 187, 194, 199.
Holcroft, Harold – 27.
Hopking, A – 62.
Hughes, Geoffrey – 37-39.
Hughes, George – 21, 22, 123.
Hughes, John – 235.

Institution of Mechanical Engineers (IMechE) – 24, 89, 91, 112, 114, 148, 210, 234.
Institution of Locomotive Engineers (ILocoE) – 24, 29, 37, 40, 62, 64, 81-83, 114, 115, 124, 139, 141, 146, 171, 211, 221, 234, 235.
Ivatt, Henry A – 25, 26.

Jarvis, Ron – 228.
Jenkins, Sam – 188-190.
Johansen, Frederick (Dr) – 56, 57, 111-118, 121-124, 126, 149, 152, 156, 180.
Jones (Fireman) – 159.

Knorr Type Valves – 48.
Kylchap Exhaust System –.120, 126, 127, 187, 224.

Lancashire and Yorkshire Railway – 7, 20, 21.
Laurel and Hardy – 109.
Lentz – 79, 80, 127, 133.
Liverpool Street to Shenfield Line – 172-174.
Lloyd-George, David (Prime Minister) – 31.
Liverpool University – 20.
LNER/GWR 1925 Comparability Trials – 43-45.
Luty, G (Fireman) – 164.
Locomotive Classes –
  BR Standard Classes – Class 4 – 226, 233.
    Class 5 – 226.
    Class 6 – 232, 238.
    Class 7 – 227, 229, 230, 232.
    Class 8 – 232.
    Class 9 – 227.
  BR Diesels - Brush Type 2 (Class 31) – 228.
    Class 42 – 234, 235.
    Class 52 – 234, 235.
    EE DP1/Deltic (Class 55) – 227-229, 231-233, 235.
    EE Type 2 (Class 20) – 228.
  BR Electrics - EMU
    (for Shenfield Line) – 228.
    EM1/EM2 – 228.

English Electric Gas Turbine 3 – 229, 235.

DRG - Class 05 – 143, 183.
    Class 06 – 183.
    'Flying Hamburger' (SVT 877) – 115, 123, 143, 148, 149.
    Scheinenzeppelin – 121, 123.
  GNR – A1/A10 – 24, 28-32, 43-49, 60, 64, 67-75, 96, 105, 120, 139, 144, 145, 150, 184, 202, 215, 236, 239.
    C1 – 139.
    Class 461 – 25, 26.
    H2/H3/H4 (later LNER K1, K2 and K3) – 25-29, 32, 45, 60, 75, 183, 184.
    J23 (later LNER J50/J51) – 32
    N2 - 60
    O1/O2 – 25, 26, 28, 29, 32, 60, 77, 80, 184,
  GWR – Castle Class – 43-45, 47, 148, 222.

Class 2800 – 25.
King Class – 66.
Pacific (The Great Bear) – 148, 149.

LMS – Black Five – 176.
  Diesel Co Co (10000-10001) – 232.
  Princess Royal – 116, 120, 122, 145, 148.
  Princess Coronation – 187, 191, 192, 222, 229, 230, 238.
  Royal Scot Class – 108, 120, 222.
  Turbomotive – 145, 180.
  2F – 227.
  4F – 227.
  8F – 209.
LNER – A1 (Peppercorn) – 219, 224.
  A1/1 (ex A1) – 217.
  A2 (Peppercorn) – 219, 224.
  A2/1 (Thompson) - 215-217, 224.
  A2/2 (ex-P2) (Thompson) – 215-217, 224.
  A2/3 (Thompson) – 215-217, 221, 224.
  A3 – 49, 72, 73, 118, 120, 131, 139, 144, 150, 153, 175, 176, 184, 185, 212, 215, 236, 239.
  A4 – 49, 115, 119, 123, 124, 145, 149-157, 161-170, 176, 180-192, 194, 197, 202, 207, 212, 215, 218, 221-223, 236, 239, 240.
  B1 – 202, 216, 217, 221, 227, 229.
  B12 – 75, 127, 195, 210.
  B17 – 80, 112, 121, 144, 145, 171, 175, 176, 180-184, 195, 212.
  C7 – 77-79, 127.
  D49 – 75, 79-81, 127, 144, 171, 185.
  J38/J39 – 75, 79, 144, 171.
  K4 – 183, 184.
  P1 – 64, 75, 77, 78
LNER proposed designs – 4-8-2 – 182, 183, 195.
  4-8-4 – 183, 195.
  'Super A4' – 103.
  P2 – 65, 93, 96, 110, 113, 121, 123-140, 142, 144, 148, 149, 176-180, 182, 197, 202, 208, 213, 215.
  V1/V3 – 144-146, 171.
  V2 – 121, 124, 139, 171-173, 176, 177, 192, 193, 198, 209, 215, 229.
  V4 – 176, 193, 192-194.
  W1 – 88-96, 110, 112, 119-121, 134, 142, 144, 176, 178, 180, 182.

LSWR/SR – N15/H15 – 148, 149.
NER - Pacific (under LNER became A2) - 32, 60.
SNCF - 241 – 134.
  242A1 – 183.
SR – Diesel Co Co – 231.
  Leader Class – 88.
  Merchant Navy – 229.

Massey, W – 38.
Maunsell, Richard – 233.
Matthews, Ronald (Sir) – 208, 240.
McCosh, Andrew – 212.
McKeen, W – 113.
Metropolitan-Vickers – 173.
Mitchell, R J – 113
Monobloc Casting – 176, 177.
Morris, R E (Driver) – 159.
Mount, Lt Col – 158.
Mozley (nee Spencer), Elsie – 35, 36, 42, 105, 203, 241.
Mozley, William – 36.
Muhlfield, J E – 86.
Mutton, Harry (Fireman) - 71 .

National Physical Laboratory (NSP Teddington) – 56, 111, 115, 118-120, 154, 156.
Nationalisation (1948) – 218-221.
Newsome, Norman – 107, 154, 160, 188-190, 202, 203.
Newton, Charles (Sir) – 213, 214.
Nicholson Thermic Syphon – 192.
North British Locomotive Company – 80.
North Staffordshire Railway – 122.

Paris-Orleans Line – 127, 135, 136, 138.
Place, Pierre – 133.
Peppercorn, A H – 8, 35, 145, 199, 201, 210, 215-220, 223-226, 236.
Pibworth, Alfred (Driver) – 71.
Pugson, Ernest – 226.

Raven, Vincent (Sir) – 32, 40, 60, 61, 95, 171.
Reeves, Luther – 225.
Remnant, Patrick – 162-164.
Richards, Henry – 38, 61, 172, 199.
Riddles, Robert – 217, 226, 228, 233.
Robinson Superheater – 69, 127.

Rogers, H C B – 62.
Rotary Cam Poppet Valves – 80.
Royal Aircraft Establishment
  (Farnborough) – 121.
Rugby Test Centre – 223, 228-230.

Sparshatt, William – 105, 150.
Spencer, B –
  Family – 10-16, 55, 234-237.
  Education – 14, 16, 17.
  Apprenticeship – 17-23.
  With L&Y Railway – 20-23.
  Draughtsman at Doncaster – 23-35.
  At King's Cross with Gresley – 37-95, 105, 109, 114, 117, 118, 120-128, 131-147, 153-160, 162-173, 176-188, 190-198, 200, 201.
  Long Lap Valve Issue – 41, 44-49, 68, 239.
  Doncaster with Thompson – 202-219.
  Doncaster with Peppercorn – 220-226.
  Doncaster with British Railways – 226-233.
  Retirement – 234-241.

Second World War – 194-200, 203-206, 210.
Sheldon, R (Driver) – 54.
Smeddle, R A – 201.
Smith (Fireman) – 105.
Stamer, Arthur – 82, 88-90, 143, 195, 198.
Standardisation of steam locomotives – 62, 214, 215, 219.
Stanier, William (Sir) –69, 88, 122, 141, 161, 171, 176, 180, 187, 218, 233, 234, 240.
Stanton, Thomas (Sir) – 112.
Steadman, C M – 151.
Steam Speed World Record
  (1938) – 187-190.
Stirling, Patrick – 19.
Streamlining – 28, 111-122, 124,140, 180-182, 196, 216, 217, 239.
Street, T – 8, 108, 156, 173.

Superheater Company – 69.
Swift, Harry – 61

Taylor, A (Driver) – 164.
Thom, R A – 8, 70, 123, 127-130, 133, 142, 145, 153, 161, 167, 191, 198, 240.
Thompson E – 8, 35, 54, 95, 123, 161, 167, 177, 183, 191, 195, 196, 198-211, 213, 215-218, 224-226, 231, 236.
Trask, Eric – 168.
Turbine Locomotives – 83, 88, 145.
Turner T H – 142, 225.
Turner T (Prof) – 56.

Uniflow Engine – 81, 82.
Urie, Robert – 148.

Vitry Test Centre – 133-135, 184.

Wagner, R P (Dr) – 56, 57, 171, 183, 187.
Wall Street Crash (1929) – 141, 172.
Walschaert Valve Gear – 37, 46, 80.
Webster, Robert (Fireman) – 150
Wedderburn, T (Driver) – 54.
Wedgwood, Ralph (Sir) – 44, 56, 58, 125, 150, 187, 188.
Welwyn Rail Crash (1935) – 157-161.
Werry, William – 83-86.
Westinghouse – 59, 78, 162, 188.
Whitelaw, William – 44, 60, 129, 145, 168.
Willetts, Alfred – 35, 36.
Wilson, Ernest – 113.
Wilson (Major) – 195.
Windle, Edward – 8, 108, 117, 134, 156, 177, 185, 201, 202, 210, 213, 215-217, 220, 225, 226, 234.
Wintour, Francis – 35, 44, 47.
Women's Social and Political Movement
  (WSPU) -13, 14.
Woodhead to Manchester Line – 172-174.

Yarrows – 87, 88.